1997

# THE HEALTHCARE SUPERVISOR

# PROFESSIONAL NURSING MANAGEMENT

D1710378

Edited by

*Charles R. McConnell*

Vice President for Employee Affairs

The Genesee Hospital

Rochester, New York

AN ASPEN PUBLICATION®

Aspen Publishers, Inc.

Gaithersburg, Maryland

1993

Library of Congress Cataloging-in-Publication Data

The health care supervisor on professional nursing management/
[edited by] Charles R. McConnell.
p. cm.
Includes bibliographical references and index.
ISBN: 0-8342-0369-3
1. Nursing services— Administration. I. McConnell, Charles R.
[DNLM: 1. Nursing—organization & administration.
2. Nursing, Supervisory—organization & administration.
3. Professional Competence. WY 105 H4335 1993]
RT89.H4 1993
362.1'73—dc20
DNLM/DLC
for Library of Congress
93-197
CIP

Aspen Publishers, Inc. grants permission for photocopying for limited personal or internal use. This consent does not
extend to other kinds of copying, such as copying for general distribution, for advertising or promotional purposes, for
creating new collective works, or for resale. For information, address
Aspen Publishers, Inc., Permissions Department, 200 Orchard Ridge Drive, Suite 200,
Gaithersburg, Maryland 20878.

Editorial Resources: Barbara Priest

Library of Congress Catalog Card Number: 93-197
ISBN: 0-8342-0369-3

Printed in Canada

1  2  3  4  5

# Contents

## Part III   Tools and Defenses

# Part IV  Other Nursing Management Concerns

# Preface

## INTRODUCTION

*The Health Care Supervisor* is a cross-disciplinary journal that publishes articles of relevance to persons who manage the work of others in health care settings. This journal's readers, as well as its authors, come from a wide variety of functional, clinical, technical, and professional backgrounds. Between the covers of a single issue of *HCS*, for example, you can find articles written by a nurse, a physician, a speech pathologist, a human resource specialist, an accountant, a nursing home administrator, and an attorney. These authors, and the numerous others who write for *HCS*, write with a single purpose: To provide guidance that all health care supervisors, regardless of the occupations or specialties they supervise, can use in learning to better understand or fulfill the supervisory role.

In the more than 10 years that *The Health Care Supervisor* has been published, a number of nursing managers and educators have contributed to its pages, some, as in the case of Helen Yura and Ruth Davidhizar, a number of times. All of these nursing contributors have had something of relevance to say to supervisors of all disciplines, but primarily they have written to and for nursing supervisors and nurses who would be supervisors.

In *The Health Care Supervisor on Professional Nursing Management* we bring together 21 articles for the nursing supervisor, whether practicing or aspiring. Based largely on the experiences of professional nursing managers and educators, these articles contain practical advice and insight for nursing supervision.

## THE NURSING MANAGEMENT ARENA

With "Needed Now: A Hospital Partnership for Patient Care," Sovie introduces the nursing management arena as one in which all contributing parties are necessary parts of a cohesive team. Yura prepares us to understand and thus motivate employees as well as ourselves with "Human Need Theory: A Framework for the Nurse Supervisor," and emphasizes the importance of a career-long learning posture in "The Nurse Supervisor as Scholar."

## ON BECOMING A NURSE MANAGER

The crucial transition from clinical specialist to manager is introduced by Rotkovich in "The Head Nurse as a First-Line Manager." DiMarco, Goodson, and Hauser offer a highly practical prescription for the education of the new nurse manager in "A Situational Approach to Developing Head Nurse Management Skills." In consideration of the pressures to be encountered by the newer nurse manager, Turner offers "The Psychological Impact of the Head Nurse Manager in Transition: Organizational Roles for Minimizing Stress."

In "Orientation and Training of Nurse Managers: A Case Study," Roach and Smith present an innovative approach used by one hospital for training new nurse managers. Yura-Petro and Brooks, in "Congruence Between Nursing Education and Nursing Service: A Common Conceptual/Theoretic Framework for Nursing Units," show how to make the transition from the theory of the classroom to the actual practice of nursing management.

## TOOLS AND DEFENSES

As we are reminded by Tabeek in "Communication: The Critical Link in Nursing Middle Management," communication between organizational levels and between and among individuals is at the heart of effective management. And in "A Common-Sense Survival Strategy for Nursing Supervisors," Nail and Singleton suggest that one remains capable of long-term effectiveness by knowing how to cope with daily pressures and unexpected events.

In "Confrontation: An Underused Nursing Management Technique," Davidhizar and Bowen promote the value and effectiveness of a direct approach with staff and others. The less quantifiable but frequently more troublesome elements of decision making are addressed by Gearhart and Young in "Intuition, Ethical Decision Making, and the Nurse Manager." The practical aspects of intuition and its development are further explored by Davidhizar with "Intuition and the Nurse Manager," and, working again with Bowen, Davidhizar suggests in "Intimidation and the Nurse Manager" that even a practice whose mention inspires negative reactions can have its positive side.

Humor can often serve as the caregiver's—and surely the manager's—medicine, as Yura-Petro suggests with "Humor: A Research and Practice Tool for Nurse Scholars–Supervisors, Practitioners, and Educators." In "An Approach to Nurse Managerial Reporting: An Essential Task," Nail and Singleton provide an introduction to necessary management documentation, and with "A Proactive Approach to Computerizing Nursing Process: A Management Perspective," Shannon, Dextrom, Fuhrhop make the nurse manager a participant in the process of system design.

## OTHER NURSING MANAGEMENT CONCERNS

In a comprehensive two-part presentation, "Enhancing the Image of the Nurse: The Role of the Nurse Supervisor," Yura tracks the history of the nursing image and proscribes the role of the nurse manager in fostering an image of today's nurse as an educated, caring professional. Yura furthers recommendations for continuing improvements in "Nursing Leadership Evaluation," and, with Young, defines the role of the nurse manager as a vital agent of change in "The Nurse Supervisor Charged With Change."

## CONCLUSION

Today's professional nurse is a highly trained specialist in a clinical discipline that is becoming steadily more complex and is seeing its incumbents called upon to bear continually more responsibility. Today's professional nursing manager must combine the education and outlook of the patient care specialist with the manager's broader understanding of the health care delivery environment. In brief, the professional nursing manager must be both a professional nurse and professional manager.

# Acknowledgments

It would not have been possible to assemble this book without the active involvement of the members of the guiding boards, past and present, of *The Health Care Supervisor*. As of this writing some of these valued advisors and authors are well into their second decade of service to *HCS*.

Our sincere thanks to the following past members of the *HCS* Editorial Board, the present *HCS* Advisory Board, and the present Board of Contributing Editors.

## Past Members of *HCS* Editorial Board

Steven H. Appelbaum, Zeila W. Bailey, Claire D. Benjamin, Marjorie Beyers, Philip Bornstein, Leonard C. Brideau, Robert W. Broyles, Joy D. Calkin, Kenneth P. Cohen, Joseph A. Cornell, Darlene A. Dougherty, Kenneth R. Emery, Valerie Glesnes-Anderson, Lee Hand, Allen G. Herkimer, Jr., Max G. Holland, Bowen Hosford, Charles E. Housley, Loucine M. D. Huckabay, Laura L. Kalick, Janice M. Kurth, Marlene Lamnin, Joan Gratto Liebler, Ellyn Luros, Margeurite R. Mancini, Robert D. Miller, Joan F. Moore, Victor J. Morano, Harry E. Munn, Jr., Michael W. Noel, Rita E. Numerof, Samuel E. Oberman, Cheryl S. O'Hara, Jesus J. Pena, Donald J. Petersen, Tim Porter-O'Grady, George D. Pozgar, Ann Marie Rhodes, Edward P. Richards III, James C. Rose, Rachel Rotkovich, Norton M. Rubenstein, Edward D. Sanderson, William L. Scheyer, Homer H. Schmitz, Joyce L. Schweiger, Donna Richards Sheridan, Margaret D. Sovie, Eugene I. Stearns, Judy Ford Stokes, Thomas J. Tenerovicz, Lewis H. Titterton, Jr., Dennis A. Tribble, Terry Trudeau, Alex J. Vallas, Katherine W. Vestal, Judith Weilerstein, William B. Werther, Jr., Shirley Ann Wertz, Sara J. White, Norman H. Witt, and Karen Zander

## Present *HCS* Advisory Board

Addison C. Bennett, Bernard L. Brown, Jr., Karen H. Henry, Norman Metzger, I. Donald Snook, Jr., and Helen Yura-Petro

## Present Board of Contributing Editors

Donald F. Beck, Robert Boissoneau, Jerad D. Browdy, Vicki S. Crane, Carol A. Distasio, Charlotte Eliopoulos, Howard L. Lewis, R. Scott MacStravic, Leon McKenzie, Jerry L. Norville, Stephen L. Priest, Howard L. Smith, and John L. Templin, Jr.

Our sincere appreciation as well to those who, in addition to several persons mentioned above, participated in creating the articles that make up this present volume:

Margaret Bown, Judith Brooks, Nancy Dextrom, Nicholas DiMarco, Marcia Fuhrhop, Sharon Cranendonk Gearhart, Jane Goodson, Henry Hauser, Frankie C. Nail, Bonnie L. Roach, Marcia Shannon, Enrica K. Singleton, Laurie MacLeod Smith, Eleanor A. Tabeek, Barbara A. Turner, and Sue W. Young.

# Part I
# The Nursing Management Arena

# Needed now: a hospital partnership for patient care

*Margaret D. Sovie*
*Associate Dean for Nursing*
*Practice*
*School of Nursing*
*University of Rochester*
*Rochester, New York*

HOSPITALS ARE UNDER increasing pressure to control the costs of patient care. The reasons are obvious as vividly illustrated by two examples. First, according to the Health Care Financing Administration (HCFA), in 1981 hospital care alone consumed $42 billion of the $62.3 billion federal expenditure for Medicare and Medicaid, that is, 67.4 percent of this category of available health dollars was spent exclusively on hospital care.[1] The second example emanates from the corporate sector, and was reported at a Blue Cross/ Blue Shield of Illinois symposium. Ray Humpke, Vice-President of Personnel for Illinois Bell, Chicago, discussed corporate America's concerns with rising health care costs, and reported that health care represents 5 to 15 percent of industry's payroll costs nationally.[2]

The growing costs of health care, to both the public and private sectors, have produced intensified demands to control and reduce the rates of in-

*Health Care Superv*, 1984,2(2),27–39

crease in hospital costs. Extensive controls on hospital utilization and reimbursement are already in effect, with additional constraining regulations positioned or planned for implementation. The messages are clear. Hospital costs must be controlled and reduced at the same time hospitals are expected to continue to meet communities' increasing demands for quality patient care services.

This challenge of meeting increasing demands while controlling and reducing costs has produced a "fiscal crisis" environment for hospitals. Hospital management must take this challenge and use it to convert the financial crisis into an "opportunity environment" through the creation of new partnerships in the business of hospital health care. There are multiple professional groups and services that should share in a partnership designed to maximize the potential contributions of all members of the hospital organization. For the purposes of this article, however, the partnership concept is explored primarily as it relates to the professional nursing staff.

## PROFESSIONAL NURSES: PARTNERS IN THE BUSINESS OF HEALTH CARE

Professional nurses constitute the single largest group of health care providers in the hospital work force. Registered nurses are one of the constant groups in the hospital, and the largest group with the responsibility for caring for patients 24 hours a day, 7 days a week, throughout the year. Wherever patients are, the hospital's nurses are there to care for them and to ensure that their needs are met. Registered nurses can become the newest partners in the challenging business of hospital health care. Since nurses provide 95 percent of all the care rendered in hospitals,[3] they are one of the most influential groups, next to physicians, in identifying approaches that can control or reduce costs while simultaneously ensuring the quality of care for patients.

*Nurses are one of the most influential groups, next to physicians, in identifying approaches that can control or reduce costs while simultaneously ensuring the quality of care for patients.*

The costs of nursing personnel usually constitute 25 to 30 percent of a hospital's operating budget, and nursing is most commonly the single largest personnel cost center in any hospital organization. As a result, hospitals facing financial difficulties are frequently tempted to approach the narrowing of budget gaps by reducing the costs of nursing personnel. However, hospitals that take this approach to reducing health care costs may prove to be short-sighted and can be making serious strategic errors. Wise administrators will reject such a "quick fix" approach to solving what may be the most serious organizational challenge facing hospitals—that is, financial stability. Instead, these administrators will recognize professional nurses as one of the groups in the hospital who are always present with patients and who, given the necessary information, challenge and opportunity, can identify new opportunities for controlling and reducing costs through changes in procedures, systems, equipment, supplies, and work organization and relationships. Future-oriented administrators know that nurses need to be brought into the management of the hospital as partners in the corporate enterprise. Nursing staff need to participate in the management of the organization's affairs, and be given the opportunity to share their knowledge and expertise in creating an efficient and effective organization in which quality patient care at controlled costs is an attained objective.

Creating a visible partnership in the business of the hospital can result in improved patient care; increased satisfaction of the participating professionals; controlled and, most importantly in many instances, reduced costs in an organization that will be able to continue to meet its objectives in serving the health care needs of its citizens.

## MANAGEMENT'S ROLE IN CREATING NEW PARTNERSHIPS IN HOSPITALS

Creating an organizational climate that promotes and nurtures the concept of a partnership between the hospital, the medical staff and the nursing staff for delivering quality patient care at controlled costs is a shared responsibility of three groups: hospital administration, the nursing staff and medical staff. Top administrators from each of these groups have to accept and visibly support the position that patient care and hospital operations will benefit significantly by extending the partnership concept to key groups in the institution and that this is an essential step in achieving control or reduction of costs. They have to agree that the professional nursing staff is one of these groups and proceed to manage the hospital operations accordingly. Components of the plan to promote a partnership concept and the associated relationships include the following:

- creation of a supportive climate, collegial relationships and participative management within nursing;
- creation of an organizational environment of shared ownership in which nurses, as well as other professionals, perceive the hospital as their business and see quality care at controlled costs as their shared responsibility;
- actualization of the concept of the nursing staff as partners in the hospital enterprise by including nurse members on committees and groups involved in governance, planning and control;
- establishment and support of joint practice committees to address patient care issues and con-

cerns that affect both medical and nursing practice;

- promotion of the concept of lateral relationships between interacting departments serving patients, with the responsibility for resolving problems delegated to the levels in the organizational structure where the problems are experienced.

## INTRAPROFESSIONAL COLLEGIALITY, MUTUAL SUPPORT AND PARTICIPATIVE MANAGEMENT

Nursing administration has a major responsibility in helping to achieve a partnership concept for the professional nursing staff within the hospital. The nursing service department must be seen by the nursing staff as "our department" and nurses must experience a feeling of "shared ownership" within nursing. A partnership in hospital affairs will not be possible if the nurses are not already participating in a partnership within nursing.

Nursing managers and administrators have to conduct nursing affairs with staff recognized and valued as colleagues in the business enterprise. The traditional view of staff nurses occupying the entry position in a hierarchical nursing structure has to change. Staff nurses are the key providers of patient care in hospitals and must be viewed as occupying central positions in the nursing organization with managers and others there to as-

sist and support them in their caregiving activities.

A participative management structure needs to exist within nursing service. Through significant involvement of the nursing staff in decisions relative to the standards of nursing practice and the policies and procedures concerned with the nursing care of patients, the concept of shared ownership is made real. The members of the nursing staff need to be actively involved in establishing, implementing and evaluating the objectives of the nursing department. There must be easy access and free exchange of data relevant to the management and evaluation of nursing activities. Opportunities must be available for staff to participate in nursing matters that extend beyond their assigned patient units. They must be provided with sufficient information and organizational experience to develop corporate knowledge and an institutional perspective. Without the latter, they cannot be expected to assume a partnership role in hospital affairs.

Interested nurses need to be guided through a series of developmental stages in which they can progress from active participation on nursing committees to membership and active participation on hospital committees. Preparation of nursing staff for the responsibilities of institutional committee membership must be a responsibility shared by the interested nurses and their nurse managers. Too frequently, an individual is appointed to represent colleagues and a discipline or unit on a committee, but the representation is not fully executed.

Committee members have an obligation and responsibility to share information with their constituency and to keep information flowing between the groups. Participative management can succeed only if individuals representing others keep communications open and information is freely and continuously exchanged. Nursing managers can help staff achieve this objective of effective representation. Opportunities can be planned for committee reports at each staff meeting. Committee minutes can be circulated or posted and committee structure and membership can be publicized throughout the organization. If the multiple approaches for participative management are known to the staff, and trust is built through ensuring consultation in decisions that significantly affect nurses and patient care, the staff will view themselves as partners in the nursing organization. The latter is an essential condition and a prerequisite to extending the partnership role to the broader corporate entity of the hospital.

## A HOSPITAL MILIEU OF SHARED OWNERSHIP

Creating an organizational environment or hospital milieu of shared ownership is an important management responsibility. In conducting the daily operations of the institution, as well as in planning for the future, the messages transmitted by management must be consistent. The hospital is the business of the nurses, as well as other professionals practicing within its walls, and quality care at controlled costs is a shared responsibility of all these individuals and groups.

Participative management, coupled with a partnership concept in a milieu of shared ownership with supportive relationships can result in the following:

- high performance goals established through group decision making in multiple overlapping groups;
- high productivity with controlled costs;
- mutual trust and confidence between the multiple groups and levels in the organization;
- high reciprocal influence among the members of the hospital structure—the various partnership groups;
- an organizational or corporate pride and loyalty, as well as peer group loyalty;
- low absenteeism and turnover;
- excellent care delivered to patients; and
- professional and personal satisfaction of staff.[4,5]

A true partnership environment, with its associated concept of shared ownership, will help create an open, supportive hospital structure conducive to finding opportunities to work better and smarter. A norm of professional behavior should be a demonstrated concern with the costs as well as the quality of care and services rendered. Nursing staff, for example, can be expected to suggest varying approaches to meeting patient care requirements. In turn, managers must be receptive to suggestions and supportive of staff so that exploration of alternative approaches is comprehensive and completed in a climate of mutual problem solving. To succeed in this important endeavor, management has the responsibility of building high levels of organizational trust.[6]

Suggestions for controlling or reducing costs will not become normative behavior unless members in the organization are kept well informed about the financial management program and the current operational status, along with the immediate and long-range plans of the hospital. Periodic reports, on a bimonthly or quarterly basis, of the health of the hospital should be given to the staff. These reports should include volume statistics, productivity indices and budgetary status, along with quality assurance reports and patient and family evaluation of care data. Knowledgeable partners who are kept well informed regarding the corporate progress and its financial status will be better prepared to execute their expanded hospital responsibilities.

## NURSE–PHYSICIAN INTERDEPENDENCIES

The two disciplines that interact continuously in providing patient care are the nurses and the physi-

cians. Quality patient care is realized when the contributions of nursing and medicine to patient care are maximized. This nurse–physician partnership for patient care is critical. In addition, collegial relationships between nurses and physicians are an essential ingredient to professional satisfaction as well as quality patient and family care.

Nurses and physicians, working as partners in hospital health care, can effect many practice changes that will control and reduce hospital costs. It is management's responsibility to support and facilitate nurses and physicians in their collaborative problem solving.

Joint practice committees, in which nurses and physicians address mutual problems and concerns in patient care, have demonstrated what can be accomplished when these two professional groups form a partnership directed at improved patient care and collegial relationships. It is now time to broaden the scope of responsibility of these committees and have them study approaches to patient care that may result in cost reductions. Certainly the opportunities are expansive. Together nurses and physicians can examine a wide array of practices

*Together nurses and physicians can examine a wide array of practices and procedures with the objective of maintaining quality care while reducing costs.*

and procedures with the objective of maintaining quality care while reducing costs. The outcomes could be significant.

Joint practice committee members can and should solicit the views of their colleagues and all suggestions should be carefully evaluated for their merit relative to reducing or controlling costs. When hospital and patient care practices are examined in an atmosphere of mutual respect and cooperation, no partner will become defensive. The objective should be known by all participants. How can things be done better while reducing costs? The examination of potential opportunities should proceed with a full review of relevant information, and hospital management staff have the responsibility to make requested data available for committee review. In addition, managers may suggest other known data sources that are available and from which additional opportunities for cost reduction may be identified.

## DEPARTMENTAL INTERDEPENDENCIES AND LATERAL RELATIONSHIPS

Patient care requires the collaborative effort of many hospital departments. Opportunities abound for promoting and encouraging mutual problem solving among these participating departments. Managers in each area have to support the philosophy that quality patient care at controlled or reduced costs is the major objective and that hospitals must find

ways to reduce costs. No department or division should be allowed to make unilateral decisions that affect patient care without consultation and involvement of the users. The concept of problem solving at the source of the problem should be promoted. Lateral relationships should be facilitated. Nurses working directly with supporting services can expedite patient care and problem resolution. In too many situations, hospital organizations have become too tall, with too many layers of management and supervision. It is time to flatten the organization by removing layers of supervision and promote and encourage multiple direct interdepartmental relationships, with the professional staff of each department viewed as partners in the enterprise who are charged with preserving quality while reducing costs. These lateral decision processes, once created, can succeed in expediting the solutions to problems. Decision making should be brought to the level in the organization where the problems exist.[7] Professional staff, those with the greatest knowledge of the situations, should be given the responsibility to resolve the problems and maximize the productivity of each group in the hospital business of patient care.

Clinician I's (head nurses) are a key group of nursing managers. They are responsible, in collaboration with their nursing staff, for the delivery of nursing care and the management of patient care on discrete units. As first-line managers, the clinicians are instrumental in establishing effective lateral relationships between hospital departments for efficient problem solving relative to the patient's total care. When there is a patient need that must be met with the assistance of ancillary or support services, the networks of lateral relationships should be so well established that a telephone call to the respective department's manager results in a satisfactory resolution of the patient's need or provides the resources required for the nurse to meet those needs. Eventually, if the concept of shared ownership is successfully implanted, all staff members in collaborating patient care departments will respond to each other's requests to meet patient and family needs in a quality, cost-effective and efficient manner. There will not be a need for manager-to-manager consultation, and efficiency as well as effectiveness will be enhanced.

## PROGRAM MANAGEMENT

The full implementation of the concepts of shared ownership in the hospital and partnerships for patient care may well be expressed in program or matrix management. In the latter, nurses, physicians, other providers and administrators are given the delegated responsibility to manage a patient care program in its entirety. Management teams are created to deal with the affairs of specific patient care programs and are responsible for program planning, budget formulation, operations, and their

control and evaluation.[8] These teams of professionals consider themselves partners in the hospital organization and in the management and operation of its programs. Finding ways to achieve program objectives within available resources are the teams' responsibility. Program management teams will conduct their operations in concert with the hospital's and the program's long-range plans while achieving current institutional objectives. Differentiated programs that are integrated through effective administration can result in successful accomplishment of the hospital's mission and goals, which include quality care at controlled costs.

## RESULTS OF THE PARTNERSHIP CONCEPT

An important result of the act of establishing the partnership concept for hospital nurses in the business of patient care is a significant change in how the nurses will perceive themselves in the organization. Nurses who are treated as equal professionals in the hospital business will want to shed the cloak of hourly employees and move to full professional status, in salaried positions. Already this is becoming apparent in selected institutions. Health care providers are well into the process of creating an explicit partnership in the business of quality patient care at controlled costs. As a part of fiscal control, increasing attention is directed to reducing overtime expenses. Nurses on the staff are reacting. They maintain that they are the best judges of when patient care requires more of their time, and perhaps the answer is to move them to salaried positions so they will not have to worry about overtime. Their view should be supported, and they should be encouraged to move forward. Nurses functioning as salaried professionals is a logical extension of professionalism and of the partnership concept, and this type of arrangement should be tested and evaluated.

Members of a partnership expect to participate in the matters that constitute the business of the organization. Consequently, nurses expect to participate in determining the standards of patient care in the hospital and in formulating procedures and policies that will facilitate the meeting of these standards. Nurses' expertise in the selection and use of patient care supplies and equipment is particularly important and can result in significant cost reductions. For example, in one institution, nurses participated in an evaluation of linen supplies and their usage. The nurses' observations were that the majority of patients did not require hospital-furnished robes since they brought these in from home, as instructed in the preadmission information materials. Simultaneously, managers in support services suggested the elimination of a flannel incontinent pad, and the nursing staff agreed to use disposable underpads only. These two suggestions combined have resulted in a projected annual cost savings of $50,000,

with no alteration in the quality of patient care services.

The quality assurance programs in hospitals also have produced excellent examples of improvements that can be made in patient care and hospital processes when health care providers collaborate on identifying and resolving problems with potential negative impact on patient care. In a majority of quality assurance studies, the consistent finding is that multiple groups or departments are involved in ensuring the delivery of quality care at established standards. The interdependencies in the hospital organization are extensive. Patient care requires the coordinated efforts of many individuals in many departments. In most of these patient care activities, nurses are directly or indirectly involved. If managers succeed in making nurses explicit partners in the hospital business of patient care, they can expect significant returns to the business.

Satisfied nursing staff participating as partners in the hospital enterprise will want to stay with the organization. Patient care will benefit by having experienced nurses on the staff. Productivity will be higher and costs will be reduced. Dollars directed to recruitment can be diverted to other important hospital programs. Resources that had gone to repetitive orientation programs can be routed to inservice and continuing education programs to increase the knowledge and skills of the staff. When well-qualified, experienced nurses give high quality patient care, patients and families will be satisfied and pleased with the services of the hospital. Risk management costs may be reduced. When qualified, experienced nurses are available to care for patients, a total care concept can be effectively implemented and fragmentation of services eliminated. Many hospitals, for example, have the professional nurses and physicians share the responsibilities for intravenous therapy, eliminating the costs of special IV teams.

A knowledgeable group of experienced nurses can participate significantly in nursing and hospital affairs. To maximize the potential contributions of a large number of new partners, nursing and hospital management will have to ensure that accurate and complete information on the state of the business is disseminated. For example, the fiscal problems that hospitals are experiencing will have to be shared in detail. If fiscal survival is at stake, the partners in the business must be informed in order to participate maximally. If the nursing staff know the facts of the financial situation facing hospitals, they can actively participate in finding solutions. Quality patient care is the bottom line. However, managers can and must find ways in which nurses and others can deliver the same quality at reduced costs. It cannot be hospital business as usual. They must find ways to conduct the business of patient care in a more effective and cost-efficient manner. If nurses view themselves and are viewed by significant others as part-

ners in the enterprise and if they are given essential management information, they will actively participate in finding new approaches to quality patient care at lower costs, and they will ensure that the changes get implemented.

Hospital administration and management personnel must increase the flow of management information if they are to succeed in creating these new partnerships. To promote and facilitate cost reductions, nurses and physicians must know the costs of the various components of patient care, including supplies and equipment items. For example, what are the costs of the individual linen items used multiple times each day—a sheet, a pillow case, a gown, an incontinent pad, a bath blanket? Perhaps if the costs were itemized and visible in each patient care area, conservation and discriminating utilization would be facilitated. What are the costs and what is the specific relevance to patient care management of frequently ordered diagnostic or monitoring examinations, such as the CBC and WBC differential, the type and hold, the urinalysis or a routine chest X-ray? In collaboration with managers in the ancillary services, data relative to indications, usefulness and costs of tests can be prepared and disseminated to ensure quality care at controlled cost. Newsletters from these departments can be effective tools in reaching this objective. One such example is a newsletter from Clinical Pathology Laboratories which featured "The WBC

Differential—How Useful?"[9] The concluding statement in this article illustrates the point:

The indications for a CBC (Hemoglobin, Hematocrit, WBC count, RBC indices) and a WBC differential count (with blood smear examination) should be considered separately based on the patient's clinical status rather than ordered together in a routine fashion. This should allow for the most efficient and appropriate utilization of these commonly ordered laboratory tests. (P. 2)

Another important area is the costs of drugs. What do specific drugs cost? If lists of drug charges were readily available throughout the patient care areas, physicians and nurses would become more diligent in ensuring the daily review of all orders to ensure their continued relevance to the management of the patients' care.

The opportunities for revising practices and procedures are extensive. Administrators and managers have to create the organizational environment in which hospital staff perceive themselves and are perceived by others as partners in the enterprise. It may be necessary to find new ways of rewarding partners for excellent contributions that result in

---

*Administrators and managers have to create the organizational environment in which hospital staff perceive themselves and are perceived by others as partners in the enterprise.*

---

significant cost reductions. Z-type organizations, according to Ouchi, provide bonuses to all employees based on the firm's total accomplishments.[10] Perhaps hospitals could consider the bonus concept if financial expenditure targets within established volume projections are maintained. Employee suggestion programs can also be considered in which individual employees can be rewarded for recommending approaches to doing business that result in significant cost savings.

Innovative programs in personnel management also should be explored and tested. For example, employee absenteeism results in significant institutional costs and potential disruptions in levels of services provided. Incentive programs that financially recognize the employee's consistent attendance in performing responsibilities may hold the potential for additional significant dollar savings for the institution. Other personnel programs with high potential for contributing to ensuring quality care at controlled costs include a longevity benefits program for nursing staff and clinical advancement systems.

A longevity benefits program can be particularly attractive to members of the nursing staff whose careers in direct patient care traditionally have meant a life-long commitment to rotating shifts and weekend work. Longevity benefits can be designed that reward nurses whose goals are to continue in direct patient care practice throughout their career. One such program includes shift of choice after ten years of service and every weekend off after 15 years of service. Such a program means that nurses who elect careers in hospital nursing practice can look forward to working straight days, Monday through Friday, by the time they reach the age of 35 to 40 years, or about the beginning of their mid-career phase. This approximates the time when individuals in other careers are getting the perquisites relative to advanced status in an organization. Such a program may provide sufficient incentive to help hold well-qualified, expert staff in hospital nursing. These experienced individuals will then be available to contribute their knowledge and skills in meeting institutional objectives. Furthermore, dollars and nursing care hours formerly spent on recruitment and orientation programs can be directed to other important nursing and patient care programs. In addition, productivity is enhanced as a result of the continuous availability of experienced nurses who are skilled in administering complex patient care and who are thoroughly familiar with the hospital, its staff, their practices and the expected standards of care.

Clinical advancement systems also recognize nurses who intend to make direct patient care a life-long career. As the nurse advances in knowledge, in expertise and in the contributions made to patient care, nursing practice and the entire organization, opportunities are made available for promotion with increasing financial rewards, expanding professional re-

sponsibilities and continuing professional enrichment. Such programs also contribute to the retention of a critical mass of well-qualified, expert nurses who have increasing corporate knowledge and who make extensive contributions to quality patient care and the mission of the institution.

Hospital managers must listen to their staff and continually encourage their suggestions, directly posing such questions as the following: How can we make this a better place for patient care and for staff to receive personal and professional satisfaction? Can you identify ways for us to streamline our procedures to save money? Are we judiciously ordering and using supplies? Are there other products that we could use to deliver the same quality of care at reduced prices? Are there different approaches we should be investigating to deliver patient care services?

Different participative management techniques need to be explored and tested to optimize staff participation. Quality circles, where interested staff members of a unit or department regularly meet to explore better ways of doing things, have resulted in noteworthy improvements and cost reductions in many industries. With hospitals emphasizing quality assurance in every department, a logical extension may be the initiation of quality circles.

Various scheduling approaches should also be investigated. When a staff's attention is directed to measures that can improve productivity, a frequent outcome is a revision of schedules that results in a better distribution of staff to meet patient care and institutional demands. Again, a service and institutional perspective is important. Staff will then appreciate the need to "float" to another area in times of high patient care demands and will know that reciprocity is expected to ensure quality and control costs.

A centralized approach to some services may also result in significant cost savings. For example, a nutritional support service was created in one institution, and within a year significant reductions in costs were realized as a result of standardization of enteral and parenteral nutrition products used. In addition, a home total parenteral nutrition program was successfully implemented, with significant reductions in the costs of managing complex nutritional problems.

In institutions that operate within the philosophy of participative management, and implement the concept of shared ownership amongst partners in the corporate enterprise, many additional program opportunities will be generated. The total number and the best approaches have yet to be determined. However, full participation of employees, opportunities for advancement, personnel recognition programs, along with the concept of incentives are important aspects for hospitals to consider, evaluate and, where feasible, implement.

Extending the partnership concept to the members of the nursing staff is one step in involving key hospital staff in achieving the objective of quality care at reduced and controlled costs. Creating an organization in which all employee groups perceive the institution as their own, that is, incorporating the view of shared ownership, may be the critical ingredient in helping hospitals get control of spiraling costs. This is the challenge of the 1980s for hospital managers.

## REFERENCES

1. Lesparre, M. "Synopsis '82 Budget Battles Dominate Congress." *Hospitals* 56 (December 16, 1982): 69.
2. "Coalitions Called Key to Health Care Reform." *Hospitals* 56 (December 16, 1982): 20.
3. American Hospital Association. *Hospital Nurse Recruitment and Retention, A Source Book for Executive Management.* Chicago: AHA, n.d.
4. Likert, R. *The Human Organization: Its Management and Value.* New York: McGraw-Hill, 1967, pp. 136–38.
5. Ouchi, W.G. *Theory Z.* New York: Avon Books, 1982.
6. Barnes, L.B., "Managing the Paradox of Organizational Trust." *Harvard Business Review* 56 (March/April 1981): 107–16.
7. Galbraith, J. *Designing Complex Organizations.* Reading, Mass.: Addison-Wesley, 1973, p. 18.
8. Davis, S., and Lawrence, P.R. *Matrix.* Reading, Mass.: Addison-Wesley, 1977.
9. *Clinical Pathology Laboratories Newsletter* 8, no. 3. Rochester, N.Y.: Strong Memorial Hospital, April 1983.
10. Ouchi, *Theory Z,* pp. 20–21.

# Human need theory: a framework for the nurse supervisor

*Helen Yura*
*Graduate Program Director*
*Department of Nursing*
*Old Dominion University*
*Norfolk, Virginia*

CONCEPTUAL AND theoretical frameworks for nursing practice have been the focus of nursing practitioners for more than a decade. Conceptual–theoretical systems of knowledge are required for clinical nursing practice, nursing education, nursing service administration, and nursing research. These frameworks facilitate nursing decisions and provide the substantive knowledge base for research validating that the prescribed nursing interventions have made a difference. The data generated by using the conceptual–theoretical frameworks for nursing contribute to the discovery of new nursing knowledge and, particularly, nursing theory development. The nurse supervisor has sought and is influenced by current conceptual–theoretical developments in nursing. Albert Einstein tells us that "creating a new theory is not like destroying an old barn and erecting a skyscraper in

*Health Care Superv,* 1986,4(3),45–58
© 1986 Aspen Publishers, Inc.

its place. It is rather like climbing a mountain, gaining new and wider views, discovering unexpected connections . . . . But the point from which we started out still exists although it appears smaller and a tiny part of our broad view."[1] Hersey states that a theory helps to explain and interpret why things happen as they do. "Theories deal with insight."[2] For the nurse supervisor, using a conceptual–theoretical framework for the application of the supervisory process can broaden the view of the self as a supervisor as well as of the persons being supervised. This heightened view of the work environment and of the relationships between and among coworkers, colleagues, those supervised, those who direct the supervisor, and the nurse supervisor contributes to improved communication, improved problem solving, prevention of crisis states in the work environment, and self-fulfillment. It provides the rationale for actions and prepares the supervisor to anticipate the human responses to the world of work. In fact, it gives the nurse supervisor the know-how to anticipate and influence future events.

Considering that the actions of the nurse supervisor are closest to the organizational level where the specific client nursing services are rendered and the organizational objectives are realized, and considering that the nurse supervisor is responsible for a larger number of persons than the administrative persons at higher levels in the hierarchical structure, the sup-

port for the supervisor's use of a conceptual–theoretical framework for action is well placed. Human need theory is a theory that has considerable utility for the nurse supervisor. It consists of knowledge to assist the nurse supervisor to explain, interpret, and predict the behavior of the nursing staff, coworkers, colleagues, and the self in the work setting. It contains the basis for the deciding, relating, influencing, and facilitating behaviors of the nurse supervisor required for goal achievement—effective, economical, person–family centered nursing care.

## ELEMENTS OF HUMAN NEED THEORY

Human need theorists view the person as an integrated, organized whole who is motivated toward meeting human needs. "A human need is viewed as an internal tension that results from an alteration in some state of the system. This tension expresses itself in goal-directed behavior of the person that continues until goal satisfaction (freedom from tension) is achieved."[3] Two significant concepts of human need theory are need satisfaction (gratification) and need fulfillment deprivation. A person is motivated to fulfill human needs; these human needs are met through a variety of societal structures—through families, communities, groups (including the work place), states, the nation, and the family of nations.

Abraham Maslow is generally recognized as a prominent contemporary need theorist in the United States. His works would be most familiar to the nurse supervisor. However, since the mid and late 1970s, human need theory has taken on international significance; scholars from varying nations have come together to develop a framework for action in meeting the human needs of the developed and developing nations of the world. Cleveland, in a 1977 report to the United Nations Environment Programme,wrote that the appearance of human needs at center stage begins "a new act in the continuing drama of world development."[4] Decisions of an international nature based on a human needs framework would recognize and account for the cultural heritage and diversity of the peoples of the world with the goal of maximal satisfaction of the biosocial, psychocultural, and spiritual needs of human beings.[5] Specifically, the theoretical contributions of a few human need theorists comprise what is known today about human needs. For example, Clayton Alderfer has a three-fold conceptualization of human needs, namely, existence, relatedness, and growth. Key words that round out his ideas are desire, frustration, and satisfaction.[6] Combs, Richards, and Richards propose one major human need—the need for adequacy. Adequacy is the force by which the self continually seeks to become more adequate to cope with life. It is akin to self-fulfillment and self-actualization.[7] Four categories of human needs that are the indispensa-

ble ingredients for human, national, and international development have been contributed by Johan Galtung. These are security (survival), welfare (sufficiency), identity (closeness), and freedom. Galtung believes human beings develop their need consciousness in a social context and most are met in a social context. When human needs are not met, some kind of disintegration takes place.[8]

Otto Klineberg states that social and cultural factors play an important part in the expression of biophysical needs. He suggests that need satisfaction must account for differences in age, gender, socioeconomic status, occupation, and educational levels. According to Klineberg, the person is like any other person as determined by a common biological heritage or universal features of social life. The person is like some other persons if he or she belongs to a cultural group but is unique because no other person experiences the same sequence of human experiences.[9] Maslow's contribution is the establishment of a five-level hierarchy of human needs consisting of physical needs (first level), safety needs (second level), belonging and love needs (third level), esteem needs (fourth level), and self-actualization (fifth level). The arrangement in a hierarchy is based on the state of power and strength of these needs. Higher needs emerge when physical needs are reasonably well satisfied.[10] A different theoretical point of view is offered by McHale and McHale, who invented a method of analysis to operationalize the new imperative of meeting human needs for the world community. They emphasized that personal and collective values have a powerful impact on the way human needs are defined and satisfied. Their idea of a human needs framework is comprised of two elements—biophysical and psychosocial—with further categorization of each element based on deficiency needs, sufficiency, and growth needs.[11]

Another categorization of human needs is supplied by Ashly Montagu, that is, vital and nonvital basic human needs. For Montagu, all needs are dependent and must be satisfied by some object(s) in a manner in which they are structured.[12] Lastly, Oscar Nudler views human needs as a dimension of an open system that he refers to as sophisticated holism. He believes there are three fundamental needs: (1) maintenance of an identity, (2) the need to grow, and (3) the need to transcend. Identity and growth needs are viewed as characteristic of all living beings but the need to transcend is specifically a human need.[13]

In conjunction with these theoretical developments, Yura and Walsh have developed a framework of 35 human needs to be used with the nursing process—a problem-solving process applied to nursing. No attempt was made to categorize these needs because it was felt that a particular need could be viewed from a variety of perspectives. For example, the human need for nutrition could have physical, psychological, reli-

gious, cultural, emotional, and social dimensions. Furthermore, it was believed that although human needs can be dealt with as discrete entities, the person must be viewed holistically with the goal of nursing to foster the integrity of the person whether this person be client, staff nurse, or nurse supervisor.[14] The human needs framework can be used with other broad theoretical frameworks such as systems, organizational, change, and leadership theories. In nursing, human needs supply the theoretical substance of the nursing process.

The human needs proposed for use by practitioners of nursing (including nurse supervisors) are the need for acceptance of self and others, by others; for activity; for adaptation and stress management; for air; for appreciation and attention; for autonomy; for choice; for beauty and esthetic experiences; for belonging; for challenge; for conceptualization, rationality, and problem solving; for confidence; for fluids (intake); for nutrition (intake); for elimination; for humor; for interchange of gases (cellular level); for effective perception of reality; for personal recognition, esteem, and respect; for protection from excessive fear, anxiety, and chaos; for rest and leisure; for safety; for self-control, self-determination, and responsibility; for self-fulfillment—to be and to become; for sensory integrity; for sexual integrity; for skin integrity; for sleep; for spiritual integrity; for structure, law, and limits; for tenderness; for territoriality; to love and be loved; for wholesome body image; for challenge; and for a value system.[15]

It is believed that the "preservation of, the fostering of, the maintenance of, and the facilitation of the integrity of all the human needs of person(s) is the territory of nursing."[16] It is within this context of nursing service that the nurse supervisor functions, whether in an acute care or long-term health care setting, an ambulatory care setting, a hospice service, or in home care service.

## HUMAN NEEDS AND THE NURSE SUPERVISOR

The literature abounds with suggestions about supervision, the supervised, and the supervisor. Information is available, for example, about how to delegate, how to negotiate, and how to budget. Yet the theoretical substance for all these efforts is rarely seen. Most often these activities are viewed as discrete processes, in and of themselves, rather than contributing processes within a specified conceptual–theoretical framework.

Human need data can be used successfully by the nurse supervisor to enhance morale and to provide an environment in which quality person- and family-centered nursing care can be provided. These data foster a holistic view of the nursing staff with needs, wants, and aspirations that are met in the work place. In addition, overdependence on the work place as the source (even the exclusive source) for meeting the person's hu-

*Human need data can be used successfully by the nurse supervisor to enhance morale and to provide an environment in which quality person- and family-centered nursing care can be provided.*

man needs can be identified and corrective problem solving initiated.

Human needs can serve as a focus for policy development, review of existing policies, the reward system, and for review of interpersonal and organizational protocols to ensure that nursing staff need fulfillment is facilitated rather than jeopardized. Because the nursing process is the core of nursing practice, the human need framework is already known by the nursing staff. Staff often realize that others (clients) require need fulfillment but are less likely to realize it is also necessary to fulfill their own needs.

A human needs assessment scale has been developed that can be used to provide data about how the staff nurse views the work place. It can provide an idea of the motivation the person has relative to work and can serve as a tool to resolve interpersonal conflicts and goal conflicts, and to handle problem staff members.

The Human Needs Assessment Scale (HNAS) was developed by Linda Lilley as part of a master's thesis at Old Dominion University in Norfolk, Virginia. It is used to establish a rating of importance for the 35 human needs specified earlier. Content and face validity were established. Internal consistency was ascertained using Chronbach's alpha test (.95 reliability coefficient). The scale has been used effectively in a number of nursing research studies. None of these reflected use of the tool by the nurse supervisor to provide human need data suitable to facilitate nursing staff motivation and to understand work behaviors of the staff and self. To determine the extent to which nursing staff members viewed the work place as a source for human need fulfillment, a pilot survey using the HNAS was conducted. Eighteen nursing staff members in an acute care setting and a long-term care setting participated; 14 were registered nurses and 4 were licensed practical nurses. Participants were asked to rate the level of importance of each of the 35 human needs in relation to their work experience. Ratings were made on a 4-point scale with number 1 standing for little or no importance, number 2 for average importance, number 3 for very important, and number 4 for critically important. Nine participants had a bachelor's degree in nursing, three had a master's degree in nursing, two possessed a diploma in nursing, and four had practical nurse education. Survey results indicated that three human needs were rated as either very important or critically important (number 3 and number 4) by all respondents (100 percent): (1) self-control and self-determination; (2) protection from excessive fear, anxiety, and

chaos; and (3) acceptance of self and others. Ninety-four percent of the respondents designated the human needs for appreciation and attention; for personal recognition, esteem, and respect; and for adaptation and stress management as very important or critically important in relation to the work experience. Table 1 includes the percentages for human needs designated as very important and critically important.

This pilot survey suggests nursing staff do identify human needs as important in the work experience. A much larger study is needed to further validate this database. It would be interesting to learn the rationale for the designations of level of importance and how the staff viewed specific need fulfillment in the work place. For example, the nurse supervisor can develop a profile of questions and circumstances relating to the 35 human needs to use in facilitating appropriate human need fulfillment in the work place and to strengthen the power, influence, and facilitating bases for the supervisor. Rewards and constructive problem interventions can be developed within the human need framework to motivate staff. Hersey acknowledges that nothing by itself is rewarding or punishing. "What's rewarding for one person might be seen by someone else as punishing. It depends on a person's *need satisfaction*"[17] (italics added).

It would be interesting to use the HNAS as a data gathering device when new staff has been appointed and then use the results for staff as-

**Table 1.** Percentages of very important (no. 3) and critically important (no. 4) responses for 35 human needs*

| Percent | Human needs |
| --- | --- |
| 100 . . . | Self-control, self-determination; protection from excessive fear, anxiety, chaos; acceptance of self and others |
| 94 . . . | Appreciation, attention; personal recognition, esteem, and respect; adaptation, stress management |
| 89 . . . | Interchange of gases (cellular level); confidence; to love and be loved; skin integrity |
| 88 . . . | Air |
| 83 . . . | Humor; beauty and esthetic experiences; safety; belonging; conceptualization, rationality, problem solving; self-fulfillment, to be, to become; autonomy, choice; wholesome body image |
| 78 . . . | Freedom from pain; effective perception of reality; tenderness; challenge |
| 76 . . . | Fluids |
| 72 . . . | Rest and leisure; elimination; value system; sensory integrity |
| 71 . . . | Nutrition |
| 67 . . . | Territoriality; sleep; activity |
| 55 . . . | Structure, law, limits |

* Adapted with permission from Linda Lilley. Information and permission to use the Human Needs Assessment Scale can be obtained from Linda Lilley, Department of Nursing, Old Dominian University, Norfolk, Virginia 23508. The author acknowledges Linda Lilley and Mary B. Walsh for providing data from the nursing staff pilot survey using the Human Needs Assessment Scale.

signment. For example, if nursing staff in an intensive care unit see higher importance in physically or biologically related human needs, the nurse supervisor might seek and assign a staff member who sees psychosocial–spiritual needs as critically important to balance the human need focus for the clients receiving care.

The following profile can provide a start for the nurse supervisor's application of the human need theory framework.

- *Acceptance of self:* Do the staff members approve of their own conduct and the conduct of others in the work setting? Are they accepting of individual capabilities and limitations? Do evaluative procedures reflect that capabilities are expected but that areas of limitations require identification, acceptance, and a protocol for offsetting these limitations?

- *Activity:* Are staff members encouraged to maintain an effective exercise program to maintain healthy function? Do these persons have options on an exercise program in the work place? Are facilities and safe areas available if staff choose to exercise during breaks or at mealtime? Is the layout of the work setting and the availability of supplies and equipment such that energy of staff is not wasted? Are there mechanical aids and sufficient personnel available to help in lifting, moving, and transporting clients?

- *Adaptation, stress management:* Is the staff member able to cope with the stresses and strains of the work situation? Are schedules and assignments appropriate to the preparation and competencies of the person? Is the workload fair and equitable? Are staff conferences planned periodically to explore solutions for stressful work situations? Does the staff member resort to chemical agents to ease stress?

- *Air:* Is air quality controlled so that staff members will maximize aeration? Is smoking allowed in the work place? Are policies in place regarding the handling and administration of gases (as oxygen) for therapeutic purposes? Is aseptic technique used to minimize transfer of airborne diseases for staff and clients?

- *Appreciation, attention:* Is the staff member capable of putting his or her mind to thought or to matters related to determining, planning, implementing, and evaluating nursing care? Does this person show ability to be aware of what is happening in the work place? While at the work place, does this person give full attention or is this person merely there physically, prone to distractions? Does the work environment lend itself to maximizing attentiveness of the staff? Are distractions and interruptions

kept to a minimum? Do staff members think well of themselves? Are they thought well of by colleagues, coworkers, and supervisors?

- *Autonomy, choice:* Is the staff member expected to make personal decisions and to accommodate the choices inherent in role(s) and responsibilities? Do policies and procedures in the work place allow autonomy and choice or are they restrictive, particularly for well-educated, highly competent staff? Do evaluative procedures expect and account for autonomy and choices inherent in one's role and the organizational structure?

- *Beauty and esthetic experiences:* Is the environment in which the staff member works attractive and pleasant? Are colors, architectural design, windows, and furnishings placed for maximum esthetic effect and effective use of available space? Is the work place clean and orderly? Are paintings and flowers selected with care and arranged for positive healing impact? Do color and arrangements for administrative quarters convey power and authority as well as beauty? Does the staff member take time to acknowledge this beauty and to arrange for esthetic experiences for self?

- *Belonging:* Does the staff member experience a sense of collegiality in the work setting? Do policies and schedules promote the establishment of working relationships? Are staff assignments constantly in a state of flux so that little sense of belonging and loyalty can be developed?

- *Challenge:* Is the staff member expected to strive to provide a high standard of nursing care? Are administrative support and resources available to facilitate meeting this challenge? Is the staff member challenged to acquire advanced educational preparation in nursing so that improved and expanded levels of nursing service can be rendered?
- *Conceptualization, rationality, problem solving:* Is the staff member expected to apply knowledge and continue to expand his or her professional knowledge base? Does the staff member demonstrate mastery of the nursing process? Is this person capable of using research results to enhance nursing practice? Does the staff member use common sense? Does this person participate in idea development and idea analysis as a means of improving the nursing service rendered and the overall setting in which care is given? Does this person know that priority is given to providing nursing care to clients? Is this priority fostered rather than having priority taken by organizationally related activities?
- *Confidence:* Is there evidence that the staff member is capable and confident in the role(s) ful-

filled in the work setting? Do personnel policies and evaluation procedures enhance the confidence of the staff member who is goal directed, appropriately productive, and competent? Is there a system of rewards (monetary, verbal, written) with established criteria for staff members?

- *Excretion, ingestion:* Does the staff member have appropriate breaks to handle elimination? Is the temperature and humidity of the work environment appropriate so that elimination through skin and lungs are not compromised? Does the staff member have the opportunity to take in liquids, such as water, in the amounts required for normal body function? Do policies and staffing patterns facilitate breaks and mealtimes? Is there evidence of a "drinking problem" (i.e., abuse of alcohol or other substances that might impair functioning in the work place)?
- *Freedom from pain:* Can the staff member work in relative comfort without undue experience of strains, back injury, or accidents? Are mechanical devices available to help in the lifting and transporting of incapacitated clients? Are inservice education programs planned to update staff members on techniques and procedures to protect against bodily injury? Are staff members treated fairly and considered as persons with both strengths and limita-

tions to minimize emotional pain?

- *Humor:* Does the staff member experience laughter that has a positive effect on state of mind? Does this sense of humor enhance relationships and aid in coping with frustration?
- *Interchange of gases (cellular level):* Is the physical condition of the staff member such that the workload can be accomplished? Does the staff member enjoy good health? Is an annual physical examination with appropriate laboratory studies a requirement?
- *Nutrition:* Does the staff member take responsibility for keeping well by maintaining adequate nutrition? Does this person maintain adequate weight and appropriate energy level to fulfill role(s) and responsibilities? Does the staff person refrain from taking in harmful substances (chemical abuse) that would diminish intellectual, interpersonal, and technical functioning? Do work schedules and staffing patterns allow for sufficient time for meals?
- *Effective perception of reality:* Does the staff member make accurate judgments about the persons and circumstances of the work place? Do evaluation protocols and the database reflect what is reality concerning the staff member? Do evaluative decisions about staff take into account these realistic data?

- *Personal recognition, esteem, respect:* Is the staff member given recognition for fulfilling the professional role? Is this person held in high regard in the work place? Is this person recognized when meritorious service is rendered? Is this recognition verbal, written, and conveyed to the staff of the total organization with a copy in the person's personnel file?
- *Protection from excessive fear, anxiety, chaos:* Is the work setting appropriately staffed? Is the manner of supervision such that motivation, not fear or anxiety, is the outcome? Is the unit well organized with space, material, and human resources available to meet clients' nursing care requirements? Does the design of the work place minimize distractions and errors?
- *Rest and leisure:* Does the staff member make appropriate use of breaks and rest periods so that energy levels and coping ability are replenished and performance is maintained throughout the work period? Does this person allow for self-rest and leisure so that he or she comes to the work place with enough energy to complete the professional role? Is time allowed for vacations, holidays, and special days? Are staffing patterns such that days off are reasonably placed—no persons work for prolonged periods of time without time off?
- *Safety:* Is the environment of the work place free of hazards from

electricity, radiation, chemicals, and noxious substances? Are policies formulated and carried out rigidly to protect staff members from pathological organisms, communicable diseases, and work-related infections? Are policies for sick leave fair and available so that staff members ill with infectious and communicable diseases can stay home from work to recover?

- *Self control, self-determination:* Does the staff member have power over his or her actions in the work place? Is this person capable of professional decision making? Does this person know the parameters of the professional role, and can he or she implement this role?
- *Self-fulfillment—to be, to become:* Does the staff member have a well-defined set of short-, intermediate-, and long-range goals for the self? Do these goals incorporate career development and expanded roles and responsibilities in the work setting? Does the staff member invest time, energy, and talent in the work place so that a sense of fulfillment from work accomplished can be experienced?
- *Sensory integrity:* Is the staff member free of visual and hearing problems? If impairments exist, are corrective measures taken to ensure sensory acuity? Are the senses of smell, touch, and taste functional? Can the staff member collect data through use of the senses and provide information, value, and healing in the practice of nursing? Is the staff member able to use data obtained through the senses or conveyed to clients through the senses in an effective, goal-directed, professional manner? Does the staff member maintain the health of the senses and refrain from abuse of the senses while in the work place through neglect, carelessness, or drugs? Does the work place have the lighting, soundproofing, humidity, and temperature to facilitate maximum sensory function of the staff member?

- *Sexual integrity:* Does the staff member feel stigmatized by gender-related stereotypes? Is the staff member accepting of his or her masculinity or femininity? Is this person valued, promoted, and compensated for professional competencies unrelated to gender? Is the work place free of evidence of sexual harassment? Is this person restricted from power positions within the health care organization solely on the basis of gender?
- *Skin integrity:* Are staff members expected to maintain personal hygiene and follow rules of asepsis in caring for clients? When skin injuries occur in the work place, are staff expected to seek treatment, and is treatment readily available? Is the environment evaluated for places, things, and substances that could be injurious to or compromise the skin of

staff and clients? Are products available for use by staff in caring for clients tested for allergic reactions? Are gloves and other bodily coverings available in the work place to protect staff?

- *Sleep:* Does the staff member come to the work setting alert and capable of fulfilling professional role(s) and responsibilities? Do staffing patterns take into account the biological rhythms of the staff? Are shift changes made considering sleep needs of the staff and the amount of time needed to change and adjust to a new sleep pattern? Are staff expected to work longer shifts or are new staff hired to accommodate an increased workload or changes in the amount of work to be done? Does the staff member show evidence of the aftermath of drug-induced sleep or take drugs to stay awake?

- *Spiritual experience:* Is fulfillment of personal spiritual needs expected of staff members? Does the staff member have the opportunity to fulfill religious obligations through scheduling adjustments, requested days off, and so forth? Are religious dietary expectations considered in planning meal offerings available for purchase in the work setting? Are resources available on which the staff member can draw for assistance in aiding clients to meet clients' spiritual needs?

- *Structure, law, limits:* Does the staff member function within the organizational structure and follow established lines of communication and formulated policies? Is the organizational structure reviewed periodically to ensure that it facilitates service goal achievement? Are policies reviewed to keep them current and to facilitate the rendering of service to clients? If policies are restrictive, vague, or discriminatory are they changed or eliminated? Is priority in use of staff time within the organization's structure, law, and limits given to nursing care of clients? Or is this priority organizationally related or related to servicing persons holding power and authority?

- *Tenderness:* Is the staff member receptive to acts of kindness in the work place? Does this person portray kindness in dealing with colleagues, coworkers, clients and their families, and administrative personnel?

- *Territoriality:* Does the staff member know and control the work space? Is the personal territory of the person respected? Is the staff member's right to privacy and protection from unlawful disclosure respected? Does the staff member respect the territory and privacy of others, particularly clients? Can this person distinguish between and among data that must be disclosed or reported and that which should be kept confidential? Does the staff member know how to present personal data—to whom, when, in what manner, how much, and where?

- *To love and be loved:* Does the staff member feel that the work environment fosters wholesome collegial relationships? Are the interpersonal relationships that prevail sensitive to the needs, feelings, and aspirations of co-workers, colleagues, staff, and supervisory personnel?
- *Wholesome body image:* Is the staff member expected to portray the image of the healthy person—in appearance and practice? Do policies refrain from restricting height and weight as an employment condition if there is no basis for such restrictions? Is the overall grooming and appearance of the staff member, including hair style and nails, appropriate for the work place to prevent injury to self or to clients? Is the garb that is worn reflective of the special requirements for the client or necessary for the safe use of therapeutic equipment, for example, asepsis garb or nonconductive shoes?
- *Value system:* Does the staff member have a well-developed ethical sense? Can this person set priorities that reflect the importance and worth of persons and their human predicament? Is the staff member considerate of the varying value systems of clients?

The human need framework can also be serviceable for the nurse supervisor in developing the self—the

*A supervisor whose human needs are reasonably well met will more likely facilitate the human needs of those being supervised and will be able to identify and use problem solving when the nursing staff overuse the work place and colleagues and coworkers for need fulfillment.*

self replenished away from as well as in the work place. A supervisor whose human needs are reasonably well met will more likely facilitate the human needs of those being supervised and will be able to identify and use problem solving when the nursing staff overuse the work place and colleagues and coworkers for need fulfillment. These abilities are strategic to successful supervision and leadership. Judicious use of need fulfillment strategies can serve to reward or punish through knowledge of a staff person's need fulfillment vulnerability—a challenge for the nurse supervisor. Because the nurse supervisor's human need fulfillment in the work place is dependent not only on those supervised but also on the supervisor's superior, the nurse supervisor is more able to reap particular rewards for self-motivation, thereby enhancing need fulfillment and, as a result, job satisfaction. The supervisor's superior can apply the human need theory framework to foster the nurse supervisor's role development. The profile of human needs presented earlier can be useful to the nurse supervisor who merely substitutes *nurse supervisor* wherever *nursing staff* occurs in the statement.

•   •   •

Human need theory has significant utility for all persons involved in health care, not only in nursing. Members of health disciplines can collaborate with nursing staff to provide a collective environment for effective and fulfilling productivity. Human need theory application, as a common ground, can enhance communication between and among interdisciplinary members and promote understanding of each discipline's unique role as well as those areas where role functions may overlap. When the focus for the client of health services, including nursing, is on meeting human needs, the actions of health workers can be more goal directed—to improve the client's health through need fulfillment. In addition, attention by interdisciplinary members to meeting human needs in the work place can promote personal and professional satisfaction.

## REFERENCES

1. Sutterley, D., and Donnelly, G. *Perspectives in Human Development: Nursing Throughout the Life Cycle*. Philadelphia: Lippincott, 1973, p. 25.
2. Hersey, P. *The Situational Leader*. New York: Warner Books, 1984, p. 10.
3. Yura, H., and Walsh, M.B. *The Nursing Process*. East Norwalk, Conn.: Appleton-Century-Crofts, 1983, p. 79.
4. Ibid., 89.
5. Ibid.
6. Ibid.
7. Ibid.
8. Ibid.
9. Ibid.
10. Ibid.
11. Ibid.
12. Ibid.
13. Lederer, K. *Human Needs*. Cambridge, Mass.: Oelgeschlager, Gunn & Hain, 1980.
14. Yura and Walsh, *The Nursing Process*.
15. Ibid., 94.
16. Ibid., 79.
17. Hersey, *The Situational Leader*, 106.

# The nurse supervisor as scholar

*Helen Yura*
*Eminent Professor*
*School of Nursing*
*Old Dominion University*
*Norfolk, Virginia*

THE NURSE supervisor is more likely to be viewed as an administrator in the work setting than as a scholar. However, opportunities for scholarliness abound for the nurse supervisor, and the benefits from scholarly efforts accrue to the nurse supervisor, as well as to his or her colleagues, coworkers, and clients. It is assumed that the nurse supervisor has the minimum academic preparation of the baccalaureate degree in nursing with the expectation of a Master's degree in nursing. Doctoral preparation, too, should be included as a future goal by the nurse supervisor.

The scholarliness of the nurse supervisor permeates all dimensions of professional function within the formal organization as well as professional and community activities external to it. Scholarliness incorporates the following:

*Health Care Superv*, 1987, 6(1), 66–77
© 1987 Aspen Publishers, Inc.

- active involvement in research to promote nursing theory development and improved nursing services to clients and their families;
- application of research results to nursing practice and administrative problems;
- sensitivity to and determination of problem statements for research stemming from nursing roles, relationships, and services;
- accommodation of nurse researchers through the approval mechanism and population selection;
- acceptance of adjunct professor status in college and university nursing programs;
- acquisition of nurse scholars to serve as consultants to nurse supervisors and nursing staffs;
- facilitation of collaborative practice arrangements with nurse scholars in academic settings;
- presentation of scholarly papers within and outside the formal organization;
- publication of papers, chapters, articles, and books stemming from the research and practice of the nurse supervisor: and
- informal and active participation in professional nursing, interdisciplinary, and community organizations to improve nursing and health services to clients and to enhance the image of nursing.

A scholar can be simply described as a learned person—a person who has significant knowledge in a prescribed area of learning, is capable of critical thinking, and is creative. The scholar is a person who values thinking as a prelude to doing and as concomitant to doing. The scholar is a problem solver. A scholar encourages and values scholarliness in himself or herself as well as in others. A scholar is appreciative of the time required for thinking and the amount of time that can be saved through thinking. The scholar knows that scholarliness entails enormous efforts.

From where was this professional model of the scholar and of scholarliness generated? The literature abounds with descriptions of scholars, the fruits of scholarly efforts, and scholarly advice. The substance of scholarliness, gleaned from the words of scholars who have made pronouncements about thinking, follows.

## SUBSTANCE OF SCHOLARLINESS

Howard Mumford Jones states that ours is an age that is proud of machines that think and suspicious of any person who tries it. Allen follows with "to begin to think with purpose, is to enter the ranks of those strong ones who only recognize failure as one of the pathways to attainment; who make all conditions serve them, and who think strongly, attempt fearlessly, and accomplish masterfully."[1] He believes doubts and fears should be rigorously excluded because they are the great enemies of knowledge. The scholars who encourage doubt and fear thwart themselves at every step.[2] The higher the scholars aim their thoughts, the more righteous and successful they become and the more valued and enduring will be their accomplishments.[3]

"Intellectual achievements are the results of thought consecrated to search for knowledge"[4] or the truth in life experiences and in nature. Allen cautions that "humanity cannot forget its dreamers; it cannot let ideals fade and die; it lives in them; it knows them as the *realities* which it shall one day see and know."[5] He believes dreams are the seedlings of realities.[6] Allen is explicit when he says that into our hands will be placed the exact results of our thoughts—we receive exactly what we earn; no more or less. "Whatever your present environment may be, you will fall, remain, or rise with your thoughts, your visions, your ideal."[7]

Scholars become known through their triumphs. Often little is seen of the trials, failures, and struggles that the person has voluntarily encountered to gain the experience and complete the work or idea. Furthermore, the scholar's public frequently has little or no knowledge of the sacrifices made, of the perseverance employed, of the faith exercised so the often insurmountable could be overcome to achieve the scholar's vision and goal. "They do not know the darkness and the heartaches; they only can see the light and joy, and call it 'luck'; do not see the long and arduous journey but only behold the pleasant goal, and call it 'good fortune'; do not understand the process, but only perceive the result, and call

it 'chance'."[8] Allen concludes by stating that in all human affairs there are efforts and results. The strength of the effort is the measure of the result. Chance is not involved. " 'Gifts,' powers, material, intellectual, and spiritual possessions are the fruits of effort; they are thoughts completed, objects accomplished, visions realized."[9]

Leslie Stephen believes that a person can only exert influence by encouraging another person to think for himself or herself as opposed to having that person merely accept the opinions of others. Thoughts are considered the predecessors of ideas that can lead to action and results. Henry Ford emphasized that people who have no time do not think because by thinking more you give yourself more time. John Hancock Field has pointed out that while many people formulate ideas, few people act on their thoughts. Richard Guggenhumer cautions that most of us splash about in our thinking and mistake the ripples of our noisy commotion with real movement.

Thus, the substance of scholarliness can be characterized by critical thinking, goal orientation, idea generation, dreaming, and persevering. Translating thinking and ideas into purposeful human-oriented action is the hallmark of scholarliness.

## NURSE SUPERVISOR AS SCHOLAR

The role of scholar is a difficult one for the nurse supervisor and other practitioners of nursing who are often heavily pressured to do more and more for consumers of nursing with fewer and fewer human resources. This situation is imposed on the nurse scholar more by circumstances than by choice. But there are choices, and the nurse supervisor scholar should dwell on these.

Drawing further on the words of the scholars who have made pronouncements about thinking, the following excerpt, adapted from a speech to the American Law Institute on May 7, 1936, has merit for the nurse supervisor scholar.

How amazing is it that, in the midst of controversies on every conceivable subject, one should expect unanimity of opinions upon difficult law questions. In the highest ranges of thought . . . we find differences of view on the part of the most distinguished experts. . . . The history of scholarships is a record of disagreements, and when we deal with questions relating to principles of law and their application we do not suddenly rise into a stratosphere of icy certainty.[10]

The word "nursing" can be substituted for the word "law," and the same argument applied to the field of nursing.

This lack of unanimity of opinion about difficult nursing questions applies directly to efforts to develop nursing theory. Nursing scholars in academic and practice settings are immersed in theory development and, as theoreticians or as contributors, draw heavily on data from nursing practice. Nursing as a practice discipline must concern itself with the development of theory that will assist nurses in using relevant knowledge to guide actions. The quality of nursing actions is directly related to the level of the individual's knowledge and understanding. It is through nursing theory that this level of knowledge and the depth of understanding can be increased so that the quality of nursing care will be enhanced. It is the nurse supervisor scholar who draws on a theoretical base to guide practice so that time spent with the nursing staff and consumer of nursing practice is purposeful and goal directed.

The nurse supervisor is a professional person and, as such, has competency in the intellectual, interper-

*The nurse supervisor is a professional person and, as such, has competency in the intellectual, interpersonal, and technical skills that constitute nursing.*

sonal, and technical skills that constitute nursing. These skills flow from and are supported by a fund of knowledge that has been organized into an internally consistent system called a body of nursing theory. A profession's underlying body of theory is a system of abstract propositions that describe in general terms the classes of phenomena comprising the profession's focus of interest. Theory serves as a base in terms of which the professional rationalizes his or her operations in concrete situations. Acquisition of the professional skill requires a prior or simultaneous mastery of the theory underlying that skill. Preparation for a profession, therefore, involves considerable preoccupation with systematic theory.

The importance of theory promotes a form of activity normally not encountered in a nonprofessional occupation, that is, theory construction by way of systematic research. Treatises have been written on political theory, musical theory, nursing theory, social work theory, and drama theory, for example, but no books have been written on the theory of punch pressing, pipefitting, or machine tending. To generate a valid theory that will provide a solid base for professional nursing practice, research and problem solving must be applied to the service-related problems of the profession. Continued employment of these methods are nurtured by, and in turn reinforce, the element of *rationality*. Rationality is the antithesis of traditionalism. The spirit of rationality in a profession encourages a critical, as opposed to a reverential, attitude toward the theoretical system. It implies a perpetual readiness to discard any portion of that system, no matter how time-honored it may be, with a formulation demonstrated to be more valid. The spirit of rationality generates group self-criticism and theoretical controversy. Professional members of associations convene regularly to learn and to evaluate innovations in theory. These meetings produce an intellectually stimulating milieu that is in marked contrast to the milieu of a nonprofessional occupation.[11]

If the nurse scholar is to practice at the highest possible level with consumers of nursing service, both well people and ill people, and in a variety of settings, mastery of the available nursing theory and active pursuit of theoretic developments are expected. It is in the day-to-day, goal-directed interactions with consumers of health and nursing care that the scholarship of the nurse supervisor is most evident and continually expanded. Scholarship involves assessing the level of satisfaction of a client's human needs, validating his or her state of wellness, or precisely designating potential obvious alterations in the fulfillment of the client's human needs. Nursing diagnosis and scholarship also involve fostering the design of nursing strategies planned for and with the consumer to enhance the state of wellness, to offset potential alterations in human need fulfillment, or to reverse an obvious alteration. Nursing scholarship is evident in creatively supporting the nursing staff's planning of nursing strategies that take into account the humanity of consumers—their ages, their gender, their life styles, their periods of growth and development, and their level of pathophysiology or psychopathology. It is evident in holding nursing staff accountable for specifying the outcome expected for the consumer or the goal to be achieved— the highest level of human need fulfillment along with the expected time of fulfillment. Scholarship is manifested in the view of nursing diagnoses as a hypothesis to be tested by the nursing staff and the nurse supervisor. It is in implementing a plan of care while monitoring the encounter between the nurse scholar and consumer. Scholarship involves evaluating the status of goal achievement based on data and making revisions as needed in the consumer's plan of nursing until the specified goal is achieved. Scholarship involves being a partner with the consumer to enhance or establish wellness.

Scholarliness demands sharing effective consumer responses to nursing strategies and sharing the unique strategies designed by the staff nurse scholar with the nurse supervisor scholar to ensure a person- and family-centered nursing service. The nurse supervisor scholar consults with other nurse scholars and with members of the interdisciplinary health team as needed to ensure goal-directed consumer health and nursing care.

The nurse supervisor may choose to blindly or uncritically accept the views or opinions of others. However, the nurse supervisor scholar selects those ideas and dimensions of knowledge that have the most utility in the practice setting and decides what to accept based on data and sound research. Nurse scholars are intellectually aware of the acquired body of knowledge that directs their practice. They glean the literature for new and different ideas and new and different ways to use the knowledge they have. They need not take sole responsibility for the generation of nursing theory, but they are obligated to share observations, relationships among data, and human responses to nursing interventions so that nursing theory development can proceed.

The nurse supervisor scholar requires time for thinking. The day's experiences with the consumers of the service (both administrative and nursing) provide a rich source for gathering data, perceiving human responses to illness and maintaining wellness, and understanding the predicament of learning roles and relationships. The nurse scholar is one who refrains from automatic responses to the human being encountered. The scholar experiences the moment—extracting from this moment the data that have been exposed and then analyzing and giving these data meaning. The nurses who are all hands and feet when providing and supervising nursing services deprive themselves of the thinking and perceiving experience that adds meaning to each encounter. Thinking is hard work. Time must be planned to think, and high value should be placed on thinking, as a product, and on the person who does the thinking—in this case the supervisor of nursing who is the scholar.

Scholarliness is manifested through the nurse supervisor scholar's research orientation. The scholar's effort to be personally involved in a research project to improve the administration of nursing services is but one example. The nurse supervisor scholar is in a strategic position to support and suggest research opportunities for the generalist and specialist practitioners of nursing functioning in the responsibility area of nursing supervision. Assistance with proposal generation and approval is a valued service. The nurse supervisor scholar should be alert to research possibilities that could involve nurse educator scholars from college and university nursing programs. Important liaisons can be developed that not only have benefits for the consumers of nursing practice but also the consumers of nursing education. The nurse supervisor scholar may be an early contact for research opportunities for graduate nursing students who will benefit from guidance in population selection and management of the research approval protocol in the formal organization. The nurse supervisor is the key person to diminish data collection abuse of the nursing staff, who are often put upon to collect data for health workers with no benefit to the nursing care of clients and no staff support to handle the data collection load. The preservation of client time for the nursing staff can be accomplished by the alert and sensitive nurse supervisor who requests that health care workers provide their own research assistants for their data collection.

The flow of nursing staff and client data in any 24-hour period can generate a myriad of research questions for nurse supervisor scholars to solve themselves, to delegate to qualified nursing staff, to forward to the nursing research unit, or to submit to the nearby college or university nursing program for resolution. Collaborative research efforts between nurse supervisor scholars and nurse educator scholars can be particularly productive and result in long-term professional relationships. From these efforts, adjunct appointments usually ensue with the supervisor receiving a joint appointment in the academic setting and the educator receiving one in the service setting. Staff in both nursing settings become beneficiaries by appreciating each other's roles, strengthening relationships, and sharing information and talent.

## PROPAGATING SCHOLARLINESS

Nurse supervisor scholars bear a responsibility to publish the fruits of a careful and critical thought process. Samples of publishing possibilities are sharing the problem, design, and results of research; proposing a model to facilitate the nursing staff's engagement in research; propagating the design and test results of nursing process strategies, administrative strategies, and experiences in facilitating the research of health-related professionals. In addition, concepts, theories, and conceptual or theoretical frameworks and models in nursing are popular topics to which the nurse supervisor scholar can contribute.

Why should the nurse supervisor scholar assume responsibility for propagating scholarliness? Foremost is the opportunity to disseminate an idea. Bridgman said, "There is no defense, except stupidity, against the impact of a new idea."[12] While this comment seems harsh, it is worthy of reflection. An idea remains unknown to all but the originator unless it is revealed through the spoken or written word. It is only then that its value can be judged, its impact experienced, its development nurtured, and its incorporation in nursing education and practice realized. Cousins indicated that "an idea does not have to find its mark in the minds of large numbers of people in order to create an incentive for change. Ideas have a life of their own. They can be nourished and brought to active growth by a small number of sensitive vital minds which somehow respond to the needs of the total organism [for us, nursing], however diffused its parts."[13] He stated further that effective oral or written communications absolutely depend on a clear understanding of one's purpose, clearly identified. The purpose should not be cluttered with extensive comment or side excursions, but it should be developed "point by point, with the rigorous attention to sequence and gradations of a professional bead-stringer at work."[14]

Generating ideas, researching problems, and publishing the results are evidence of ongoing development of the self and the profession of nursing. Through this scholarly activity, the nurse supervisor scholar validates the specialized practice of administering nursing. Publishing provides an outlet for the scholar's creativity, plus the basis for joy, exhilaration, and a boost in professional self-confidence. When one's name and work are published, the possibility for immortality for one's name and contribution is real. As Cousins stated, "The writer is a creator of options. The writer enables people to discover new truths and new possibilities within themselves and to fashion new connections to human experience."[15]

The moment of triumph for the author occurs when an important idea is born and the creativity spills over, demanding release. Cousins stated, "It is also a moment of commitment, for the writer knows that the idea will possess him and hover over him until he puts down the words that will set him free again. If it is self-tyranny, it is at least the tyranny of purpose."[16]

As a reader reviews the publication, reactions in the form of verbal comments, letters, and invitations to present more elements of the author's ideas or research to professional groups may be forthcoming. The nurse supervisor scholar may be sought out by other prospective authors who wish to draw on the published content so that they, too, may have a successful publishing experience. Stimulating discussions may ensue that may challenge the scholar's work, show uses never dreamed possible, and add dimensions to expand the work. Nurse supervisor scholars may feel very proud to see their work footnoted or to have the publisher convey to them a request for permission to publish a portion of the work in someone else's publication. This may mean that the scholar has developed the missing piece in someone else's work.

What about the cost in time, energy, material, and relationships? Huxley responded to this concern by telling us "there is a well-worn adage that those who set out upon a great enterprise would do well to count the cost. I am not sure that this is always true. I think that some of the very greatest enterprises in this world have been carried out successfully simply because the people who undertook them did not count the cost; and I am of the opinion that, in this very case, the most instructive consideration for us is the cost of doing nothing."[17]

Cousins reminded us that "anything that ignites the human mind, anything that sets the collective intelligence to racing, anything that creates a new horizon for human hopes, anything that helps to enlarge the vocabulary of common heritage and common destiny—anything that does this is of incalculable value."[18] A published idea may do just that. He continued, "The creative process depends least of all upon accident. It requires that the mind be properly worked and tended, that it be given the blessing of silence and the gift of sequence, whether the moment of triumph produces a spark or a thunderbolt, it is certain to have lasting effects. It can generate the carrying power to sustain an author through a thousand nights of torment at the writing desk."[19] Publishing ideas facilitates their dissemination and contributes to the knowledge and prac-

tice expectations of the generalist and specialist practitioners of nursing, with goals of improving the provision and supervision of nursing service to clients. Nurses so engaged are in a position to influence the human condition in a positive way. Their astute, first hand observations over time, their sensitivity to the human needs and wants of persons and families, their hunches about what should be done and the outcome to be expected are unique and valuable. It is in this very arena that nursing knowledge is deficient; the nursing know-how deficits are starkly exposed. But in this very arena are the data for the resolution of these deficits. The problems must be identified first, then researched and solutions sought. The deficits, the resolutions, the research results, the solutions gained through problem solving—these efforts are all publishable. A scholar does not have to wait for the solution before publishing. It is possible to publish the problems, the problem statements, and the preliminary research, too. Publishing researchable ideas, potential designs, and possible and actual results will generate more opportunities for publishing by stimulating potential authors to try, verify, and expand what is in print. Some of these ideas may not only improve nursing services but may also enhance the development and the direction of nursing as a profession.

With the publication of a work comes added responsibility to continue the scholarly activity. This publication may be a springboard for

> **With the publication of a work comes added responsibility to continue the scholarly activity.**

other publications or even a lifelong pursuit. Thomas Carlyle was eloquent when he said a "well-written life is almost as rare as a well spent one."[20] Will his comment hold true for the nursing supervisor scholar?

It is recommended that prospective authors develop a mentor relationship with a seasoned author. It might be possible to coauthor a work for publication with one's mentor. This would not only be a valuable learning experience, but it might facilitate a publishing experience sooner. Working with a nurse supervisor or nurse educator colleague with a compatible style, goal, and approach to an idea may generate fruitful results and bring an idea to fruition much sooner.

There are risks involved in publishing one's thinking and ideas. Nurse supervisor scholars must know this. They should expect respect for their ideas as they respect the ideas of others. Partial ideas, when shared, may be completed by one's professional colleagues.

Is there fear of risk taking? Publishing does expose one's ideas and work to peers, colleagues, the nurse population at large; however, this could be a positive experience. Often suggestions to strengthen the work accompany the return. It is also a good idea to have a sense of history and knowl-

edge of the literature of the field. This will help offset returns due to duplication of an idea already published. Emerson wrote that, "Bad times have a scientific value. These are occasions a good learner would not miss."[21] Jonas Salk says that life is an error-making and error-correcting process, that nature in marking our papers will grade us for wisdom as measured by both survival and the quality of life of those who survive— for nursing it is the authors, the readers, and our clients.[22] The nurse scholar could receive validation and encouragement for his or her ideas as well as useful criticism—the kind that criticizes the idea without criticizing the person. The scholar may get some direction, if needed, or learn of additional ways the ideas can be used. It can be expected that publication may bring communication from others who are struggling with similar ideas. Networks of colleagues develop in this way.

Publishing captures the history of nursing and enhances the author's nursing image. What is written in the present will eventually be preserved as the past. Both past and present ideas, events, results, and their developers can be influential in the future. Nurse supervisor scholars can connect and expand on what has gone before to reflect new thinking and the new times. Published ideas can be picked up by other professional and public presses, thus maximizing their value. If nurse scholars do not publish, nursing's image may be diminished and the world of nursing, particularly the clients of nursing, will be deprived.

How do nurse scholars maintain themselves as learned persons, as persons of thought and action? It can be accomplished through membership in professional nursing associations, particularly honor societies, in idea sharing, in critical analysis of nursing theory development, in research generation and discussion, and in recognition of scholarly effort. Opportunity for and support in sharing differing and opposing views on scholarly nursing topics should be available through workshops, seminars, and research symposiums. In addition, opportunities should be created in the work setting. For example, nurse supervisor scholars could design inservice programs to enhance theory development and its propagation for nursing practice, seek out and collaborate with other nurse scholars in the practice environment, and negotiate time for scholarly discussions and the conduct of research that enhances nursing service to the consumers. Staying current with the scholarly nursing literature and pursuing advanced education in nursing are two more ways to maintain scholarliness.

## PAYOFFS FOR SCHOLARLY ENDEAVORS

It is obvious that scholarship permeates the role and responsibilities of the nurse supervisor. Involvement in scholarliness enhances the supervisor's sense of self and professional self-concept. Professional and personal enrichment come with idea generation, problem-solving activities, and goal designation and achievement. Positive responses from nursing staff and clients come from good ideas put into practice with fruitful results.

Increased nursing staff satisfaction with their service to clients may be a direct result of recognition by the nurse supervisor of their competency. Maximizing competency by valuing thinking and other intellectual and interpersonal efforts can translate into effective technical effort. Taking time to think about goals and strategies may require more time initially but may actually save time, in the long run, for the nursing staff and clients. The expectation that the nurse supervisor and qualified nursing staff base their practice on a strong theoretical base can also have positive results for the nursing staff and clients.

The goal of the nursing staff and the nurse supervisor scholar is the client's achievement of optimal wellness. The achievement of this level of wellness in a reasonable time, with a person- and family-centered approach, and with minimal possibility of loss of the optimal state, will engender increased satisfaction of client and family. Clients will be the beneficiaries of the nurse supervisor scholar's efforts to research and problem solve the human experience of wellness and illness and the elements of the nursing process.

Finally, the formal organization for

health and nursing that promotes the scholarliness of the nurse supervisor and rewards these efforts will be viewed by nursing staff and clients in a positive manner. The possibility of maintaining the status quo or perpetuating inefficiency is minimized. A formal organization is more an idea than a tangible entity. The tangible portion is the people of the organization—the nurse supervisor, the qualified nursing staff, and the consumers of nursing services.

The nurse supervisor should be viewed as a nurse scholar—a *learned person,* a person whose scholarliness is lifelong, a person whose scholarship is demonstrated by systematized knowledge of nursing; a person who exhibits the ability to *think* critically, accurately, and thoroughly. Christopher Morley, who wrote the following, would have supported this view: "Read every day something no one else is reading. Think every day something no one else is thinking. It is bad for the mind to be always a part of a unanimity."[23]

## REFERENCES

1. Allen, J. *As a Man Thinketh.* New York: Grosset and Dunlap, 1984, p. 44.
2. Ibid., 45.
3. Ibid., 52.
4. Ibid., 53.
5. Ibid., 59.
6. Ibid., 61.
7. Ibid., 63.
8. Ibid., 65–66.
9. Ibid., 66.
10. Bartlett, J. *Familiar Quotations.* 14th ed. Boston: Little, Brown, 1968, p. 864b.
11. Greenwood, E. "The Elements of Professionalization." In *Professionalization,* edited by H.M. Vollmer and D.L. Miller. Englewood Cliffs, N.J.: Prentice-Hall, 1966, pp. 10–19.
12. Gardner, J., and Reese, F.G. *Know and Listen to Those Who Know.* New York: W.W. Norton, 1975, p. 63.
13. Cousins, N. *Human Options.* New York: Berkley Books, 1981, p. 52.
14. Ibid., p. 179.
15. Ibid., p. 175.
16. Ibid., p. 177.
17. Gardner and Reese, *Know and Listen to Those Who Know,* p. 58.
18. Cousins, *Human Options,* p. 164.
19. Ibid., p. 177.
20. Gardner and Reese, *Know and Listen to Those Who Know,* p. 163.
21. Ibid., p. 86.
22. Ibid., p. 29.
23. Abromson, H., ed. *Prefaces Without Books: Prefaces and Introductions to Thirty Books.* Austin: University of Texas, 1970.

# Part II
# On Becoming a Nurse Manager

# The head nurse as a first-line manager

**Rachel Rotkovitch**
*Vice President for Nursing*
*Yale-New Haven Hospital*
*New Haven, Connecticut*

THE COST OF health care in this country is rising at an inflation rate that outstrips the annual increase in the cost of living. There is not a branch of the media that has not publicized this fact. It is widely believed that the current diversion of a substantial portion (10 percent) of our gross national product to health care cannot be sustained without hurting other aspects of the good life that all people want. Because of this, government, industry and health insurance companies are asking for economies, constraints and new and innovative methods of providing health care services from all who are involved in the health care industry. Since the cost of providing nursing services accounts for a substantial part of hospital expenditures—in some hospitals as much as 40 to 70 percent of payroll—it is imperative that these expenditures be closely examined to determine whether they are warranted.

*Health Care Superv*, 1983,1(4),14–28
© 1983 Aspen Publishers, Inc.

The country's health care bill amounted to 286 billion dollars in 1980 and 287 billion dollars in 1981. According to a survey conducted by the Research Triangle Institute, the head nurse and assistant head nurse force numbered 90,203 in 1980.[1] Assuming the average salary of a head nurse today to be about $20,000 yearly plus 20 percent fringe benefits, the yearly cost of maintaining this force is about 1.6 billion dollars. Are hospitals getting their money's worth for this expenditure? To find out, the following must be examined:

- Who is the head nurse?
- What is the head nurse's role?
- What qualifies a nurse to become a head nurse?
- What effect does the head nurse have on achieving the purpose of the organization?
- What kind of support needs to be provided to the head nurse?

## WHO IS THE HEAD NURSE?

In some hospitals, head nurses are called nursing care coordinators; in others they are called teachers or clinicians. Regardless of title, these are the registered nurses who are assigned the responsibility for the quality of nursing care given to a number of patients located in a defined physical area for 24 hours a day, seven days a week.

The defined area is usually called a patient care unit, a nursing unit (a misnomer, since the area is not set up to serve nurses but to serve patients) or a ward (a leftover from days gone by when hospitals were built with large rooms without partitions and 40 to 50 patients lay side by side). The capacity of the patient units in most hospitals today is about 20 to 30 beds, and the patients are accommodated in single or double rooms.

## WHAT IS THE ROLE OF THE HEAD NURSE?

To discharge his or her responsibility, the head nurse must have the authority for (1) selecting the nursing staff assigned to his or her unit, (2) assigning staff to days and hours of the workweek, (3) assessing staff's knowledge and skills, (4) matching assignments with complex patient needs for nursing care, (5) evaluating staff performance, (6) making recommendations for promotions or severance, (7) authorizing overtime, (8) coping with staff turnover (which is greater in nursing than in most professions) and (9) improvising when the unexpected occurs.

The head nurse is also responsible for requesting the nursing personnel needed to accomplish the foregoing tasks. As the head nurse assumes responsibility for his or her unit's approved payroll budget, he or she becomes accountable for its judicious management to ensure that expenditures do not exceed allocations.

Many believe that the head nurse's job is the most difficult job in the hospital setting. The position's responsibilities may be enough to tax the physical, intellectual and emotional resources of any individual. In addition, the head nurse is responsible for work done on his or her unit 24 hours a day even though he or she is off the premises for two-thirds of that time.

---

*The head nurse's responsibilities may be enough to tax the physical, intellectual and emotional resources of any individual.*

---

To maintain excellence, the head nurse must create an environment and atmosphere on his or her unit that is conducive to the self-motivation and self-direction of the staff. The head nurse must accomplish this while assuring patients and their families humane, safe and competent nursing care and while keeping an eye on the judicious use of resources. Achieving this in a working environment laden with pain, sorrow and tension (the usual diet of all who work in close proximity to the ill and disabled) makes the head nurse's job a most difficult and challenging undertaking.

Some duties of the head nurse may vary from hospital to hospital, whereas some aspects of the role may be the same everywhere. The differences in the role in various hospitals is a result of the nursing philosophy, which determines the structure within which nurses provide care. The head nurse's role will differ in the traditional, team and professional models within which nursing care is provided. All three of these nursing care delivery structures or their variations continue to exist today. To clarify what is meant by structure, it is necessary to review the historical background of the practice of nursing in the hospital setting.

## Historical background of nursing practice

It may be hard to believe that 40 years ago medical knowledge and practice were essentially primitive. Patients were dying from a simple streptoccocal blister on the foot or from tuberculosis, malaria, typhoid or septicemia. There were no antibiotics; sulfa drugs were the only weapons against fever-causing bacteria. Sometimes these drugs helped, but more often than not, physicians simply stood helplessly by. The other member of the hospital team who provided care was the nurse, or rather the student nurse. In those days, almost all nursing education took place in nursing schools affiliated with hospitals.

In light of today's knowledge, technology and expectations, one would hardly consider the student nurse who spent three years in a hospital nursing school as being adequately educated. It was an apprentice kind of preparation for the practice of nursing. While lectures on anatomy, physiology, and other subjects were given to the students by physicians, nurse instructors taught bedmaking, bathing, giving injections and enemas and making the patients comfortable.

The greater part of a student nurse's three years at nursing school consisted of working on the patient care units under the supervision of the head nurse, who may also have been the instructor. In addition to teaching the student nurses nursing arts and skills, head nurses taught them how to make a soft-boiled egg or mashed potatoes and how to clean the patient's environment. This included terminal cleaning of beds, washing the walls of the patient's room (only to the windowsills) and cleaning the patient's bedside table. The hospitals rewarded these students for the cheap labor they provided by furnishing them room and board and, of course, classroom activities.

Of 1,400 diploma schools of nursing active in the 1940s and 1950, only a handful (about 300) are currently operational. Some of these schools added college-affiliated courses to their curricula. Others are closing at the rate of approximately 6 percent yearly.[2] In some cases, the sole reason for their continued existence is loyalty to the school by its alumni, the public and the hospital administrator. Indeed, some hospitals cling to their schools of nursing for the same reasons they did so in the 1940s.

Did patients receive good care in hospitals in those days? As one who lived through that era as a student nurse, I would say, yes, patients received very good nursing care in those days. Patients may have been dying for lack of medical knowledge, but they were dying with dignity and with the knowledge that the nurses loved them and cared enough to make them as comfortable as possible.

World War II brought many changes in the use of hospitals. It stimulated the development of medical knowledge and the use of the most sophisticated technology in the diagnostic and treatment activities that take place in the hospitals of today. Hand in hand with these changes, the demands on the knowledge and skills of nurses have become such that the apprentice-type preparations that hospital schools of nursing were providing have proven to be inadequate. Four years in a college school of nursing is considered to be the minimum requirement for the practice of modern nursing.

In 1965, the ANA made the four-year degree requirement a goal to be achieved by 1985.[3] However, not one state has yet passed legislation that would make a B.S. degree in nursing a requirement for practice.

### Educational background of nurses

This is not the place to discuss all the actions, reactions and positions of nurses, hospital administrators and physicians on the subject of nursing education. However, many health care providers continue to resist the need to bring the education of nurses into the twentieth century.

Holding on to diploma schools will perpetuate a situation that not only will continue to provide technically prepared nurses at a time when the need for professionally prepared nurses is greater, but also will continue to confuse persons who interact with nurses as to what the nurse's role is.

Today, nurses who graduate from associate degree, diploma or baccalaureate programs all take the same licensing exam and are all considered legally and literally to be professional nurses. In many hospitals the salaries they earn are equal. In spite of the many stumbling blocks nurses encounter on the road to professionalism, about 23 percent of the nursing work force, or 96,000 nurses, have earned a baccalaureate or higher degree in nursing.[4]

Since two out of three working nurses practice in the hospital setting, the number of nurses on the hospital scene with baccalaureate or master's degrees has increased dramatically. The effect on nursing practice in hospitals has been equally dramatic. These nurses have brought with them not only a solid theoretical background in nursing practice but also an inquisitive intellect, a daring to question old practices, and a desire to use their knowledge, skills and dedication to ensure that patients receive competent nursing care.

## Models of nursing practice

### Traditional model

The practice of hospital nursing that today's new graduates have been questioning is the traditional industrial or assembly-line model of assigning nurses. In this model the role of the head nurse is considered by all who interact with him or her to be that of a master sergeant. The head nurse sits behind the "nurses" desk and from that place manages the unit. At the beginning of the shift (7:00 or 8:00 A.M.), when the nurses come to work, the head nurse and all the other nurses listen to the night shift nurses' report.

The shift report is lengthy and detailed concerning every patient. When it is completed, the head nurse hands out assignments to the nursing staff. One nurse is to take and record vital signs on all patients; another is assigned to do treatments and prepare patients for surgery. Still another nurse's assignment is the administration of medicine to all patients; this is the famous "medication nurse."

Actual bedside care is assigned to LPNs and nurse aides. Patients assigned to nurse aides are usually ambulatory, since they, it is believed, are "easy patients" who can help themselves with dressing, walking, toileting, and so forth. Unfortunately, this is not true. Many patients who are not bedridden nevertheless bring with them fears and concerns that, if not identified and treated by a competent therapist or a professional nurse, may cause delayed recovery, if not make recovery unachievable.

As is illustrated in the job assignment process, the care of patients is fragmented, disjointed and at variance with the philosophy about people, patients and the role of nurses that the new generation of professional nurses bring with them to the hospital. An example of a philosophy expressing the new professional role of the nurse is presented in the appendix. Nurses are questioning the functional nursing model. This prompted a search for a structure within which nursing care could be provided on the basis of a belief in the totality of a human being, especially when the person is unwell and unable to cope with the health problems, which results in hospitalization.

### Team model

For a while, team nursing was believed to be the solution to the problem. The patients on a unit were divided among two or three groups of nursing staff, with each group composed of LPNs, aides and one or more RNs. The most senior or most competent RN would be designated as the team leader. He or she would give treatments, distribute medicine and supervise the nursing care provided by support staff.

The team model, although similar to the traditional one, had its merit at the time it was introduced—in the immediate post–World War II years, when there was a great shortage of RNs and they had to be spread thinly.[5] In this model the role of the head nurse was similar to that in the traditional model except that in the team model the head nurse relied on the team leader to provide assistance in supervising the nursing staff.

In comparison with the traditional model, the team model created an environment more conducive to the provision of nursing care. The head nurse in the traditional model was almost glued to a desk and had little time to observe, teach and supervise the care givers. The team model, although still requiring the head nurse to be behind a desk, provided two or three RNs in the patient rooms at frequent intervals to supervise and occasionally provide care.

### Professional model

Today neither the traditional model nor the team model is viewed by nurses as conducive to the provision of high quality care. In neither of these models is the nursing care of each patient in the hands of a registered nurse who has the knowledge and the skills to:

- assess the nursing needs of each patient through a medical history and physical examination of the patient;
- make a nursing diagnosis, that is, decide what health problem the patient has that can be handled with competency;
- write a nursing care plan;
- provide care to the patient and the family as needed;
- evaluate the patient's response to the medical and nursing regimen;
- modify the care plan as needed; and
- teach patients how to care for themselves when at home (i.e., plan the patient's discharge).

*Today neither the traditional model nor the team model is viewed by nurses as conducive to the provision of quality care.*

The foregoing are the steps in the nursing process followed by the nursing staff in what is known as the professional nursing model. At times, the professional nursing model is referred to as the primary nursing model. In this model an RN is, at all times, responsible for the total nursing care of a patient and for coordinating the care provided by other members of the health care team. This includes coordination of the medical regimen.

Although the professional and primary models are viewed by some as different only in name, there are substantial differences in their implementation. The most pronounced variation between the professional model and the primary model is the number of hours the nurse is responsible for the assigned groups of patients each day. In the professional model, the RN has 8-hour responsibility; in the primary model, he or she has 24-hour responsibility.

The role of the head nurse in the professional model is different from that in the previous two models discussed. To begin with, in this model the head nurse will seldom be found behind a desk. Answering telephones, giving information and collating charts are functions performed by secretaries. Secretaries also transcribe and expedite doctors' prescriptions (sometimes referred to as doctors' orders). In this model, the management of the hotel-type services and the interaction with the various support services are often delegated to unit service managers. (The role of unit service managers and other support staff is addressed in another part of this article.)

In the professional nursing model, if the head nurse is not behind the desk, where is the head nurse? Most of the time he or she will be in the patients' rooms. While there, he or she is in a position to evaluate the staff nurses' abilities and strengths and weaknesses, function as a role model by laying hands on patients and, through judicious assignment of a reasonable number of patients to be cared for by one nurse, assure patients the quantity and quality of nursing care they need. When a head nurse performs all of these functions, the quality of nursing care is superior. This is what all persons working in hospitals want—excellent care for patients.

## WHAT QUALIFIES A NURSE TO BECOME A HEAD NURSE?

One may wonder what kind of person possesses the qualities and preparation needed to do justice to the head nurse position.

### Education

From the description of the role of head nurse in the professional model, one can easily see that to be able to provide the needed assistance to the nursing staff, the head nurse must have expertise in nursing care in a particular clinical area. Such expertise can be acquired through experience, but the modern way of internalizing the knowledge of the many specialties and subspecialties in which patients are cared for is to learn it in nursing schools and in graduate educational programs.

The head nurse in today's hospital would benefit by being a graduate of a master's degree nursing program. This is achievable because now, more than ever before, schools are preparing nurses at this level, and there is a large pool of nurses with M.S. degrees.

Nursing schools across the country graduate 5,000 nurses every year in medical, surgical, pediatric, obstetric, psychiatric and community health specialties.[6] Why then not place such nurses on patient care units to help the nursing staff provide competent nursing care while encouraging professional growth? There are several answers to this question.

- There may not be enough applicants with master's degrees for head nurse positions.
- These nurses may hesitate to assume head nurse responsibilities in a hospital in which support services, such as those provided by unit service management, are not ensured.
- The financial compensation for master's degree nurses often is not considered by the applicants as adequate.

- The directors of nursing may not believe in the need for such nurses in head nurse positions. It is likely that such directors will maintain the past premise and past practice of appointing head nurses.

### Promotions

In the past, nursing directors promoted the best staff nurses to head nurse positions. This meant that nurses who distinguished themselves as excellent providers of bedside care were shown gratitude for such performance by being promoted. Wherever this practice is still followed, it may be to the detriment of all involved—the nurses, the patients and the hospital.

Excellent staff nurses who love what they are doing, as evident in the excellence of their practice, are being taken out of direct nursing care. They are being deprived of the pleasure and satisfaction of doing what they excel in. The patient loses the competent and excellent nurse, and the hospital is often stuck with a first-line manager who has had no preparation for a managerial position.

One possible justification for perpetuation of this detrimental practice may be the lack of another resource for compensating excellence in nursing practice. However, as the saying goes, "For every ill there is a remedy." Some nursing services have introduced programs designed to remedy this situation. They have instituted merit programs, which provide financial compensation for those staff nurses who have been recognized as excellent care givers by their head nurses and a review committee. Since most nurses choose nursing as a profession because they want to take care of patients, this program has been effective in keeping these nurses at the patient's bedside, the place where the quality of the nurse counts most.

Regardless of frequent problems, however, one should not always assume that excellent care givers cannot become excellent head nurses. But when they *do* assume head nurse positions, these nurses must exhibit the abilities expected of managers, because the head nurse is the first-line manager in the nursing department. Recognizing this, many nursing directors carefully scrutinize prospective candidates for head nurse positions. This is commendable and practical; the nursing director knows that the choice of a first-line manager affects the effectiveness and efficiency of all nursing service.

## Evaluating head nurse candidates

In weighing the decision to appoint or not appoint a candidate to the head nurse position, a director of nursing is keenly aware that the candidate must be an expert in the nursing care of the clinical area under consideration and that he or she must also demonstrate leadership and management abilities and possess certain basic managerial qualifications. To be qualified for such a position, a nurse should have some years of experience in the setting in which

he or she is being considered for promotion to head nurse. The nurse should also have a B.S. degree in nursing (and preferably a master's degree) and should have had courses in management in either formal or nondegree programs.

The head nurse candidate should be a master in interacting with people and should possess excellent communication skills, maturity and good physical health. Most of all, he or she should have a great desire to take on the position. It is a good practice to ask the applicant to put in writing his or her qualifications for the position, his or her perception of the position and how he or she hopes to go about achieving the requirements of the position. The candidate should also be able to articulate his or her reasons for seeking such an appointment.

---

*The head nurse candidate should be a master in interacting with people and should possess excellent communication skills, maturity and good physical health.*

---

## Administrative requirements

It is regrettable that most graduate nursing programs designed to prepare nurses for administrative positions have not included in their curricula a sufficient number of courses related to the head nurse's role as first-line manager or other administrative nursing roles. Instead of courses in finances, budgeting, labor relations, legal aspects of hospital practice, statistics, computer technology and theory of organizations, these programs have an abundance of courses that deal with the pathophysiology of illness and modes of therapy.

Some nurse administrators, as well as students, presently enrolled in master's programs designed to prepare them for administrative positions in the hospital setting have expressed their disenchantment with curricula in which the balance of courses is geared toward clinical practices. Some schools have noted this criticism and are revamping their programs to meet the needs of their graduates in practice. Some nurses have turned to graduate programs in health service administration or even business administration to acquire the needed knowledge. Such graduates often do very well as nursing managers in both first-line and higher positions.

The most important benefit that graduates of programs that also prepare hospital administrators have gained is the knowledge they share with those administrators. Whether in head nurse positions or higher positions, nurses must be able to speak the language of their peers and superiors. The essential vocabulary includes such terms as *budget, overspending, variance, income, expense, cash flow, cash disbursement,* and *depreciation.*

Not being able to converse with peer managers in their language can put nurse managers at a disadvantage in that they may lack credibility in their ability to discharge the responsibilities of a manager. There is no doubt that the responsibility for the judicious use of all resources put in the hands of a manager and the accountability for same has always been and will continue to be important in evaluating the manager's performance.

Head nurses are charged primarily with responsibility for the quality of nursing care on their units, and their clinical expertise is of paramount importance. However, this does not diminish their responsibility and accountability for the budgets they have been appropriated. Most of the funds are intended for payroll purposes, including overtime, vacations and paid sick time for staff. If head nurses do not know how to control these variables and disregard the fact that they cannot spend what they do not have, a negative variance will occur. A director of nursing who permits his or her head nurses to create such a problem may have to look for another position.

## WHAT EFFECT DOES THE HEAD NURSE HAVE ON ACHIEVING THE PURPOSE OF THE ORGANIZATION?

Suppose a person well prepared for the head nurse position and desirous of taking on the responsibilities of the position is found and given the assignment. What effect will this head nurse have on achieving the purpose of the hospital? It is well accepted by those who manage hospitals, those who actively provide the services and those who are admitted to hospitals that the purpose of the hospital is to provide episodic care to people who may need it and cannot get it elsewhere.

Naturally the administrators, the providers and the receivers of hospital services wish these services to be of the highest possible quality and available at reasonable cost. If this is the expectation of the hospital, then the head nurse is the "quarterback" of the hospital team. He or she leads and directs the nursing staff. It is this nursing staff who actually translate the hospital's reason for existing into the tangible acts that take place where patients are—on the units, in their rooms, in the operating room, in intensive care and in classrooms in which patients and their families are taught how to live with disabilities or residual deficiencies.

The head nurse also coordinates the activities of other hospital staff who provide direct and indirect services to patients. Foremost among these activities is the care provided by physicians. In hospitals in which nursing care is being provided within the structure of the professional model of nursing, physicians work more closely with staff nurses who care for patients than they do with the head nurse.

In spite of this, physicians still tend to identify the overall responsibility for patient care with the head nurse. They will seek out the head nurse if they have complaints or when they wish to sing the praises of a particular nurse. Other hospital staff who "lay hands" on patients while they provide specialized services, such as physical therapists, respiratory therapists, lab technicians, dietary staff, social workers, chaplains and volunteers, also look to the head nurse for help, clarification and guidance.

## WHAT KIND OF SUPPORT NEEDS TO BE PROVIDED TO THE HEAD NURSE?

What kind of support must the head nurse receive to make it possible to discharge his or her responsibilities effectively and efficiently? There is a caricature in literature that depicts a head nurse with many arms; with each hand he or she touches and interacts with the various hospital departments that provide services to patients. Thus the head nurse reaches out to:

- the laundry department—to request additional linen to change patients' beds or give baths;
- the dietary department—to inform them of changes in patients' diets, to request additional nourishments or to complain that the trays were not collected promptly after meals;
- the laboratories—to inquire why the reports did not arrive on the units or why the stat requests have not been done;
- the housekeeping and maintenance departments—to check why patients' rooms and bath-

rooms have not been cleaned promptly, wastepaper baskets have not been emptied, faucets are leaking or light bulbs have not been changed.

As previously mentioned, the strategic base from which the head nurse accomplishes all of his or her tasks is the unit station. The telephone is there, the patient records are there, and all paperwork connected with the operation of the unit is there.

### The role of unit service management

The foregoing represent just a few of the constant and irritating interactions that the "multiarmed" head nurse is involved in every day. Unfortunately, in hospitals in which support services on patient units are deficient, the head nurse, to the detriment of his or her true responsibilities, is forced to devote much time to activities that nonnurses can perform. In a number of hospitals, unit service managers and support staff have been placed on patient units for the purpose of relieving head nurses of many of the aforementioned involvements.

Twenty years ago the concept of unit service management was nonexistent. Today many hospitals have such a department. Most hospitals have at least provided clerical assistance on the units; this is a great help in that it frees the head nurse from the desk and makes it possible for him or her to attend to responsibilities related to direct patient care and the supervision of nursing staff.

Some hospitals have taken an additional step in providing support to the head nurse by placing unit service managers in patient areas. Thus the unit secretaries assume the chores of the desk (answering the telephone, giving out information and taking care of paperwork), and the unit service managers circulate, enter patients' rooms to check on the environment and interact with support departments as needed.

Unit service managers are also responsible for instituting and directing systems to ensure that the staff on the units have an adequate supply of needed materials and equipment. The absence of such supplies as linen, drugs, IV solutions and nourishments causes anger and frustration for staff and patients alike. It is the unit service manager's job to prevent this.

To meet the hospital's objectives, the staff need calm working conditions that promote mutual respect and collaboration. Thus the role of unit service management in the hospital structure can be considered to be of great importance. Those who contend that the unit service management department should report to an administrator other than the director of nursing run the risk of creating an environment on the patient units laden with finger pointing, hostility and inefficiency.

### Coordination of unit service management and nursing service

The work of the nursing staff and that of the members of unit service management is so intertwined that drawing administrative lines between these two groups of employees can be disastrous. In hospitals in which such reporting systems have been introduced, they have proven to be costly in both goodwill and money. Montefiore Hospital in New

---

*The work of the nursing staff and that of the members of unit service management is so intertwined that drawing administrative lines between these two groups can be disastrous.*

---

York and Massachusetts General in Boston are hospitals that tried the two-administrator concept and failed. They then switched to the reporting relationship described here—both nursing and unit service management reporting to the same person.

Since, according to the standards of the Joint Commission on Accreditation of Hospitals, nursing must report to a nurse, the person to whom unit service management should report must be the nursing administrator, who may have nonnursing departments reporting to him or her as well. The Long Island-Jewish Hillside Medical Center in New York, Yale-New Haven Hospital in Connecticut and Long Island College Hospital in New York are hospitals in which such a reporting relationship has proven successful, not only in creating an

amiable working relationship on the patient care units but also in controlling the nonpayroll budget.

The responsibility for the nonpayroll budget rests with unit service management, yet the items in this budget are used by nurses on the patient care units. The nurse administrator has the overall responsibility for this budget. What this means is that the responsibility and ultimate accountability for the dollars in both the payroll and nonpayroll budgets are in the same hands—the nurse administrator's.

The use of unit service management benefits all support departments. Since a unit service manager usually bears responsibility for several patient units, one communication from such a person to a support department may cover the requests of several units. It makes it easier on the managers of support departments to deal with one person instead of getting short-tempered calls from four or five head nurses each asking for the same thing. In light of all this and more, one may wonder why more hospitals are not adopting unit service management.

## ARE HOSPITALS GETTING THEIR MONEY'S WORTH IN MAINTAINING THE HEAD NURSE FORCE?

Whether hospitals are getting their money's worth in spending 1.6 billion dollars a year to maintain a head nurse force depends on what services directors of nursing expect head nurses to provide and on the ability of nursing directors to create the proper environment for head nurses to fulfill the responsibilities of their positions.

An environment conducive to goal achievement by head nurses includes the following elements.

- a philosophy of nursing service;
- the organization and process of the delivery of nursing care;
- measurement of the success of nursing practice based on outcomes, when possible;
- selection criteria for nurses to fill head nurse positions; and
- support from nursing directors and assistants in promoting growth and development for head nurses as first-line nursing managers.

In summary, a director of nursing usually expects the head nurse to:

- assure patients an acceptable level of nursing care;
- use the human and other resources at his or her disposal in an efficient and effective way;
- interpret the philosophies of nursing and of the hospital to patients, nurses and others;
- maintain compliance with hospital rules and regulations; and
- maintain an environment conducive to esprit de corps among all members of the hospital staff.

In how many of the country's 7,000 hospitals these conditions are met is not known. What is known, however, is that in hospitals in which head nurses do not function in the roles described, their talents, commitments and abilities are being misused or not used at all. How much of the 1.6 billion dollars the country spends on maintaining this head nurse force is wasted is anybody's guess. At this time, when financial resources and qualified head nurses are both in short supply, a waste of either must be corrected.

## REFERENCES

1. U.S. Department of Health and Human Service. Public Health Service. *Registered Nurse Population: An Overview from the National Sampler Survey of Registered Nurses*. Division of Health Profession, Analysis Report No. 82-S. Washington, D.C.: Government Printing Office, 1982.
2. National League for Nursing. *NLN Nursing Data Book*. New York: NLN, 1981.
3. American Nurses' Association. *Educational Preparation for Nurse Practitioners and Assistants to Nurses: A Position Paper*. New York: ANA, 1965.
4. U.S. Department of Health and Human Service. Public Health Service. *Registered Nurse Population*, 82.
5. Lambertson, E. *Team Nursing: Organization and Functioning*. New York: Teachers College Press, 1953.
6. National League for Nursing, *NLN Nursing Data Book*, 19.

# Appendix

# Yale-New Haven Hospital
# Philosophy of nursing service

The Nursing Service of Yale-New Haven Hospital supports the mission of this hospital in offering to the community the benefits of expanding health services, teaching and research.

The philosophy of nursing within this setting is based upon the belief that each individual is a unique human being who possesses basic rights and responsibilities and whose values and circumstances command respect at all times.

Utilizing the Professional Model, nursing provides individualized and comprehensive care directed toward health maintenance, health restoration or dignified death.

A collaborative relationship among the members of the health care team is a must in the provision of quality health care. We believe that patients/clients are significant members of the health care team and therefore should participate in decision making regarding their health care regimen.

We believe that the continuous scientific advancements and the increasing complexity of the health care systems demand an ongoing learning process and research endeavors, which can only be facilitated in an environment which promotes professional growth and creativity.

While Nursing Service is responsible for creating that environment for professional development, it is the individual nurse's responsibility to seek out those opportunities which meet his or her own needs.

# A situational approach to developing head nurse management skills

**Nicholas DiMarco**
*Associate Professor of Management*
*School of Business*
*Webster University*
*St. Louis, Missouri*

**Jane Goodson**
*Associate Professor of Management*

**Henry Hauser**
*Associate Professor of Management*
*School of Business*
*Auburn University of Montgomery*
*Montgomery, Alabama*

ONE OF THE MAJOR problems the nursing profession faces is lack of effective leadership training, training that can enable head nurses or charge nurses to enhance the effectiveness of their individual units.[1,2] The highly technical skills required of nurses dominate the nursing curriculum, leaving little room for teaching the skills nurses will need in managerial roles. According to Nowell, inadequate preparation for the leadership role has created a sense of frustration and dissatisfaction among head nurses and has produced unsatisfactory results for hospitals.[3] It is becoming increasingly apparent that the delivery of efficient and high-quality patient care will depend on the effective use of leadership and supervisory techniques.

Most writers on management development agree that the solution is twofold: (1) selecting better head nurses and (2) implementing programs designed to teach nurses leadership and management techniques.

*Health Care Superv*, 1989, 7(4), 57–65
© 1989 Aspen Publishers, Inc.

However, not everyone agrees on what specific skills a head nurse should acquire. Some view the head nurse management role to be one of support and advancement of staff nurses: others think the head nurse should maintain control and ensure compliance. As a result, many programs for management development have been prescribed.[4,5]

The "prescription approach" (take a week of leadership training and see you back at work) assumes that all head nurses manage the same situations and are faced with the same set of needs. That approach contradicts the model every nurse is exposed to during professional training. The first step in any type of development process is diagnosis: before one can prescribe a solution, one needs to assess the needs of the situation. The approach to management development should be no different than the approach taken to the nursing role. Current thinking in the area of leadership and management development favors a situational approach.[6,7] This approach asserts that the best way to manage or supervise depends on the environment in which a manager functions. When the situational approach is used, the management situation is first assessed, and then various managerial behaviors are prescribed.

A situational management training program for head nurses was developed at a 170-bed midwestern hospital. The program included a situational assessment of the management needs from the perspectives of head nurses and staff nurses, assessment of the present skill levels of head nurses (again from the perspectives of head nurses and staff nurses), and identification of areas in which head nurses' management skills needed development.

## SITUATIONAL ASSESSMENT

A model developed by Yukl provided the framework for determining the management needs of the head nurses.[8] This model builds on and takes into account the shortcomings of earlier models and provides a more comprehensive approach to situational management development. In this model, factors important in determining the needs of a particular situation include the nature of the people managed (e.g., staff nurse skills and staff nurses' understanding of job duties and responsibilities), the nature of the tasks performed (variety in tasks and structure in task assignments), the type of organizational structure (e.g., authority and discretion of the individual head nurse), and the nature of the organizational climate (e.g., relationships between head nurse and staff nurses and intra- and interstaff relations).

A detailed analysis of these factors disclosed 19 "needs" that the head nurse might be required to manage (see box, "Situational Need Dimensions").

The Situational Assessment Questionnaire (SAQ) was used to determine the magnitude of each need. The SAQ was administered to both head nurses and their subordinate staff nurses. Each head nurse–staff nurse team was coded, scores were computed, and the average score for all the staff nurses reporting to a given head nurse was used in the analysis. Items used to assess the performance emphasis need dimension (the first of 19 items in the box, "Situational Need Dimensions") are presented in Figure 1; the more the conditions described in Figure 1 were present in the environment, the higher the scores, indicating a need for head nurse management skills

## Situational Need Dimensions

1. **Performance emphasis:** the need to emphasize the importance of subordinate performance, improve productivity and efficiency, keep subordinates working up to capacity, and check on performance.

2. **Consideration:** the need to be friendly, supportive, and considerate toward subordinates and to be fair and objective.

3. **Inspiration:** the need to stimulate enthusiasm among subordinates for the work of the group and to say things that build confidence in the subordinates' ability to perform assignments successfully.

4. **Praise–recognition:** the need to provide praise and recognition to subordinates who perform effectively, to show appreciation for their efforts and contributions, and to make sure they get credit for their helpful ideas and suggestions.

5. **Structuring reward–contingencies:** the need to reward effective subordinate performance with tangible benefits such as pay increases, promotions, more desirable assignments, better work schedules, more time off, and so forth.

6. **Decision participation:** the need to consult with subordinates and otherwise allow them to influence managerial decisions.

7. **Autonomy–delegation:** the need to delegate authority and responsibility to subordinates and allow them to determine how to do their work.

8. **Role clarification:** the need to inform subordinates about their duties and responsibilities, specify the rules and policies that must be observed, and let subordinates know what is expected of them.

9. **Goal setting:** the need to emphasize the importance of setting specific performance goals for each important aspect of a subordinate's job, measure progress toward the goals, and provide concrete feedback.

10. **Training–coaching:** the need to determine training needs for subordinates and to provide any necessary training and coaching.

11. **Information dissemination:** the need to keep subordinates informed about developments that affect their work, including events in other work units or outside the organization, decisions made by higher management, and progress in meetings with superiors or outsiders.

12. **Problem solving:** the need to take the initiative in proposing solutions to serious work-related problems and act decisively to deal with such problems when a prompt solution is needed.

13. **Planning:** the need to organize efficiently and schedule the work in advance, plan how to attain work unit objectives, and make contingency plans for potential problems.

14. **Coordination:** the need to coordinate the work of subordinates, emphasize the importance of coordination, and encourage subordinates to coordinate their activities.

15. **Work facilitation:** the need to provide subordinates with necessary supplies, equipment, support service, or other resources; eliminate problems in the work environment; and remove other obstacles that interfere with the work.

16. **Representation:** the need to establish contacts with other groups and important people in the organization, persuade them to appreciate and support the work unit, and influence superiors and outsiders to promote and defend the interests of the work unit.

17. **Interaction–facilitation:** the need to encourage subordinates to be friendly with each other, cooperate, share information and ideas, and help one another.

18. **Conflict management:** the need to restrain subordinates from fighting and arguing, encourage them to resolve conflicts in a constructive manner, and help to settle conflicts and disagreements between subordinates.

19. **Criticism–discipline:** the need to constructively criticize or discipline a subordinate who shows consistently poor performance, violates a rule, or disobeys an order (disciplinary actions include an official warning, reprimand, suspension, or dismissal).

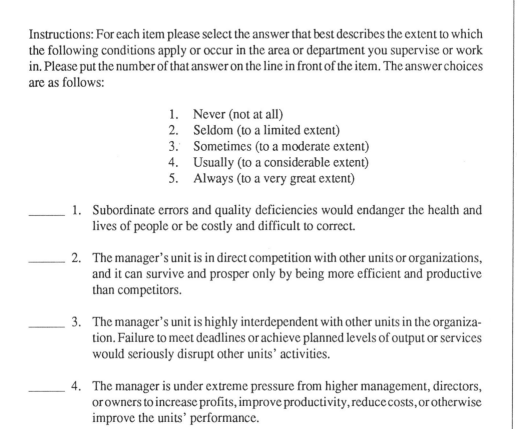

Instructions: For each item please select the answer that best describes the extent to which the following conditions apply or occur in the area or department you supervise or work in. Please put the number of that answer on the line in front of the item. The answer choices are as follows:

1. Never (not at all)
2. Seldom (to a limited extent)
3. Sometimes (to a moderate extent)
4. Usually (to a considerable extent)
5. Always (to a very great extent)

_____ 1. Subordinate errors and quality deficiencies would endanger the health and lives of people or be costly and difficult to correct.

_____ 2. The manager's unit is in direct competition with other units or organizations, and it can survive and prosper only by being more efficient and productive than competitors.

_____ 3. The manager's unit is highly interdependent with other units in the organization. Failure to meet deadlines or achieve planned levels of output or services would seriously disrupt other units' activities.

_____ 4. The manager is under extreme pressure from higher management, directors, or owners to increase profits, improve productivity, reduce costs, or otherwise improve the units' performance.

_____ 5. Subordinates are not highly motivated to do the work and are likely to "slack off" if not prodded and encouraged.

**Figure 1.** Items used to assess the performance emphasis need.

in the area. The remaining 18 need dimensions were similarly assessed.

## ASSESSMENT OF PRESENT SKILL LEVELS

The second step in the situational management development model was to evaluate how well the head nurses were performing on the 19 dimensions identified in the situational assessment. This was determined by having the head nurses and their subordinate staff nurses complete the Manager/Supervisor Behavioral Description Questionnaire (BDQ). Figure 2 presents the items relevant to the first of 19 items, performance emphasis. The BDQ has two components: one to be completed by the head nurse and one to be completed by his or her subordinates. (A third form, which can be completed by the head nurse's superior, was not used in this study.) The performance emphasis scale

Managerial-supervisor form—to be completed by supervisor/manager

Instructions: For each item please select the answer that best describes your supervisory behavior. Please put the number of that answer on the line in front of the item. The answer choices are as follows:

1. Never (not at all)
2. Seldom (to a limited extent)
3. Sometimes (to a moderate extent)
4. Usually (to a considerable extent)
5. Always (to a very great extent)

**Performance emphasis**

_____ 1. I emphasize the importance of achieving a high level of performance.

_____ 2. I try to keep subordinates working at their maximum level of performance.

_____ 3. I push for increased productivity and efficiency.

_____ 4. I encourage subordinates to do high quality work.

**Subordinate form—to be completed by a sample of 3–5 subordinates**

_____ 1. My supervisor emphasizes the importance of achieving a high level of performance.

_____ 2. My supervisor tries to keep subordinates working at their maximum level of performance.

_____ 3. My supervisor pushes for increased productivity and efficiency.

_____ 4. My supervisor encourages subordinates to do high quality work.

**Figure 2.** Manager/supervisor behavior description questionnaire items (assessing performance emphasis).

represents those management behaviors necessary to ensure high productivity, efficiency, and quality (see Figure 2). The remaining 18 dimensions were similarly assessed.

By combining the results of the situational needs and managerial behavior skill level assessments, areas were identified where change or development was most needed. Three outcomes were possible for each dimension: (1) behavior or skill level was less than the need level and should be improved, (2) behavior or skill level was greater than need level and should be de-emphasized, (3) behavior or skill level matched need level and required no change.

## RESULTS

As part of the training effort, the head nurses were encouraged to share the results of the study with their staff nurses. All head nurses were given the results of their own staffs.

Table 1 shows the means and standard deviations for the need scores for both the

*By combining the results of the situational needs and managerial behavior skill level assessments, areas were identified where change or development was most needed.*

head nurses and their subordinate staff nurses and T-values for the comparisons between groups. The T-values indicated that the head nurses and staff nurses perceived their situation differently on only the inspiration dimension. The head nurses saw more need for inspiration than did their staff nurses. An examination of the items consti-

**Table 1.** Situational need dimension scores for head nurses and their staff nurses

| Dimensions | Head nurses (N=13) | | Staff nurses (N=52) | | T-value |
|---|---|---|---|---|---|
| | Mean | Standard deviation | Mean | Standard deviation | |
| 1. Performance emphasis | 3.6 | .7 | 3.6 | .7 | .0 |
| 2. Consideration | 3.9 | .5 | 3.8 | .6 | .3 |
| 3. Inspiration | 4.0 | .4 | 3.7 | .5 | 4.0* |
| 4. Praise–recognition | 3.5 | .3 | 3.4 | .5 | .5 |
| 5. Structuring reward–contingencies | 3.2 | .6 | 3.3 | .8 | .2 |
| 6. Decision participation | 4.1 | .4 | 3.9 | .5 | 1.8 |
| 7. Autonomy–delegation | 3.5 | .3 | 3.5 | .4 | .0 |
| 8. Role clarification | 2.8 | .5 | 2.8 | .4 | .0 |
| 9. Goal setting | 3.5 | .5 | 3.4 | .6 | .3 |
| 10. Training–coaching | 3.5 | .6 | 3.3 | .6 | 1.2 |
| 11. Information dissemination | 4.0 | .6 | 3.9 | .7 | .2 |
| 12. Problem solving | 3.0 | .7 | 2.9 | .5 | .4 |
| 13. Planning | 3.5 | .5 | 3.3 | .5 | 1.7 |
| 14. Coordination | 3.4 | .7 | 3.7 | .7 | 1.9 |
| 15. Work facilitation | 3.4 | .9 | 3.2 | .8 | .6 |
| 16. Representation | 3.1 | .6 | 3.1 | .7 | .0 |
| 17. Interaction–facilitation | 3.8 | .6 | 3.9 | .6 | .3 |
| 18. Conflict management | 2.1 | .6 | 2.2 | .7 | .2 |
| 19. Criticism–discipline | 4.3 | .4 | 4.1 | .5 | 1.8 |

*P<.05

**Table 2.** Skill behavior scores for head nurses and their staff nurses

| Dimensions | Head nurses (N=13) | | Staff nurses (N=52) | | T-value |
|---|---|---|---|---|---|
| | Mean | Standard deviation | Mean | Standard deviation | |
| 1.  Performance emphasis | 4.2 | .6 | 4.2 | .8 | .0 |
| 2.  Consideration | 4.5 | .5 | 4.2 | .7 | 2.2 |
| 3.  Inspiration | 3.6 | .6 | 3.5 | .8 | .2 |
| 4.  Praise–recognition | 4.2 | .4 | 3.8 | .7 | 3.9* |
| 5.  Structuring reward–contingencies | 4.1 | .5 | 3.6 | .7 | 5.8** |
| 6.  Decision participation | 3.8 | .8 | 3.6 | .8 | .7 |
| 7.  Autonomy–delegation | 4.9 | .7 | 4.1 | .5 | .4 |
| 8.  Role clarification | 4.3 | .6 | 3.9 | .7 | 3.6 |
| 9.  Goal setting | 3.8 | .7 | 3.7 | .8 | .2 |
| 10.  Training–coaching | 4.1 | .6 | 3.5 | .9 | 5.2* |
| 11.  Information dissemination | 4.2 | .5 | 3.8 | .8 | 2.9 |
| 12.  Problem solving | 4.2 | .5 | 3.9 | .7 | 2.1 |
| 13.  Planning | 3.6 | .7 | 3.6 | .8 | .0 |
| 14.  Coordination | 3.6 | .9 | 3.4 | .8 | .6 |
| 15.  Work facilitation | 4.3 | .7 | 4.0 | .6 | 2.4 |
| 16.  Representation | 4.3 | .6 | 4.0 | .6 | 2.6 |
| 17.  Interaction–facilitation | 4.5 | .5 | 4.1 | .8 | 2.9 |
| 18.  Conflict management | 4.0 | .8 | 3.7 | .9 | 1.2 |
| 19.  Criticism–discipline | 4.3 | .6 | 3.6 | .9 | 7.0** |

*P<.05  **P<.01

tuting this need dimension indicated a significant difference in how the two groups perceived whether staff nurses were discouraged by temporary setbacks and lack of progress resulting from the difficult and frustrating nature of their work.

Table 2 shows the scores for the head nurses and their staff were significantly different on four dimensions. The head nurses reported engaging in more praise–recognition, structuring reward-contingencies, training–coaching, and criticism–discipline behavior than their staff perceived them engaging in. The head nurses were again encouraged to share their

results with their staff, especially when results differed by one point or more. The scores for specific items in each dimension were provided to help the head nurses pinpoint differences between themselves and their staff.

Table 3 presents the rank orders of the mean need and behavior scores and the differences between the need and behavior ranks for each group. Each dimension was placed in one of the three categories (behavior greater than, less than, or matching need) on the basis of the differences between the need and behavior rankings. The criterion used was the mean difference for the rank

**Table 3.** Dimensional need and behavioral skill scores for head nurses and their staff nurses

| Dimensions | Head nurses (N=13) Rank order | | | Staff nurses (N=52) Rank order | | |
|---|---|---|---|---|---|---|
| | Need | Behavior | Difference | Need | Behavior | Difference |
| 1. Performance emphasis | 7 | 8.5 | 1.5 | 8 | 1.5 | 6.5 |
| 2. Consideration | 5 | 1.5 | 3.5 | 5 | 1.5 | 3.5 |
| 3. Inspiration | 3.5 | 18 | 14.5 | 6.5 | 17.5 | 11 |
| 4. Praise–recognition | 10 | 8.5 | 1.5 | 10.5 | 9.5 | 1 |
| 5. Structuring reward–contingencies | 15 | 11.5 | 3.5 | 13 | 14.5 | 1.5 |
| 6. Decision participation | 2 | 15.5 | 13.5 | 3 | 14.5 | 11.5 |
| 7. Autonomy–delegation | 10 | 13.5 | 3.5 | 9 | 3.5 | 5.5 |
| 8. Role clarification | 18 | 4.5 | 13.5 | 18 | 7.5 | 10.5 |
| 9. Goal setting | 10 | 15.5 | 4.5 | 10.5 | 11.5 | 1 |
| 10. Training–coaching | 10 | 11.5 | 1.5 | 13 | 17.5 | 4.5 |
| 11. Information dissemination | 3.5 | 8.5 | 5 | 3 | 9.5 | 6.5 |
| 12. Problem solving | 17 | 8.5 | 8.5 | 17 | 7.5 | 9.5 |
| 13. Planning | 10 | 18 | 8 | 13 | 14.5 | 1.5 |
| 14. Coordination | 13.5 | 18 | 4.5 | 6.5 | 19 | 12.5 |
| 15. Work facilitation | 13.5 | 4.5 | 9 | 15 | 5.5 | 9.5 |
| 16. Representation | 16 | 4.5 | 11.5 | 16 | 5.5 | 10.5 |
| 17. Interaction–facilitation | 6 | 1.5 | 4.5 | 3 | 3.5 | .5 |
| 18. Conflict management | 19 | 13.5 | 5.5 | 19 | 11.5 | 7.5 |
| 19. Criticism–discipline | 1 | 4.5 | 3.5 | 1 | 14.5 | 13.5 |

differences for each group: 6.4 for the head nurses and 6.7 for the staff nurses.

**Dimensions requiring increases in skill level**

A dimension was placed in this category if either the head nurses' need rank score was 6.4 or *higher* than the behavior rank score or the staff nurses' need rank score was 6.7 or *higher* than the behavior rank score. Table 3 shows that the scores for both groups indicate a need for improvement in the inspiration and decision participation dimen-sions, while the head nurses' scores indicate a need for improvement in the planning dimension, and the staff nurses scores indi-cate a need for improvement in the coordi-nation and criticism–discipline dimen-sions.

**Dimensions requiring decreases in skill level**

A dimension was placed in this category if either the head nurses' need rank score was 6.4 or *lower* than the behavior rank score or the staff nurses' need rank score was 6.7 or *lower* than the behavior rank score. As Table 3 shows, the scores for both groups placed the role clarification, problem solving, work facilitation, and representation dimensions in this category, as did the staff nurses' scores for the conflict–management dimension.

## Dimensions not requiring any changes in skill level

A dimension was placed in this category if either the difference between the head nurses' need and behavior rank scores was less than 6.4 or the difference between the staff nurses' need and behavior rank scores was less than 6.7. Table 3 shows that, according to the scores for both groups, no change was needed in the performance emphasis, consideration, praise-recognition, structuring reward-contingencies, autonomy–delegation, goal setting,

training–coaching, information dissemination, and interaction–facilitation dimensions.

•    •    •

A situational approach can be successfully applied to developing head nurses' management skills. Programs such as this can counteract the management crisis in the nursing profession. One hospital's application of this approach demonstrated the need for using input from both supervisors and their subordinates in designing and implementing a management development training effort. Such an approach not only provides more accurate information about areas in which management skills training and development are needed but also ensures that all parties will be receptive to the subsequent development effort.

## REFERENCES

1. Wilsea, M.M. "Nursing Leadership Crisis: Proposal for Solutions." *Supervisor Nurse* 2, no. 4 (April 1980): 47–48.
2. Westphal, B.C., Jenkins, R., and Miller, M.C., III. "Charge Nurse: Where Staff and Management Meet." *Nursing Management* 17, no. 4 (April 1986): 56–58.
3. Nowell, G. "Job Tension among Unit Managers." *Hospital Topics* 57–58 (May/June 1980): 24–28.
4. Carter, K.A. "Managerial Role Development in the Nursing Supervisor." *Supervisor Nurse* 11, no. 7 (July 1980): 26–28.

5. Smith, H.L., and Mitry, N.W. "Nursing Leadership: A Buffering Perspective." *Nursing Administration Quarterly* 8, no. 3 (Spring 1984): 42–53.
6. House, R.J., and Mitchell, T.R. "Path-Goal Theory of Leadership." *Contemporary Business* 3 (Fall 1974): 81-98.
7. Hersey, P., and Blanchard, K. *Management of Organizational Behavior*. Englewood Cliffs, N.J.: Prentice-Hall, 1982.
8. Yukl, G.A. *Leadership in Organizations*. Englewood Cliffs, N.J.: Prentice-Hall, 1981.

# The psychological impact of the head nurse manager in transition: Organizational roles for minimizing stress

*Barbara A. Turner*
*Head Nurse Manager*
*Surgical Intensive Care Unit*
*University Hospital of Arkansas*
*Little Rock, Arkansas*

T HE PSYCHOLOGICAL experiences of the novice head nurse in transition from staff nurse have a profound impact on the success or failure of that transition. While promotion elicits feelings of joy and anticipation as self-actualization is realized within the individual, it also brings high stress as the novice ventures into unknown and untested waters.

Understanding the mechanisms of stress and how they produce behavior in the individual will provide the organization with insights into problems encountered. This knowledge will enhance the development of programs designed to reduce stress and develop positive behaviors and attitudes in the novice manager toward both the role and the organization.

This article does not necessarily represent the opinions of the University Hospital of Arkansas.

*Health Care Superv*, 1991, 9(3), 23–28
©1991 Aspen Publishers, Inc.

## THE CONTEMPORARY HEAD NURSE ROLE

The role of today's head nurse manager is more demanding than ever. With the current economic climate and the critical need for cost containment within the organization, managers at all levels are being held more accountable for allocation and utilization of human and material resources.

This extension of the head nurse role has benefited both the head nurse and the organization. While decentralization is cost-effective for the organization, it has markedly increased the stress levels of those first-line managers who now find themselves responsible for the operation of the unit. Effective staffing, proper mix levels, and budget prediction are essential to effective operation. So too, appropriate coping mechanisms are essential to the successful manager, who has a direct impact on the organization's future financial viability.

## STRESS AND COPING IN THE WORK SETTING

Why do some individuals excel in management while others fail dismally? To a great extent, success or failure depends on both the individual (intrinsic factors) and the environment (extrinsic factors) in which the new manager must function.

Behavior (response) is the product of the interaction between these two sets of factors. Intrinsic factors are those innate components that make us unique and form the basis of how we perceive ourselves in relation to the world. They include educational preparation, knowledge base, values, goals, commitments, and past experiences. Confidence, adaptability, and the ability to perceive outcomes are all influenced by intrinsic factors.

Extrinsic factors arise from the situation and the environment. They include the presence and duration of stressors, the type of management practice employed by the institution, social networks, and power and political structures. Consider how a new situation confronting the manager might affect behavior. How might a novice manager react to giving employee evaluations if he or she had insufficient training on the subject?

The interaction of intrinsic and extrinsic factors causes the individual to form a perception of the environmental stimulus that may range from benign, to challenging, or even threatening. Positive stimuli are the most beneficial to effective behavior, whereas threatening ones are the most detrimental to it. Table 1 lists factors and possible outcomes or behaviors that depend on whether the perception is positive or negative.

Positive perceptions, which produce desired behaviors, are consistent with successful management. Because the head nurse manager has a profound influence on the unit's function, it is imperative that the organization develop strategies that promote positive behaviors.

## IDENTIFYING AND TRAINING THE POTENTIAL MANAGER

Unfortunately, most hospitals and other components of the health care delivery system continue to rely heavily on past performance and intuition when selecting head nurse managers. Yet to identify candidates the organization should also consider conducting simulations of tasks required of the head nurse manager and extensive interviews.

### The interview process

When reviewing a field of candidates for a manager position, the goal is selecting the

**Table 1.** Intrinsic and extrinsic factors that influence perception and response

| Factors | Positive responses | Negative responses |
|---|---|---|
| **Intrinsic** | | |
| **Past experience** | Past experience relevant. Able to perceive outcomes.<br>Uses stressor perceived as a challenge or at least benign.<br>Reinforces feelings of control and self-confidence. | Past experience not relative.May generate feelings of anxiety, helplessness, loss of control creating decreased self-confidence and esteem. |
| **Education preparation knowledge** | Adequate.<br>Has knowledge to develop useful skills which increase successes.<br>Decreased anxiety, increases job satisfaction and feelings of self-worth. | Inadequate. Insufficient knowledge to develop skills.<br>Leads to feelings of inadequacy. Unable to accurately prioritize. Heightened feelings of frustration even to hostility if unsuccessful at dealing with problems. |
| **Values and goals** | Consistent with supervisor and organization.<br>Fosters positive feelings regarding role and about organization. | Inconsistent with supervisors and organization. May cause hostility and anger toward supervisor and/or organization. Increased frustration and job dissatisfaction as individual is unable to meet own goals. |
| **Commitments** | Has role as one of personal priorities and willing to expend necessary time and energy to complete the job requirements—increases feelings of self-satisfaction. | Does not have definite commitment to role; majority of priorities elsewhere. Frustration increased when needed to spend additional time to accomplish responsibilities which may generate feelings of helplessness and hostility toward organization. |
| **Extrinsic** | | |
| **Novelty** | Tends to view new role as a challenge. Affected directly by intrinsic factors and feelings of ability to control own environment. | If inadequately prepared or has insufficient past experience, will eventually feel threatened and unable to control environment. |
| **Duration of event** | Frustration and stress significantly decrease if able to rapidly prioritize and decrease length of duration. | The longer the duration, the higher the stress. If unable to resolve expediently will produce feelings of frustration and futility. |
| **Urgency of stimulus** | Able to address situation quickly. Prioritizes effectively.<br>Perceives stimulus as a challenge. | Feels frustration at being unable to accomplish existing tasks. Produces negative feelings toward source of stimulus. |
| **Role ambiguity** | Clearly understands role and responsibilities. Able to accomplish tasks. Increased feelings of self-actualization with success. | Role ambiguity causes frustration, anger, and hostility toward the supervisor and organization. |
| **Outcome perception** | Is able to visualize possible outcomes accurately. Generates increased success rate and increased self-esteem. | Has difficulty in visualizing outcomes. Feels increased anxiety and apprehension. |
| **Social support** | Adequate social support perception increases the perception of challenge toward the event.<br><br>Tends to promote problem-solving responses. | Perceived lack of social support produces significant feelings of insecurity that significantly affect the ability and inclination to make difficult decisions.<br><br>Tends to promote emotion-solving responses. |

right person for the job. Frequently, the candidate's perception of the role of head nurse is different from what that role actually is. Clarification of the role during the interview is essential for both the interviewer and the candidate.

> *Selection of the head nurse manager on the basis of past clinical performance and interviewer intuition alone is a precarious method at best.*

The interview process should include personal interviews to determine the candidates' views, values, and beliefs. Those individuals who differ substantially from the prospective supervisor's and the organization's goals and objectives will find the role most difficult. Compatibility with organizational goals may be identified by having the candidate complete a questionnaire comprised of situational statements to which the candidate must respond or by the use of a job-center program. A job-center program, used by numerous organizations, helps identify processing and coping behaviors. In such a program, the candidates are placed in a simulated work environment and given tasks associated with the role. Their performance is evaluated by trained observers. The job center program is, however, costly. Questionnaires are more cost-efficient.

Whatever format is chosen must ultimately provide the interviewer with sufficient information about the abilities and perceptions of the candidate. All too often, head nurses are selected based only on past performance in the clinical area and a brief interview.

## Selection

Selection of the head nurse manager on the basis of past clinical performance and interviewer intuition alone is a precarious method at best. Given the impact of leadership on morale, recruitment, and retention and the critical need for cost containment, it is crucial to find a person who can assume the role quickly and effectively. Placing a novice in the leadership position of a unit experiencing difficulties with staff relations, excessive discipline, or staff shortage is questionable, for the novice may be unable to cope with the extraordinary demands required to turn the unit around. The environment and the manager must be somewhat compatible.

## Orientation

Once the candidate is chosen, the organization must provide sufficient orientation to the unit and the role. Inadequate programs do not provide the novice with sufficient opportunity to become acclimated to the role or to develop needed skills. The period should to a degree insulate the new manager from excessive demands and enable the novice to assimilate information and develop appropriate social networks. For example, a strong preceptor–mentor program would benefit both the organization and the novice by providing continuity in the organization. Areas that must be addressed during this period are: (1) administrative policies, (2) mechanisms for effecting change, (3) resocialization within the organizational structure, (4) role clarification, and (5) chain of command.

## Training

A careful review of the factors in Figure 1 shows that training may be the key to successful transition. It is certainly the most

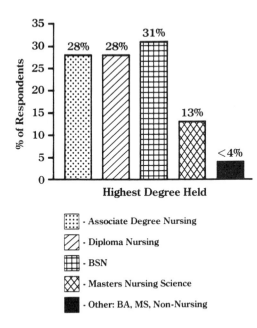

**Figure 1.** Graph showing degrees held by survey respondents.

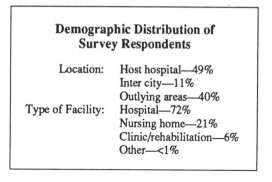

readily modifiable factor. Few nurses are trained to be managers. Managing a single shift as a charge nurse is entirely different from managing a unit on a 24-hour basis. Unfortunately many health care institutions find the initial cost of training prohibitive and thus ignore its long-term benefits.

Undergraduate training for nurses focuses primarily on the development of clinical skills and theory. At the bachelor level, if leadership theory is introduced at all, it is too brief to be of use to the practicing head nurse manager. Those who continue on to the master's level are somewhat better prepared. However, they are generally placed in supervisory roles in middle or upper management. Associate degree and diploma-prepared nurses receive no leadership training.

Head nurse positions are ideally reserved for those with at least bachelor degrees. But this is not the case in many areas, particularly because of the current nursing shortage. This was clearly illustrated in a recent survey conducted by the staff development department in the author's institution. The results were impressive in spite of the small sample size ($N$=53) of respondents and the limited demographics (surveys were sent only to institutions within the state; see the box entitled "Demographic Distribution of Survey Respondents").

Demographic information included the name of the institution and the job title and highest degree held by the respondent (see

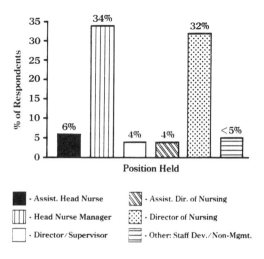

**Figure 2.** Graph showing positions held by survey respondents.

**Table 2.** Top 10 categories graded as perceived needs by survey respondents

| Category | 1 | 2 | 3 |
|---|---|---|---|
| 1. Managing change and conflict | 55% | 14% | 10% |
| 2. Managing assertively | 42 | 45 | 13 |
| 3. Legal aspects of management | 36 | 49 | 15 |
| 3. Leadership versus management | 36 | 43 | 21 |
| 4. Politics of management | 32 | 51 | 17 |
| 5. Pitfalls of management | 30 | 49 | 21 |
| 6. Motivating staff | 25 | 68 | 7 |
| 6. Organizational skills | 25 | 55 | 20 |
| 7. Problem solving | 21 | 62 | 17 |
| 8. Conducting evaluations | 19 | 23 | 58 |
| 8. Personnel development | 19 | 60 | 21 |
| 9. Business management | 15 | 38 | 47 |
| 10. Conducting interviews | 11 | 58 | 31 |
| 10. Decision making | 11 | 68 | 21 |

1 = essential; 2 = would be nice; 3 = don't need at this time.

box and Figure 1). Twenty-one managerial items were listed for evaluation of perceived need.

Of those surveyed, 56 percent were in managerial roles with associate or diploma preparation (see Figure 2). The top 10 perceptual needs include basic managerial functions (see Table 2). One interesting item not included here was the lack of perceived need for management theory (exceeded 70 percent). One wonders if this was related to confusion among respondents about the role of management and leadership theory.

Given these results, it is clear that health care delivery organizations need to address the issue of management training. Also needed is a nationwide survey of nurses' perceptions of supervisory roles.

•   •   •

The role of the head nurse continues to expand within the contemporary health care system, and the impact of that role will seriously affect the financial viability of health care organizations. Therefore, it is apparent that these organizations must re-evaluate this role in relationship to its goals and objectives. They must also adopt strategies to select the appropriate individual for the particular job and provide sufficient training for successful management behaviors. The organization that expects its novice managers to hit the ground running must prepare these managers to clear the high hurdles, endure the marathons, and sprint to the finish line.

## SUGGESTED READINGS

Billings, C. "Employment Setting Barriers to Professional Actualization in Nursing." *Nursing Management* 18, no. 11 (1987): 69–71.

Butler, J., and Parsons, R.J. "Hospital Perceptions of Job Satisfaction." *Nursing Management* 20, no. 8 (1989): 45 48.

Fein, A., and Strosberg, M. *Managing the Critical Care Unit.* Rockville, Md.: Aspen Publishers, 1987.

Hodges, L.C., Knapp, R., and Cooper, J. "Head Nurses: Their Practice and Education." *Nurse Educator* 13, no. 2 (1988): 9–11.

Hyna, W.F., and Guttman, C.M. *Management of Surgical Facilities.* Rockville, Md.: Aspen Publishers, 1984.

Massie, J.L. *The Essentials of Management.* 4th ed. Englewood Cliffs, N.J.: Prentice Hall, 1987.

Prescott, P.A., and Bowen, S.A. "Controlling Nursing Turnover." *Nursing Management* 18, no. 6 (1987): 60–66.

Raffing, K.L., Smith, H.L., and Rogers, R. "Factors That Encourage Nurses To Remain in Nursing." *Nursing Forum* 21, no. 2 (1984): 78–85.

Smith, H.L., and Piland, N.T. "Managing Organizational Aversion among Health Care Workers." *Health Care Supervisor* 7, no. 4 (1989): 1–10.

Taylor, M.S., and Covaleski, M.A. "Predicting Nurses' Turnover and Internal Transfer Behavior." *Nursing Research* 34, no. 4 (1985): 33–40.

Umiker, W. "Decision Making and Problem Solving by the Busy Professional." *Health Care Supervisor* 7, no. 4 (1989): 33–40.

Whitney, L., and Holm, K. "Nursing Care Delivery into the 1990's." *Dimensions of Critical Care* 6, no. 5 (1987): 259–60.

Young, S.W., Johnston, D., and Sweeney, C. "Excellence in Leadership through Organizational Development." *Nursing Administration Quarterly* 12, no. 4 (1988): 69–77.

# Orientation and training of nurse managers: A case study

**Bonnie L. Roach**
*Assistant Professor*
*Department of Management Systems*
*Ohio University*
*Athens, Ohio*

**Laurie MacLeod Smith**
*Human Resources Specialist*
*Exxon Central Services*
*Florham Park, New Jersey*

A MAJOR CONCERN in the health care industry is the need for competent and qualified nurse managers. Not only must these nurses be clinically competent, they must also utilize the appropriate administrative skills to perform most effectively in their roles.[1] Hospitals tend to promote their "best" nurses into these positions—nurses who were originally evaluated highly because of their clinical competence and knowledge.[1] These skills, while important for the clinician, are not enough to ensure that the nurse manager will perform with optimal efficiency.[2,3] Many nurses promoted to managerial roles are confronted with the realization that they do not have the necessary skills to perform the job.

To complicate matters even further, little information is provided to nurses entering these positions that would help them make the transition from clinician to manager. Many nurses

Portions of this article appeared in *Proceedings of the Eastern Academy of Management* 26 (1989): 127–29.

*Health Care Superv*, 1991, 9(4), 9–14
©1991 Aspen Publishers, Inc.

face the frustration of being placed in a new role for which they have no experience and few role models. The result is high turnover in these positions because many are unable to handle the stress and ambiguity associated with the new role.[1] This situation can produce serious consequences in the future because the nurse executive or manager will increasingly be recognized as an important asset to the health care profession but will be in limited supply.[4]

Part of the problem is that the nursing administrator must possess the clinical competence and knowledge essential for the field and at the same time also possess general managerial skills.[4-9] To determine what managerial skills are most useful for administrative positions, Freund sent questionnaires to chief executive officers (CEOs) and directors of nursing (DONs) of 250 university-affiliated hospitals.[4] Both groups responded that administrative positions require general managerial knowledge along with fiscal, accounting, and human management skills. Knowledge of these skills is also useful for the nurse manager. Respondents indicated that educational programs must offer their students adequate preparation in three areas to fully prepare them for administrative duties: (1) a solid base in the field of management, (2) courses dealing with organizational politics, and (3) general knowledge of nursing practice, the profession, and the health industry.[4]

Are nurses in managerial roles actually functioning as true managers? Sherman surveyed 105 nurses in supervisory positions (head nurses, nurse supervisors, assistant directors of nursing, and directors of nursing) who were employed by large (400-bed or larger) general hospitals.[10] The nurses were asked to respond whether they actually performed 101 specific tasks on a weekly basis. There tasks were formulated from seven general categories of

management—planning, organizing, staffing, leading, communicating, decisionmaking, and controlling. Responses indicated that these tasks were indeed performed on a weekly basis, and thus Sherman's study concluded that nurses in supervisory roles are true managers.[10]

It would seem logical that educational institutions would offer courses in these skills; however, many programs do not offer sufficient administrative courses to meet the needs of the nursing executives.[11] Historically, degree programs have concentrated on providing clinical rather than administrative knowledge, and administrators have only recently been required to possess advanced degrees. In the 1920s, a baccalaureate was considered sufficient for administrators in nursing service and education. The Master of Science degree for nursing first became available in the 1930s and soon became a requirement for all nurses because the knowledge required for the field was rapidly expanding. The need for highly qualified nurses, however, outnumbered the advanced degrees offered at the time, and these degrees concentrated on clinical rather than administrative skills.

In response to this problem, many graduate programs developed in the 1950s and 1960s focused on clinical nursing but not on administration. During the 1960s educational programs shifted from functional to clinical training. Administrative programs became unpopular to such an extent that they were not considered an acceptable field of study for nurses.[4] In the 1970s, more programs offered preparation for nurse administrators but only at the graduate level. Anderson, Thurkettle, and Fitzpatrick point out that continuing education programs were attempting to help the nurse administrator develop managerial skills, but even with the availability of these programs, only a minority of registered nurses (RNs) in administrative posts held advanced degrees. Of 61,000 RNs in administrative posts, surveyed in 1985, only 18 percent held master's degrees while 1.4 percent possessed doctorate degrees.[11] Furthermore, formal educational preparation for the managerial role was offered in only 18 (24 percent)[5] of the nation's 76 graduate schools of nursing.

Some evidence exists that hospitals rely on advanced educational degrees to provide nurses with adequate skills. For example, educational requirements for administrative positions have increased steadily in the last few years. Butts, Berger, and Brooten looked at recruiting advertisements in several journals of nursing for director of nursing, clinical director, supervisor, head of nursing, clinical specialist, in-service educator, and consultant.[9] Their findings confirmed that educational requirements increased for all positions except clinical specialist, which already had a high percentage of master's degrees required. In one study cited by McClosky and colleagues, a panel of national experts recommended that "95 percent of nurse administrators in major health care facilities should have master's degrees and 5 percent should have doctorates."[12(p.505)] Nonetheless, in 1981, only 8 percent of the students enrolled in 127 master's programs majored in administration and supervision while 72 percent of the sample majored in advanced clinical practice.[12]

One reason for the increased demand for advanced credentials in the service industry is the increasing complexity of the issues and problems that confront the nursing administrator.[13] Nursing administrators today must be knowledgeable about state and local regulations concerning health care because these regulations determine available resources, constraints on health care, availability of health care personnel, collective bargaining, financial budgeting, and ethical issues in health care.[11] The question remains whether these programs actually offer courses in administration or managerial skills and whether these courses are sufficient. Sherman states that the same number of administrative courses are offered in both two-year and three-year bachelor's and master's degree programs.[10] Nurses reported receiving only one or two courses in management during their entire program. Many in the profession felt that only four-year degrees provide the necessary qualifications for these positions. However, Sherman states that many prefer the four-year degree because of its perceived certification of the graduate's credentials, not because it provides better training in administration.[10]

---

*One reason for the increased demand for advanced credentials in the service industry is the increasing complexity of the issues and problems that confront the nursing administrator.*

---

A study by Duffy and Gold surveyed 76 nursing service administrators who held master's degrees in nursing administration and non-nursing administration. Most of the respondents felt that they had received only moderate preparation in managerial skills.[5] Those with degrees in non-nursing administration felt they were better prepared in budgeting, financial management, and marketing.[1] Carter recommends that nursing supervisors need adequate skills in the areas of planning (the ability to forecast the needs of the organization and develop appropriate policies to meet these needs), organizing (development of an organizational structure that describes the lines of authority and the responsibilities of each position), directing (the ability to arrive at a decision independently and implement that decision), and controlling (the development of evaluation standards of performance).[1]

Even with the increase in programs offering administrative training, it seems clear that the demand for skilled nurse managers will exceed the supply. Furthermore, because hospitals frequently promote from within, it is unrealistic to expect that these institutions are able to send their candidates to educational institutions to gain these skills. One possibility is that hospitals will rely on in-house programs to supplement the managerial needs.

If in-house training is to be effective, it must not only provide the appropriate skills but help the nurse manager make the transition from a clinical role to a managerial one. This case study looks at one hospital's methods of solving the problem and considers why this approach is consistent with the orientation and training literature.

## CASE STUDY

The target hospital is a 283-bed, full-service, fully accredited, not-for-profit, acute care hospital serving 43 counties in the midwestern United States. During monthly staff meetings, it becomes apparent that the assistant nurse managers (N=40) were encountering difficulties in their positions. The assistant nurse managers were required to have an associate's degree or diploma, although a Bachelor of Science degree in Nursing was preferred. Their degree did not appear to prepare the nurses for their new role as managers. Through informal discussions with the directors of nursing, the assistant nurse managers expressed concern that they had minimal leadership and administrative experience. It was decided that some of the problem could be alleviated by a training or

orientation program that would help define the assistant manager's role and identify management education goals.

Suggestions were passed to the nursing directors. A committee of three nursing directors was formed to investigate and create a training program for the assistant managers. Each director would be responsible for the orientation and training of all assistant nurse managers within a particular unit. The first step of the orientation process involved scheduled meetings between each assistant nurse manager and the unit director. During these meetings, the director explained and clarified the role of the assistant manager and all duties associated with the position. Furthermore, the director diagrammed how the role of assistant manager fits into the entire organizational structure as well as into the unit. The director's duty was to act as a mentor to the assistant nurse manager and assume responsibility for setting learning goals, acting as a resource person during the orientation, and monitoring the new manager's progress.

Once the assistant manager was well informed about her role, the director provided self-paced study materials, tapes, and workbooks. The self-paced modules included a policy and procedure exercise, resources (people and departments), budgeting information, personnel policies and procedures, scheduling and staffing techniques, and time cards and attendance calendars. These courses provided the trainees with three basic skills of management—conceptual, human relations, and technical.[14]

The director furnished the assistant nurse manager with the names of contact persons, their phone numbers, and an explanation of their importance to the assistant manager's unit. More importantly, the assistant manager was required to meet with people who have principle dealings with her unit—accounting, personnel, housekeeping, pharmacy, employee assistance program (EAP), quality assurance, central processing, and distribution and storeroom, for example. The purpose of these meetings was to identify individuals having close associations with the unit and to show how they can assist the assistant manager in performing the job. The director tested the trainee's knowledge by giving a list of problem questions to the assistant manager, which required that she know whom to call and what to ask for.

Once the self-paced orientation program was completed, the assistant nurse manager would then move into the management education programs available for all hospital management personnel. These programs include courses in equal employment opportunities, employment interviewing, stress management, progressive disciplinary processes, management systems, running effective meetings, and interpersonal communication, along with a management skill identification center. All of these topics would be presented in the classroom. Evaluations of the content of classes have been favorable. Evaluations collected from all participants of the classes show that 95 percent of respondents believed the classes were relevant, current, had substance, and enhanced their understanding of the topic.

• • •

The problem of recruiting and retaining administratively trained nurses in management positions is becoming a widespread concern. Educational programs are not likely to solve the problem because they do not offer the appropriate types or numbers of courses that could better prepare the nurse manager. Because the demand for nurse managers is increasing and educational programs do not provide adequate managerial training, the hospitals must assume the responsibility. By providing training, hospitals can not only ensure that their

nurses can perform more efficiently, but also help reduce the stress and possible turnover that results when untrained individuals attempt to perform unfamiliar tasks in an unfamiliar setting.

The hospital in this case study has followed a program that provides supplemental skills to the nurse manager and a thorough orientation to the managerial role. Reichers points out that a principal feature of any orientation is the socialization process of the newcomer.[15] This involves the adoption of a situational identity and making sense of the organization. The avenue by which the newcomer becomes assimilated to the environment is known as symbolic interaction, the process of attaching meaning and significance to events, practices, and procedures through interactions with others by the perceptions that arise through those interactions.[16] Assigning the new nurse manager to the director of the unit quickly provides the newcomer with a person who can provide the appropriate and immediate cognitive structure to aid in socialization. Furthermore, the director can direct the newcomer to the key people or units and appropriate sources for handling problems. This will help the newcomer to form an identity with her role as an assistant nurse manager within the context of the unit.[15] Reichers states that socialization rates are accelerated when "both newcomers and insiders act on each other and seek out interactions."[15] The consequence of the program is that the assistant nurse manager quickly adopts the identity of a manager rather than remaining a clinician trying to adopt a managerial role.

The second consequence of this type of program is that the assistant nurse manager learns the required managerial skills in a way that is likely to be retained and transferred to the job. Self-paced instruction allows trainees to obtain immediate feedback about how well they are learning and applying the material. This part of the process is similar to linear programming, which is characterized by the following criteria:

- Material is presented in small frames.
- Each frame requires a response from the learner.
- Immediate feedback is given to the learner about the correctness of the response.
- The program is designed to provide proper learning sequences.
- Each trainee proceeds at his or her individual pace.[17]

According to Goldstein, most studies show that programmed instruction does not necessarily make the trainees learn more, but it requires less time to learn the concepts than with other training methods.[18] This, coupled with the immediate reinforcement of the director, makes this an efficient and applicable program.

Future research should consider whether trainees actually experience a transition of identity from clinician to manager. This program, however, follows sound orientation and training procedures. Other hospitals may find it a viable type of program to supplement the skills of nurse managers.

## REFERENCES

1. Carter, K.A. "Managerial Role Development in the Nursing Supervisor." *Nurse Supervisor* 11 (July 1980): 26–28.
2. Buccheri, R.C. "Nursing Supervision: A New Look at an Old Role." *Nursing Administrative Quarterly* 11 (1986): 11–25.
3. Cederberg, D.M. "Changing Roles: From Nurse Educator to Novice Executive." *Nursing Management* 17 (1986): 69–70.
4. Freund, C.M. "Director of Nursing Effectiveness: DON and CEO Perspectives and Implications for Education." *The Journal of Nursing Administration* 15 (June 1985): 25–30.
5. Duffy, M.E., and Gold, N.E. "Education for Nursing Administration: What Investment Yields Highest Returns?" *Journal of Nursing Administration* 20 (September 1980): 3–18.
6. Poulin, M.A. "The Nurse Executive Role: A Structural and Functional Analysis." *The Journal of Nursing Administration* 14 (February 1984): 9–14.
7. Poulin, M.A. "Future Directions for Nursing Administration." *The Journal of Nursing Administration* 14 (March 1984):37–41.
8. Beyers, M. "Getting on Top of Organizational Change Part 2: Trends in Nursing Service." *The Journal of Nursing Administration* 14 (November 1984): 31–37.
9. Butts, P.A., Berger, B.A., and Brooten, D.A. "Tracking Down the Right Degree for the Job." *Nursing and Health Care* (February 1986): 91–95.
10. Sherman, C. "Nursing's Management Crisis." *Nurse Supervisor* 11 (October 1980): 31–33.
11. Anderson, R.M., Thurkettle, M.A., and Fitzpatrick, J. "The New Breed!" *Nursing Success Today* 2 (1985): 4–8.
12. McCloskey, J.C., Kerfoot, K., Molen, M., and Mathis, S. "Educating Nurse Administrators: One Program's Answer." *Nursing and Health Care* (November 1986): 505–08.
13. Kirk, R. "Management Development: A Needs Analysis for Nurse Executives and Managers." *Journal of Nursing Administration* 17 (1987): 7–8.
14. Fralic, M.F., and O'Connor, A. "A Management Progression System for Nurse Administrators, Part 2." *The Journal of Nursing Administration* 13 (May 1983): 32–38.
15. Reichers, A.E. "An Interactionist Perspective on Newcomer Socialization Rates." *The Academy of Management Review* 12(2) (1987): 278–87.
16, Blumer, H. *Symbolic Interactionism: Perspectives and Method.* Englewood Cliffs, N.J.: Prentice Hall 1969.
17. Bass, B.M., and Vaughn, J.A. *Training in Industry: The Management of Learning.* Belmont, Calif.: Wadsworth, 1969.
18. Goldstein, I.I. *Training: Program Development and Evaluation.* Belmont, Calif.: Wadsworth, 1974.

# Congruence between nursing education and nursing service: A common conceptual/theoretic framework for nursing units

*Helen Yura-Petro, Ph.D., F.A.A.N.*
*Eminent Professor Emeritus*
*School of Nursing*
*Old Dominion University*
*Norfolk, Virginia*

*Judith Brooks*
*Educational Nurse Specialist*
*Pitt County Memorial Hospital*
*Greenville, North Carolina*

IN HER 1893 TEXT, *Nursing, Its Principles and Practice,* Isabel Adams Hampton (Robb) expressed woeful concern about the incongruity of nursing practices among graduate nurses hired from other hospital training schools. Isabel Adams Hampton was the founding Superintendent of Nurses and Principal of the Training School for Nurses at Johns Hopkins Hospital. Her extensive writings were meant to rectify this problem and bring uniformity of practice among nurses.[1] In the 100 years that followed, concern continued to be expressed—nurse educators lamenting that graduates of nursing programs could not practice nursing as taught in colleges and universities and nurse supervisors complaining that new graduates required significant orientation to be highly productive from the start.

Debates between nurse educators and nurse supervisors have occurred over the decades. Discussions have centered upon

*Health Care Superv,* 1991, 10(2), 1–12
©1991 Aspen Publishers, Inc.

- changing the expectation that nursing students were *students* during clinical experiences and *not employees,*
- supporting the education of professional nurses in academic settings,
- upgrading the academic preparation of the nurse supervisor comparable to the expectation and preparation of nurse educators, and
- supporting the need for orientation for newly appointed nurse graduates in keeping with their education and with orientation requirements comparable to that received by other health professionals.

In the design for nursing's future from the National Commission on Nursing Implementation Project titled *Nursing's Vital Signs,* Margaret Murphy writes that over the years tension between nurse administrators and nurse educators has often surfaced over differences between the expectations of the practice sector and the outcomes espoused by the education sector.

Each group has asserted that the other has acted without being aware of the constraints of the other. Nurse administrators want educators to produce a product that is relevant to the service needs. Nurse educators want the service sector to provide adequate clinical experiences for students, to allow new graduates reasonable time to mature in their practice, and to place graduates in jobs appropriate to their educational preparation.[2(p.41)]

DeBack points out that the change in nursing education programs (from diploma to associate or baccalaureate degree) is but one aspect of the redesign process taking place in nursing education and affecting nursing practice. Outcomes of associate degree and baccalaureate degree nursing programs are being designed to approximate the practice competencies expected of nurses of the future. The changing

health care environment will require nurses who are educated differently than nurses in the past. Increased use of technology and the changes already seen in the age and health status of clients will require curricula that teach the broad life skills as well as sophisticated technical skills.[3(p.60)] Data are beginning to show that the nursing practice sector is taking responsibility for determining the abilities needed by nurses for the clients they serve and is using this information to influence educational outcomes. In addition, the deployment of nursing personnel based on education is becoming one of the factors used in creating more cost-effective, quality nursing care delivery systems.[3(p.53)]

Today, nursing education and practice systems are responding to current health and nursing care issues while anticipating future demands. The changes in society, particularly health care, have encouraged the development of partnerships and linkages within the nursing profession and between it and other disciplines. Ruth Waite observes: "Nursing's response is being reflected in the creative systems that are emerging in education and practice. Linkages and cooperative efforts are essential... to meet the challenges that face nursing now and in the future."[4(p.26)]

## A PARTNERSHIP FOR EDUCATION AND PRACTICE

Partnerships have been formed between individual schools and health care organizations to enhance the "fit" between education and practice.[2(p.42)] Such a partnership was developed between a nurse educator/consultant from Old Dominion University School of Nursing, Norfolk, Virginia, and nurse supervisors from Pitt County Memorial Hospital Nursing Unit, Greenville, North Carolina. In the past, nurse educators were (and needed to be) "future oriented" while nurse supervisors were mainly "now oriented." Through this partnership the educator and the supervisors were able to look at the future together and design the "here and now" to achieve a preferred future for nursing education and practice.

Recent developments in nursing such as the designation of four major concepts (human being, society/environment, health, and nursing)—widely used in developing nursing curriculums, such as nursing's metaparadigm (Jacqueline Fawcett, written communication, 1988), and in the development of nursing's human need theory (NHNT)[5]—provide a common framework for viewing nursing education and practice in the present state and for the future. Use of the metaparadigm (conceptual/theoretic frameworks) and NHNT by both the educator and supervisor facilitates communication and unity of purpose. Perspectives for practice, whether from an educational point of view or from the view of nursing service, begin to diverge rather than develop. Congruency becomes a reality.

## THE LIAISON PROCESS

Components of the liaison process that were used effectively to enhance congruence between education and practice involved

- preparation of statements of philosophy expressing beliefs about human beings, society/environment, health, nursing education, and nursing practice;
- incorporation of NHNT into the educational and practice documents;
- compatibility between the end of educa-

tional program behaviors for the graduate and the job descriptions for new graduate nurses; and
- incorporation of the triad of processes for professional nursing—nursing process, leadership process, and research process.

The nursing leadership group (head nurses/nurse managers, clinical nurses, nurse specialists, educational nurse specialists, nurse supervisors/coordinators, and nurse administrators) of the health care agency sought a nurse consultant and curriculum specialist from the university school of nursing. A series of consultation visits and workshops were conducted by the consultant initially with the nursing leadership group then with a selection of members of the nursing and health care staff culminating in a meeting with the entire nursing staff.

Significant nursing service documents were needed to incorporate NHNT and to achieve congruence with educational documents. These six nursing service documents included

1. *the philosophy of the nursing service unit.* The philosophy is the singular most important document developed by the nursing service leadership. All other documents stem from the philosophy statement. Beliefs about human beings and human needs, society/environmental and human needs, health (incorporating dimensions of wellness and illness) and human needs, and nursing service and meeting the human needs of the client are stated.
2. *the purpose of the nursing service unit.* It is stated in broad terms—the statement flows from the philosophy.
3. *the expectations for nursing clients.* These are specified in behavioral terms.

For example, as a result of nursing service, clients will have

- been treated with worth and dignity and as holistic beings with human needs that must be met,
- been the recipients of the application of the nursing process during illness phase of the health continuum to enhance human need fulfillment,
- been able to achieve optimal wellness in the present health state—a state of highest level of need fulfillment possible,
- been afforded the use of resources of the health care agency as needed as well as the broader community of services to enhance human need fulfillment,
- been the recipients of research outcomes having direct applicability in the plan of care,
- been able to experience the coordination of their prescribed nursing care with the services of other health professionals,
- been the recipients of information that would enhance their health and ability to care for themselves,
- had their families/significant others participate in their care and informed about how to support their recovery after leaving the health care agency, and
- left the health care agency with their health and their concept of self enhanced as a result of care and interaction with primary nursing staff.

4. *the theoretic and conceptual frameworks.* Conceptual and theoretic frameworks determine the handling of the knowledge of the field and facilitate decision making to realize client expectations. These are written in a document consisting of a preamble in which concepts (human beings, society/envi-

ronment, health, and nursing) and subconcepts (human needs, person, family, community, nursing process, and leadership and research processes) are stated. The body of the document expands upon the theoretic underpinnings of the concepts—specifically NHNT. The final portion of the document incorporates the manner in which the concepts and subconcepts along with the theory will permeate or influence all other documents and dimensions of nursing service. The conceptual/theoretic frameworks constitute the keystone for this service process and prescribe the operation of the philosophy for the nursing service unit.

5. *the behavioral expectations for the staff nurse resulting from the application of the conceptual/theoretic frameworks for nursing.* For example, as a result of application of conceptual/theoretic frameworks for nursing, the staff nurse will

- be able to apply knowledge drawn from the biological, physical, behavioral, and nursing sciences in prescribing nursing care for the client;
- apply the nursing process with the client as a person within the family and community focus to achieve optimal wellness by maintaining, fostering, and meeting human need fulfillment;
- use research results as applicable in designing and implementing the nursing care plan to enhance human need fulfillment;
- collaborate with other health professionals regarding the status of goal achievement for the client while coordinating efforts of health care professionals in meeting human needs of clients;

- draw upon community resources to enhance human need fulfillment with the goal of maintaining optimal wellness for client;
- foster the client's holism by responding to the client as an integrated composite of body, mind, and spirit;
- demonstrate leadership in promoting the level of human need fulfillment for the client by influencing health care professionals, administration, responsible groups, and organizations to obtain the required services, staff, resources, and health-enhancing information; and
- demonstrate accountability and responsibility in enhancing wellness for clients and self.

6. *the evaluative outcomes for client and nurse in keeping with the philosophy and conceptual/theoretic frameworks.* Tools and processes as well as time frames are outlined and developed to validate that stated behavioral expectations are realized.

The process outlined for the preparation of significant nursing service documents demonstrates a relationship between client outcomes and staff nurse expectations and is the

---

*The process outlined for the preparation of significant nursing service documents demonstrates a relationship between client outcomes and staff nurse expectations and is the mirror image of the critical nursing curriculum documents prepared by nurse educators.*

---

mirror image of the critical nursing curriculum documents prepared by nurse educators. The four major concepts—human being, society/environment, health, and nursing (nursing's metaparadigm)—comprise the substance for the philosophy, end-of-program behaviors, conceptual/theoretic frameworks, level and course behaviors, plus course content and teaching learning strategies. Thus, if the end-of-program behaviors for the baccalaureate program in nursing indicate that the graduate of the program will be able to

- apply knowledge drawn from the biological, physical, behavioral, and nursing sciences in prescribing nursing care for the client;
- apply the nursing process with the client as person, family, community within a human need theory framework to foster optimal wellness;
- collaborate with members of the nursing and health teams in resolving health-related problems for the clients of nursing;
- use research results as applicable in designing the nursing care plan to enhance human need fulfillment for the client;
- demonstrate accountability and responsibility in enhancing wellness for clients and self; and
- enhance his or her professional and personal development in the roles of person, scholar, and citizen.

And if the expectations of the employing nursing service unit reflect these behaviors, then congruency exists between education and service. Readers will note the consistency among behaviors stated for the client, the staff nurse, and the graduate prepared in the baccalaureate nursing program.

This congruency is critical for job satisfaction and professional and personal growth of the graduate of the nursing program and for the stability of nursing service units. The level of "culture shock"—a condition that develops when significant gaps are evident between the intellectual, interpersonal, and technical competencies achieved by the graduate of a nursing program and the opportunity to apply these competencies in the nursing service unit—is diminished. Furthermore, professional esteem is likely to be enhanced, tenure expanded, and promotional opportunities become clear and achievable. The congruency between educational and service expectations promotes the evaluation process in that expectations achieved in the academic setting can be refined and maximized in the service setting. Fairness and justice in the evaluation tools, procedures, and processes are likely to be realized.

The results of one health care agency's (Pitt County Memorial Hospital, Greenville, North Carolina) efforts to implement conceptual/theoretic frameworks are described by Judith Brooks—one of the core members of the nursing leadership team who energized the practice of nursing for themselves, the nursing staff, consumers of nursing service, and health care colleagues by developing the practice model.

## THE PITT COUNTY MEMORIAL HOSPITAL MODEL

Over the past six years, the nursing staff of Pitt County Memorial Hospital (PCMH) redefined the nursing services philosophy and developed a conceptual framework on which to base nursing practice. We used Capers's (Cynthia Flynn Capers, written communication, 1986) and Fawcett's (Jacqueline Fawcett, written communication, 1988) criteria to develop our model. Capers stated one must determine whether the nursing practice environment is conducive to using an explicit conceptual model. Other issues addressed included anticipated outcomes from the use of the model, how the staff will be prepared to use the model, how and when the use of the model will be evaluated, and financial resources required and available.

Fawcett's criteria for selecting a conceptual model for clinical practice were used as a guideline in the selection of our model. These five criteria included the

1.  nurse's statement of beliefs and values about the concepts of person, environment, health, and nursing;
2.  detailed analysis and evaluation of several conceptual models;
3.  comparison of the content of the model with the philosophical statements, the image of nursing, and the usual ways of practicing nursing;
4.  selection of the model that most closely matches these beliefs, thoughts, and practices; and
5.  use of the model in a variety of situations to determine its utility.

The responsibility and goal for the philosophy development began in 1984 when Nursing Information Systems (NIS) was first introduced at PCMH. A group of nursing service representatives were identified as the NIS committee charged with the responsibility of identifying long-range needs for NIS that would assist in both individualized patient care and the administration/delivery of nursing care. Soon it became evident that such an information system would require a framework for the way we look at nursing at PCMH. It was decided that a conceptual framework would guide the development of an NIS that acts as an automated data processing system needed to plan, implement, evaluate, and document patient care and to support the management and delivery of that care.

The original committee was comprised of a clinical instructor, clinical nurse specialist, a head nurse, the computer application coordinator, and two nursing administrators. At that time all members except the computer application coordinator had a master's degree in nursing. After clarification of the group focus, the committee was expanded to include nursing leadership and staff nurse representation from each nursing division. Nursing leadership members all had a master's degree in nursing. With committee restructuring, the committee was renamed the Nursing Philosophy Task Force. During the development and implementation process, membership changed numerous times with a core group remaining from inception to implementation kickoff in May 1987. It was viewed as a privilege to serve on the Task Force, and at times there was a waiting list for membership.

Since several committee members had previously held faculty positions, the group directed its attention toward conceptual framework development. In order to give direction to the conceptual framework development, it was necessary to clarify the nursing philosophy for PCMH.

The impact of the priority for philosophy development when using a model was recognized early and addressed. Discussion focused on how a system's philosophy will guide the institution in all directions, including standards of care, assessment tools, care planning systems, documentation systems, discharge planning, job descriptions, and the performance appraisal system.

## Defining the nursing services philosophy

The next step was to refine PCMH's nursing services philosophy. Refinement was accomplished using the Delphi technique to identify values and beliefs about nursing, management, and patient care at PCMH. All the nursing staff and nursing leadership participated in the survey. Concurrently, work was also begun to identify a conceptual framework for clinical practice, education, research, and management.

The Nursing Philosophy Task Force, using a literature review and Delphi tools, began to identify the elements of the new philosophy. The four major concepts to be defined were individual (person), environment, health, and nursing. The Delphi statements were categorized according to these concepts. Hours were spent by subgroups to develop philosophy statements for each of the concepts, which were expanded and refined in a grueling two-day retreat with an outside consultant. The group wrote the philosophy draft to reflect terminology that would not suggest nor commit to a particular theory or conceptual framework at this time. The draft would be applicable from any perspective of patient care, for management, education, or research. It would represent all ages, all areas, and a myriad of opinions. It would be global in perspective, but with enough substance that nursing services, values, and beliefs could be interpreted and implemented in a conceptual framework.

Because of the participative management style at PCMH, drafts of the proposed philosophy for nursing services were sent for divisional feedback numerous times. Finally in July 1985, with the incorporation of all the feedback received, the nursing leadership group sanctioned the new philosophy.

### Groundwork for the selection of a conceptual framework

The next step was to identify nursing theories that reflected the philosophy and could be used as a foundation for our conceptual framework. During the next five months, the Nursing Philosophy Task Force reviewed and analyzed the work of the major nursing theory scholars. This review provided a common framework of reference for all task force participants. In the conceptual framework development, members first had to differentiate between a philosophy and conceptual framework. One Task Force member was quoted as saying, "We all felt as if we were back in graduate school, except it was more fun since we weren't being graded and since we were applying the concepts." The conceptual framework served as a direct guide for implementing our philosophy in the areas of practice, management, education, and research.

---

*The conceptual framework served as a direct guide for implementing our philosophy in the areas of practice, management, education, and research.*

---

Members of the task force were divided into subgroups to examine and analyze a specific conceptual/theoretic model. Imogene King's model framework questions were used for model analysis (Imogene King, oral communication, 1987). These questions included

- What is the goal for nursing?
- What knowledge is essential for nursing practice?
- What professional values are held by nurses and the profession?
- What is the relationship of nursing to the health field?
- What is the relationship of nursing to the local community, state, nation, and the world?
- What is the relationship of nursing to other professions?
- Where do nurses perform their functions?
- For whom do nurses provide a social service called nursing?

Several emotionally draining, but rewarding and productive, workdays were spent reviewing and analyzing each model in relation to each of the above-mentioned questions. This stimulated numerous lengthy discussions and philosophizing sessions regarding the strengths, limitations, concepts, and goals of each model. It became readily apparent that the development of a list of terms requiring definitions was necessary for clarity and to facilitate progress. The models analyzed were those of King, Orem, Roy, Johnson, Rogers, Newman, and Yura and Walsh.

At this point, because of limited experience in conceptual framework development, the Task Force identified the need for consultative assistance in the analysis of the theories, in the development of our conceptual framework, and in deciding which theory best fit the expectations of PCMH's nursing services. Consultant options were explored and one finally decided upon. In the meantime numerous articles were reviewed to provide background for the conceptual frameworks under review. A significant bibliography was developing. At first, consultations with a university nurse educator were conducted via the telephone by the Task Force Chair. The nursing consultant provided guidance in how to approach a conceptual framework and the process for devising a conceptual framework.

## Conceptual framework development

In the conceptual framework development, the Task Force first identified and agreed upon the major concepts and the subconcepts, and then the theories that were evident in each of the major concepts and subconcepts. Next subgroups within the Task Force each addressed one of the four major concepts (individual, environment, health, and nursing), and the subconcepts and theories that applied to each concept. Each of the concepts and subconcepts were defined. At this step the committee's appendages had become a dictionary and thesaurus, and they became adept at finding words in the dictionary and had memorized all the concepts and subconcepts. The development of subconcept identification, subconcept/terminology definitions, and sanction from nursing leadership took approximately six months of intensive meetings and heated discussions of definitions. Sessions were growth promoting and stimulated a new look at nursing practice and its components. Communication was clearer, and consistency in interpretation of terms was evident.

A workday was instituted with the nursing consultant guiding the group in further differentiation of thoughts, concepts, and theories. After thorough analysis of concepts, subconcepts, and related theories the group decided that Yura and Walsh's NHNT best matched the new philosophy and nursing practice at PCMH.[5] This practice focused on meeting patient's needs rather than on problems. NHNT was chosen because of its applicability to daily nursing roles, its practicality as a base of practice, and its ability to function as the common language that could unify all nursing efforts and enable PCMH to deliver the best possible nursing care.

## Implementing conceptual/theoretic frameworks

Over the next several months, we acquired in-depth information about NHNT. In the fall of 1986, Dr. Yura of Old Dominion University School of Nursing was invited to PCMH to present NHNT to the nursing leadership. As a result of this program, the nursing leadership group felt that the nursing staff should have the opportunity to hear Dr. Yura. Finally, on Nurses Day in May 1987, after the culmination of years of productive work, nursing services at PCMH adopted its philosophy and conceptual framework based on Yura and Walsh's NHNT to guide nursing practice. As part of the initial implementation kickoff, Dr. Yura presented NHNT to the nursing staff. Another part of the program included the slide-tape-song presentation created and written by a talented staff nurse to reflect our philosophy and the conceptual/theoretic frameworks. (This song would later win an award from Sigma Theta Tau International Honor Society of Nursing.)

## Using conceptual/theoretic frameworks for nursing service

Using NHNT began with its incorporation into the nursing services orientation. Expected behaviors and outcomes for all levels of nursing staff were developed. Standards of performance for all levels of nursing staff were implemented. Since implementation at the staff nurse level was of utmost concern, strategies included providing each unit with a copy of the first three volumes of *Human Needs and the Nursing Process*[6] and the fifth edition of *The Nursing Process* by Yura and Walsh.[5] Monthly articles, such as "Why

Should I Care About a Philosophy and Conceptual Framework?" by Hope Sylvain Moore, were written in *Nursing Notes* (PCMH's nursing newsletter) during 1987 and 1988. The philosophy subcommittee submitted an article on "Human Need Theory and Nursing Diagnosis: Making the Pieces Fit" for publication in *Perspectives on Nursing Care* (PCMH's journal).

Excitement filled the air as communication was enhanced among nursing staff and between nursing staff members and the nursing leadership group. In addition, nursing faculty and nursing students having clinical experiences at PCMH could readily be incorporated into the intellectual groundswell energized by the application of NHNT with the nursing process.

Concurrent with other developments, in February 1987, as part of the plan to computerize nursing care plans, a task force was formed to develop structured nursing care plans in the NHNT framework. The task force was comprised of nursing leadership members. Each nursing leadership member was assigned one of the 35 human needs from which to develop a model care plan. Each subgroup, a nursing leadership member and two staff nurses, used standards of care and Yura and Walsh's *Nursing Process* to develop the nursing care plan that fit a specific format and was congruent with nursing practice at PCMH.

Within this theoretic model, nursing diagnoses were viewed as human needs which were met "too little, too much or there was a disturbance in patterns of fulfillment."[5(p.129)] The care plans were then given to two other subgroups for review and feedback. Once this was completed the nursing care plans were given to NIS for computer program development. Six months later, the clinical

instructors and the clinical nurse specialists were asked to critique the care plans according to computer criteria and consistent terminology.

Simultaneously, the clinical instructors, clinical nurse specialists, and the NIS coordinator were charged with the development of a nursing admissions assessment record that incorporated the NHNT. This was another grueling task complicated by trying to meet the expectations of acute care nursing service, rehabilitation and psychiatric nursing service, the documentation and forms committees' criteria, and the constraints of legalities simultaneously.

Finally, in the spring of 1989 an orientation was provided on the use of nursing care plans in the NHNT framework for all nursing units, followed by centralized and decentralized inservices. Also, the nursing admissions assessment record incorporating NHNT (meeting everyone's criteria) was ready to be piloted.

The enormous value of these achievements is only now being realized. Accountability and responsibility for nursing service have been strengthened; precision and consistency prevailed in documentation. Acceptance of the theory-driven assessment record and nursing care plan by nurses providing direct services to consumers contributed to enhanced personal satisfaction for both the nurse and the patient. Their use has improved

---

*Use of the theory-driven assessment record and nursing care plan has improved quality of care through more thorough recordings of patient data and outcomes.*

quality of care through more thorough re-cordings of patient data and outcomes, and they incorporate the structure and substance for quality assurance review.

In the summer of 1988, a Human Needs Steering Committee was organized to coor-dinate and oversee all related activities. A revised inservice educational plan was implemented as data from the survey of nurs-ing staff were analyzed. Introduction of the philosophy into the nursing services orienta-tion was continued. In February 1988, an implementation kickoff campaign was launched with the placement of a booth in the cafeteria and a traveling booth for those who could not avail themselves of the information provided. A button and pad that contained the NHNT logo and the phrase "Nursing Meet-ing Human Needs" plus a brochure with general information about NHNT and the educational plan for staff were distributed. Acceptance of the conceptual/theoretic framework by the total nursing staff was increasing as a common language and com-mon mode of practice brought satisfaction and valuing from colleagues, coworkers, and consumers.

In the summer of 1989 a patient and nurs-ing staff survey reflecting values about nurs-ing care and clinical nursing at PCMH was developed. Using experts in survey question-naire development and the patient education specialists, this survey assisted in evaluating the impact of the philosophy and conceptual framework. The survey focused on behav-iors that characterize most nurses who prac-tice and care for patients at PCMH. The survey was administered prior to implemen-tation of the educational plan and at various intervals afterward to reflect the use of NHNT in nursing practice. The educational plan to facilitate implementation of NHNT

was in place January to June 1989. The plan was followed by readministration of the sur-vey in winter of 1989. The results of the survey were overwhelmingly positive for nurses and patients.

Since the inception of NHNT much work continues in implementing the theory in all facets of nursing service. Incorporation of NHNT in quality assurance activities and monitors, inservice educational programs, and performance appraisals is ongoing and requires continued development or refine-ment.

•   •   •

The results of the incorporation of a con-ceptual/theoretic framework in this nursing service setting have been an improvement in the service to consumers of nursing, an effec-tive restructuring of the environment of the health care agency advantageous for the cli-ent and for nursing staff, and the differentia-tion of practice roles according to education, experiences, and client needs.[7(p.93)] It has fos-tered understanding, acceptance, and sup-port of the contribution of theory develop-ment and nursing research to nursing and health care. It brought together nurse leaders in education and service to the benefit of both and with maximum benefit to the consumer of nursing services. The specification of the philosophy, outcome behaviors, and concep-tual/theoretic frameworks has allowed nurses to have control over nursing. It has incorporated nurses in setting the pace for the future of nursing practice, promoted the de-velopment of peer activity and review, and demonstrated how nursing can make a differ-ence. The benefit for the nurse includes in-creased job satisfaction, enhanced profes-sional and personal development, increased self-esteem, and the realization that the service of nursing is a valued and valuable service to consumers.

Promotion of the image of the nurse was another outcome, as was the realization that nurse educators and nurse supervisors share common goals. The timeframe may be different in that educators see a finished product years ahead while nurse supervisors see client outcomes on a daily basis. The gap between these two efforts is bridged by the use of common conceptual/theoretic frameworks for the design and administration of both the nursing education and nursing service units. The collaborative and cooperative efforts of nurse educators and nurse supervisors will help to design a preferred future for nursing and serve as a model for application on a broader scale in nursing.

## REFERENCES

1. Spittle, L. "Classics Corner." *Bulletin of the American Association for History of Nursing*, No. 26, Spring 1990, p. 9.
2. Murphy, M. "Nursing Services Delivery Systems." In *Nursing's Vital Signs: Shaping the Profession for the 1990's.* Battle Creek, Mich.: W.K. Kellogg Foundation, 1989.
3. DeBack, V. "Nursing Education." In *Nursing's Vital Signs: Shaping the Profession for the 1990's.* Battle Creek, Mich.: W.K. Kellogg Foundation, 1989.
4. Waite, R. "The Driving Forces for Change." In *Nursing's Vital Signs: Shaping the Profession for the 1990's.* Battle Creek, Mich.: W.K. Kellogg Foundation, 1989.
5. Yura, H. and Walsh, M.B. *The Nursing Process.* 5th ed. East Norwalk, Conn.: Appleton & Lange, 1988.
6. Yura, H., and Walsh, M.B. *Human Needs and the Nursing Process.* 3rd ed. New York, N.Y.: Appleton-Century-Crofts, 1982.
7. American Organization of Nurse Executives. In *Nursing's Vital Signs: Shaping the Profession for the 1990's.* Battle Creek, Mich.: W.K. Kellogg Foundation, 1989.

# Part III
# Tools and Defenses

# Communication: the critical link in nursing middle management

*Eleanor L. Tabeek*
*Assistant Professor*
*Boston College School of Nursing*
*Chestnut Hill, Massachusetts*

THE NURSE MANAGER can and should serve as a key person in coordinating the total management of the care of clients from the moment the client enters the system. Nurses are critical resource persons at all levels of the health care system.

The role of the nurse in middle management has undergone drastic change in the past few years. Changes in society and in health care delivery, hospital organization, and nursing roles have together brought about this change in middle management.

The future of professional nursing is precarious at best. Nurses are currently experiencing, and perhaps even expediting, an image change, attempting to bury forever the handmaiden role and assume a more contributory, autonomous role in the health care system.

*Health Care Superv*, 1986,4(3),80–87
© 1986 Aspen Publishers, Inc.

Communication is the key process that enables the nurse in a middle management position to serve as a role model for exemplary care to clients, to direct his or her subordinates, to challenge his or her peers, and to support higher management and the system itself.

## FACTORS EFFECTING CHANGES IN THE ROLE OF NURSE MANAGER

### Health care as an industry

The American health care system, of which nursing is the largest subsystem of professional providers, has become one of the largest industries in the nation. This development reflects the system's change of focus from an altruistic model emphasizing the goal of service to others to an egoistic model emphasizing the survival of the system itself. The nursing subsystem views the purpose of the hospital—a major subsystem and the employer of a large percentage of nurses—as a source of caring for the sick and improving the health and welfare of the community. Other subsystems view the hospital as a source of employment for the community, as a physician's workshop, as a learning laboratory for students of various disciplines, and as a major consumer of equipment and supplies. The model of hospitals has changed from a service model to an industrial model, but the education of nurses continues in an altruistic, humanistic model.[1]

### Cost-effectiveness of the health care system

The health care industry has become more conscious of cost as a result of scrutiny by subsystems that pay the bills, particularly the government and private third party insurers. Costs are rising because of expensive medical technology, inappropriate use of services, excessive hospital beds, the practice of defensive medicine, decreases in institutional productivity, and increases in alternative health care delivery systems.

### Complexity of the health care system

While the costs of maintaining the system have been rising, the structure of the system has been increasing in complexity. The expansion of the health care system exemplifies the characteristics of complexity as discussed by Mason and Mitroff.[2] Complexity literally means the condition of being tightly woven or twined together. Three characteristics of health care system complexity are:

1. Any policymaking situation is comprised of many problems and issues.
2. These problems and issues tend to be highly interrelated. Consequently, the solution to one problem requires a solution to all of the other problems. At the same time, each solution creates additional dimensions to be incorporated in the solution to other problems.

3. Few, if any, problems can be isolated effectively for separate treatment.

For policymaking, client health care provider issues that reflect the foregoing complexities within the system are numerous, such as the cost of health care, the right to health care, and the level of care provided to clients. These issues are highly interrelated, involving direct and indirect care, and the solution to one directly influences the others. The separation and isolation of one problem within the system is impossible as each problem relates either laterally or vertically to subsystems.

Compounding the complexity issue is the autonomous functioning of each subsystem that is responsible for only a small portion of society's health care needs. A lack of balance among the subsystems has accentuated the weaknesses of the health care system in general and the nursing subsystem in particular.

Nurse managers face a most difficult task: The health care system is in a state of flux, role expectations of the nurse from both inside and outside of the nursing subsystem are unrealistic, and support for nursing as an autonomous subsystem is not readily accepted by clients or other health care professionals. Nurse managers must develop and refine their managerial skills to create a supportive, productive environment for their clients and their subordinates. Nurses need to support each other and support their managers. The nursing sub-system needs to devote more time and energy to the development of risk-taking nursing leaders.[3]

## ORGANIZATIONAL STYLES IN HOSPITALS

The dramatic changes in the health care system over the past decade have prompted reorganization within hospital administration. Traditionally, the organization chart reflected the classic pyramid structure, but this has become inappropriate for most hospitals because of the autonomy of the subsystems within the hospital structure.

Many hospital administrators have adopted the matrix organizational structure. This structure enhances the subsystem of nursing by facilitating the use of highly specialized staff, permitting flexibility in conditions of change and uncertainty, encouraging interaction between highly technical specialists, freeing top management for long-range planning, improving motivation and commitment, and providing opportunities for personal development.[4]

Rowland and Rowland state that in the matrix organization there is a smoother flow of the necessary treatment tests and services to the client, and intrusion on clients' privacy by varying types of hospital employees is reduced; nurses have a greater opportunity to optimize clinical skills and provide clients with an effective, tailored health care program.[5]

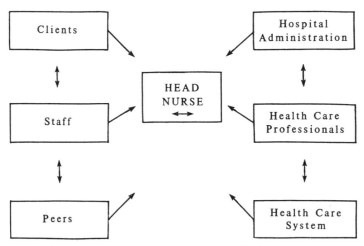

**Figure 1.** Middle management in nursing: pivotal link through communication.

## EVOLVING ROLE OF MIDDLE MANAGEMENT IN NURSING

Traditionally, the nursing supervisor in the classical pyramid structure was the key management person who reported to the director of nursing service, who in turn was responsible to the hospital administrator.

The change in the organizational structure of health care facilities has prompted change in the role of the nursing supervisor. Stevens identified the change in the supervisor's role to coordinator of nursing personnel and staff and coordinator of nursing systems.[6] This change in the nursing subsystem permits the middle management role in nursing to be invested in the team leader, the primary nurse, head nurse, or charge nurse, whichever title is preferred.

The middle manager has access to three power resources: position, clin-ical knowledge and skill, and a professional value system.[7] The middle manager is the main link between the patient care unit and the rest of the hospital. The position using the linking pin concept describes the middle management person as a connector between two member groups: the peer group and the team of care providers.

Because the prevalent model is that reflected in Figure 1, the title of the middle manager will be *head nurse* for the balance of this discussion.

The study by Jones and Jones of head nurses at Fort Worth Children's Hospital incorporated Mintzberg's framework of managerial activities to delineate what head nurses do.[8] Mintzberg separated the managerial role into three distinct categories: interpersonal, informational, and decisional.[9]

Mintzberg further identified the three interpersonal roles as figurehead, leader, and liaison person. The informational roles were classified as monitor, disseminator, and spokesperson. The decision-making activities were separated as entrepreneur, disturbance handler, resource allocator, and negotiator.

Jones and Jones observed head nurses and assistant head nurses in their implementation of Mintzberg's roles and developed a head nurse activity role model. They developed a time frame of 30 percent in interpersonal roles, 40 percent in informational roles, and 30 percent in decisional roles. The key element in all of these roles is communication. Therefore, the ability to communicate effectively is inherent in the head nurse managerial role incorporating the Mintzberg framework.

## COMMUNICATION IN THE ROLE OF MIDDLE MANAGER

One of the most complex factors in working with people is communication. Whether, by way of the spoken or written word or by sign or symbol, facial expression, or body language in any variety or form, communication poses major and continuing challenges to everyone.[10]

One reason nurses have not influenced the health care system in proportion to their potential strength may be their inability to attract an audience, to be granted credibility, or to express themselves forcefully. The ability to influence social action and

*One reason nurses have not influenced the health care system in proportion to their potential strength may be their inability to attract an audience, to be granted credibility, or to express themselves forcefully.*

change is primarily a communication process.[11] Nurses have not been educated in this process but rather have accepted a role in which all communication is downward, and are thus reluctant to speak out. The consequences of not speaking out are the restrictions of administrative credibility, and the designation of and control over care to clients. A portion of the lack of facility with communication may also be due to restrictions placed on women as well as on nurses.

An explanation of the aspects of communication is essential to a full discussion of Mintzberg's managerial roles.

### Communication is a dynamic process

The basic model of the communication process indicates a dynamic phenomenon that is constantly moving and changing.[12] The simple components of any single communication interchange consist of a sender with certain goals who forms those goals into a message that is transmitted through a medium to an intended receiver. The receiver decodes the message and responds to its content. The response is determined by the sender's perceptions. Feedback is established when response is necessary, and the process is reversed.

## Communication is a multidirectional process

The formal channels of communication are vertical and horizontal lines, and the customs and mores of the practice setting have established precedents for their use. Vertical communication originates at the top of administration and is passed downward through a hierarchy to the lowest level of authority. The head nurse, as the most accessible and conspicuous representative of the organization, is the critical link in the chain of command. Vertical communication is a two-way process; not only does the head nurse transmit information from the top to the staff, but he or she also relays information upward to administration. In horizontal communication there is collegial sharing of responsibility for quality of client care. Interaction with other head nurses and health care providers is integral to making sound professional decisions with courage, comfort, and acumen. The grapevine—informal channels of communication—is the swiftest and most persuasive model of intraorganizational communication. The communication process with clients may be horizontal to direct caregivers or vertical through the nursing staff. The channel of communication with cli-

ents should be egalitarian, but because of emotional or physical helplessness, the client may assume a subordinate role.[13]

## Communication takes many forms

The dimensions of communications and appropriate usage addressed by Allen in the management of large organizations such as hospitals are

- intentional and unintentional communication;
- verbal and nonverbal communication;
- oral and written communication;
- formal and informal communication; and
- internal and external communication.[14]

## Communication can create or destroy supporting relationships

Personal characteristics can act as catalysts for communication and can facilitate cooperation and support. Communication implies listening— which elicits a sense of worth, caring, and empathy—to client, peer, or administrator. The climate of communication demands respect for the knowledge and abilities of others.

## Communication is personal

Stone et al. identified three aspects relating to the flow of communication that indicated similar conclusions.[15] People are subjected to forces urging them to communicate with those who will help them achieve their aims, and against communicating with those who will not assist their accomplishments. People also direct their communication toward those who make them feel secure and gratify their needs, and many people in organizations are always communicating as though they were trying to improve their positions.

## Communication is susceptible to weaknesses

Middle managers must identify weaknesses in the communication system to maintain effective operatives. Rowland and Rowland developed the following five points to consider in assessing one's communication patterns.[16]

1. Do you receive information that is excessive, minimal, inaccurate, or right?
2. Do you hear complaints about information arriving too late?
3. Do you receive information that is untimely, insufficient, or imprecise?
4. Do you hear that your communications are late, unnecessarily time consuming, or in need of revision?
5. Do you send reports that are purposeless, inconsistently informative, or inappropriate?

## Communication has barriers to overcome

Barriers to effective communication must be considered in developing effective communication skills.[17] Such barriers include

- unclear self-expression;
- unawareness of peripheral barriers (noise, interruptions);
- demonstrated lack of interest in concerns of clients and peers; and
- use of too many words in the message.

## Communication is a people process

Gibb described defensive communication in which speech can be judgmental.[18] A manager attempting change can imply that the person to be altered is inadequate. Speech that is used to control a listener evokes resistance. Communication should be viewed as a people process rather than a language process. Gibb described defensive communication behavior by a listener when a message is received as possessive, evaluative, superior, or controlling; he described supportive communication behavior by a listener when a message is received as descriptive, problem-oriented, spontaneous, and equal.

The foregoing aspects of communication are vital to the role of middle manager in nursing to strengthen the critical link between the client and the health care system. Most basic nursing curricula do not include a management core; however, many nurses enter managerial roles within two years of graduation. To function effectively in the position of middle management head nurse, the communication issue must be addressed. The head nurse is indeed the linking pin between the client and the system, and all are looking to him or her for support and direction on the road to wellness and equality.

# REFERENCES

1. Hanson, R.L. *Management Systems for Nursing Service Staffing.* Rockville, Md.: Aspen Systems, 1983, pp. 4–10.

2. Mason, R., and Mitroff, D. *Challenging Strategic Planning Assumptions: Theories, Cases and Techniques.* New York: Wiley, 1981, pp. 3–16.

3. Hanson, *Management Systems for Nursing Service Staffing,* 10–12.

4. Gibson, J., Ivancevich, J.M., and Donelly, J.H., Jr. *Organizations.* Plano, Tex.: Business Publications, 1982, pp. 305–310.

5. Rowland, H., and Rowland, B. *Nursing Administration Handbook.* Rockville, Md.: Aspen Systems, 1983, p. 241.

6. Stevens, B.J. *The Nurse as Executive.* Wakefield, Mass.: Contemporary Publishing, 1975, pp. 93–95.

7. Marriner, A. *Current Perspectives in Nursing Management.* St. Louis: Mosby, 1979, pp. 109–113.

8. Jones, K., and Jones, W. "The Head Hurse: A Managerial Definition of the Activity Role Set." *Nursing Administration Quarterly* 2 (1979): 45–56.

9. Mintzberg, H. *The Nature of Managerial Work.* Englewood Cliffs, N.J.: Prentice-Hall, 1973, pp. 54–86.

10. LeRoux, R.S. "Communicating and Influence in Nursing." *Nursing Administration* 3 (1978): 51–57.

11. Yura, H., Ozimek, D., and Walsh, M. *Nursing Leadership.* New York: Appleton-Century-Crofts, 1981, p. 122.

12. Allen, R.K. *Organizational Management through Communication.* New York: Harper & Row, 1977, pp. 42–44.

13. Marriner, A. *Guide to Nursing Management.* St. Louis: Mosby, 1980, p. 143.

14. Allen, *Organizational Management through Communication,* 42–44.

15. Stone, S., et al., *Management for Nurses.* St. Louis: Mosby, 1984, pp. 25–27.

16. Rowland and Rowland, *Nursing Administration Handbook,* 241.

17. Schweiger, J. *The Nurse as Manager.* Ontario, Canada: Wiley, 1980, pp. 57–59.

18. Gibb, J.R. "Defensive Communication." *Journal of Nursing Administration* 4 (1982): 14–17.

# A common-sense survival strategy for nursing supervisors

**Frankie C. Nail**
*Nursing Consultant*
*National Medical Enterprises*
*Central and Eastern Regions*
*New Orleans, Louisiana*

**Enrica K. Singleton**
*Professor/Coordinator*
*Nursing Service Administration*
*School of Nursing Graduate*
*   Program*
*Louisiana State University Medical*
*   Center*
*New Orleans, Louisiana*

NURSING SUPERVISORS are likely to begin feeling increasing pressure as they are placed under additional stress from the nursing executive and from staff nurses because of the growing emphasis on productivity in the hospital work environment. Nursing supervisors, like middle managers in other fields, are the essential links for persons who are above and below them in the organizational hierarchy. They are also expected to communicate laterally with other persons within the nursing structure and persons who are in various positions in departments other than nursing. Supervisors are expected to be cognizant of the broad administrative perspective needed for operating a hospital and the perspective needed for developing, planning, and achieving the goals of the nursing department.

Working within the broader structure is becoming increasingly more

*Health Care Superv,* 1986,4(2),50–58
© 1986 Aspen Publishers, Inc.

difficult because internal changes are beginning to be directed by external forces. The impact of the federally imposed prospective payment system on nursing service is keenly felt by those in supervisory positions. These persons become the conduits through which nursing executives carry out financial management plans, whether they choose to use participative or autocratic approaches. Because most acute care hospitals are experiencing budget cuts, nursing, like other departments, recognizes budget cutting as a priority. The nursing department, then, establishes a goal to reduce costs while delivering effective patient care services. Toward that end, nursing executives are reexamining the role of the nurse and the domain of nursing. The traditional role of the nurse and its relevance in today's acute care setting are undergoing serious scrutiny. Often the supervisor becomes the major consultant during this examination to determine the need for change and just as often serves as the deputy for implementing decisions that result from this process. Ideally, the supervisor's input contains information acquired by consulting with the staff.

## NURSING SUPERVISION— GREAT EXPECTATIONS

The supervisor's input is expected when the executive asks whether routine activities are necessary and, if so, whether nurses or other personnel should perform these tasks. For example, the executive may ask how often a patient's temperature, pulse, and respiration should be taken, the bed changed, a condition classified, blood pressure checked, or care plan updated. The executive might ask whether these activities are necessary in their current form or whether they should be replaced by something else. If replacement is suggested, the executive might ask, "What is the nature of the replacement and the nature of the concomitant education for staff nurses and patients?" Other questions might be, "Will the changes reduce the use of resources?" "What is the nature of the reductions?" "What portion of these savings might be reallocated to other areas?"

Given the need to cut costs, the nursing executive will rely heavily on the supervisor to see that unit operation stays within established budgetary constraints. The supervisor must prudently keep staff abreast of the goals of the department and gain their support in cost-cutting efforts while seeking staff assistance in revising old policies or formulating new ones to accommodate designated changes.

Clearly, the supervisor's administrative tasks will multiply along with increased pressure to reduce costs. Studies might show that a reduction of staff is indicated. As this process is undertaken, staff nurses will experience job insecurity, will demand more information, and will require frequent reassurance from supervisors. During this period, staff nurses might be less prone to verbalize any job dissatisfaction. However, administrators and supervisors must remain keenly aware of the likelihood of this problem because it has been common among nurses. Until recently, jobs for nurses were plentiful and staff nurses often tried to resolve their conflicts or enhance job satisfaction by finding different jobs. With fewer jobs now available, flight becomes relatively less available as a solution to the problem. Therefore, dissatisfied nurses will probably remain with the institution and over time the manifestation of dissatisfaction will become more visible. The quality of a dissatisfied nurse's communications with coworkers may suffer, and the nurse may offer little beyond the minimum acceptable obligations to patients or to the organization.

The picture is further complicated because, given the prospective pricing system, the nursing executive is under pressure to provide acceptable care at a reduced cost while expediting discharge. At the same time, inpatients will be those who are very ill and who are not candidates for same-day surgery or ambulatory care provisions. Furthermore, as more information becomes available to the general public, the consumer will develop additional expectations of the health care system. With patients increasing their expectations of the institution, nurse productivity will be of major concern to middle- and executive-level nursing administrators. Their stress will increase as a result of demands made by hospital administrators, staff nurses, and patients. The supervisor, as the intermediary, is the crucial party in seeing that the needs of patients, staff, and administration are met while seeing that costs are controlled. In preparing for this stressful period, supervisors will be wise to formulate a self-survival strategy—to assess mechanisms within the system over which they have control, to determine their tolerance level of stress, to identify their personal support system, and to become conscious of their strengths. Several other suggestions for developing a common-sense strategy should be helpful.

## Facing the facts

A prospective pricing system for patients on Medicare has been created for regulating and reducing the cost of health care. Thinking that the current emphasis on reducing health care expenditures is a fad that will soon lose momentum is a delusion. The era of plentiful resources is gone, perhaps forever. Telling staff nurses not to worry or that nursing care will not be affected by the new payment system is not advisable because it is probably not true. Instead, supervisors must prepare to serve as interpreters of the prospective payment system and its influence on the actions of management. This requires sharing with staff detailed financial information about the hospital in general and about the nursing department in particular. With an adequate financial database, staff nurses would

*The era of plentiful resources is gone, perhaps forever. Telling staff nurses not to worry or that nursing care will not be affected by the new payment system is not advisable because it is probably not true.*

have a framework that could allow them to offer suggestions for change that might allow greater economy in the practice environment.

Supervisors must realize, however, that a high degree of judgment is required to determine how much information is appropriate for the staff nurse and how this information should be presented. They must remember that the objective is to help establish a realistic financial framework for nursing practice, not to create minicontrollers and business office managers.

In this day of expanded information systems, all nurses must be exposed to and accept the idea that nursing care has a price tag. Income for nurses and other personnel and money for other expenditures come from patients. If costs to patients are to be contained, then nursing must bear a part of the burden of the institutional efforts. Accepting this fact and planning accordingly will reduce the number of times the supervisor becomes frustrated about the impenetrable wall that is being established by cost containment.

## Documenting patient care

Documentation of patient care has long been considered important and it will become even more critical in the new cost-conscious environment. Supervisors must raise the awareness of staff nurses as to the value of documentation. Assiduous charting of observations, appropriate nursing intervention, and timely evaluation of nursing care represent an incomplete process unless they are accompanied by content that is concise and goal oriented or problem specific. Frequently, nurses view charting as a mundane necessity rather than as historical evidence of patients' progress and as a means by which nurses can get credit for their work. To be sure, charting takes time, but it may not take nearly as much time if nurses learn to work smarter in this regard. For example, is it not just as easy to note what part of the nursing care plan was discussed with the patient and the goal that was reached as it is to record such entries as physicians' visits and requested laboratory tests? Notations that are consistent with the care plan are especially useful in instances where care plans are preserved, updated, and maintained rather than erased and discarded. Even when plans are not preserved, such notations provide evidence that a plan existed. The physicians' progress notes or order sheets will give evidence of the physicians' visits, and the entry of laboratory test results will attest to the fact that these tests were requested, whereas nursing entries provide the major specifics about nursing care and the outcome of that care. Also, given sufficient charting, the question "What does the nurse do?" will be readily answered.

## Documenting supervisory functions

Supervisors must also document certain facts. Just as the staff nurse's documentation on the patient's record is an important statement about the contribution nursing makes in the clinical arena, the supervisor's record documents her or his contribution to the nursing department and to the organization as a whole. For example, the supervisor should maintain a record of the teaching, counseling, and evaluation periods spent with nursing staff and the outcome of those sessions. In addition, nursing supervisors often serve as resource persons to leaders in other departments in times of stress. By virtue of their educational preparation, they know how to incorporate "therapeutic use of self" in working with others. Sometimes department heads from areas such as laboratory, radiology, dietary, or housekeeping seek and rely on nursing supervisors for moral support to accomplish their tasks in a changing environment. The importance of the supervisor's role in this exchange can be compared to the importance of the group leader in a session for nurses who are experiencing burnout. If the nursing supervisor discovers that she or he is frequently sought to provide job-related counseling that impacts on the delivery of patient care, she or he should record that conference time. Of course, the recipient's privacy and confidentiality should be protected. Providing emotional support to key persons in the organization and helping them solve problems facilitate their capacity to function in the organization. Although this personal counselor role is not technically a part of the nursing supervisor's job, such counseling does take place in the practice setting, and through this activity the supervisor makes a valuable contribution to the continuity of the organization. Supervisors deserve credit for providing this support. Therefore, if nursing supervisors are filling such a role, this function should be brought to the attention of top management. Documenting this service along with those traditional functions allows the supervisor to account for use of time. If supervisors record how they use their time they will seldom say, "Today is over and I really don't know what I've accomplished." Of course, there is a subsequent benefit: The supportive supervisor will usually receive willing assistance when making extraordinary requests of personnel in other departments.

## Gluing the system together

Nursing supervisors often glue the system together. They see that the patient's hunger is eased when the dietary department is closed, that medications are secured when the pharmacy is closed, and that requests get from one department to another when there is no courier. They also plan, organize, staff, and control their sections of the nursing department. In this time of reduced resources, nursing supervisors must either stop holding the system together or receive credit for doing so. Without carefully controlling the time and energy spent on this activity, the supervisor can shortchange the nursing department while contributing to other areas. By documenting "gluing time" the supervisor not only demonstrates self-value to the organization, but she or he also evaluates personal use of time in order to maintain the appropriate priorities. To retain the gluing function, the supervisor should have the staff available to allow for achievement of that function.

## SELF-REWARDS

The literature is replete with information on burnout, with much of it stressing the importance of taking care of oneself. Supervisors should review that material, take it seriously, and reward themselves for a job well done.

The supervisors' reward comes from knowing that employees for whom they are responsible are doing a good job. Therefore, they should evaluate employee achievements as such achievements relate to the supervisors' influence. For example, positive responses should be offered to such questions as: "Did management allow the current level of staffing because the supervisor presented an excellent case supporting this need?" and "Are the patients on the oncology unit showing exceptional progress because the supervisor arranged for all of the nurses on that unit to engage in an educational program?" Supervisors should always strive to connect such positive outcomes to supervisory efforts.

In yet another example, suppose that expenditures were reduced on a unit while quality assurance standards were maintained. This might have been accomplished because the supervisor made certain changes in procedures and now fewer supplies are required on the unit. Rather than accepting this accomplishment as all in a day's work, the supervisor may wish to take credit for this, not waiting for someone else to recognize such an accomplishment. Ideally, the supervisor's superior should comment on positive achievements as well as on shortcomings, but if that does not happen—or even if it does— the supervisor should recognize her or his own worth. In another instance, suppose the supervisor hears a comment such as, "I like working on this floor." Rather than accepting that statement without further thought, the supervisor should make a mental note, acknowledging the part she or he plays in creating an environment that is valued by staff. An environment that is conducive to nursing practice is no accident; it must be cultivated and it rarely develops without concerted effort on the part of the leader.

The supervisor should establish a "Supervisor's Day." Occasionally, when an especially noteworthy goal is reached, she or he should go out to dinner or to a theater, buy a gift, or spend the next day off in the park. The important thing is to do something to recognize and reward oneself. This professional worker will return to the job feeling much better.

The supervisor should be realistic in self-evaluation, acknowledging areas that need to be improved and working on these. However, less-than-perfect outcomes should not be allowed to consume the thoughts. To be sure, there will be enough people in the organization who are willing to point out supervisory deficiencies. It is usually unnecessary for the supervisor to spend more than one half of one percent of time in self-criticism, but it is time productively applied. Based on a forty-hour week, that amounts to a maximum of twelve minutes per week. Time is much better spent working toward goal accomplishment that includes attention to self-development.

## THE POSITIVE CONFERENCE

In addition to recognizing her or his own strengths, the supervisor should recognize strengths in persons being supervised. In most situations, nursing supervisors spend a majority of their conference time with poor performers. Perhaps this

needs to change. One approach that has been used successfully is to schedule a positive employee conference each week. Have an employee who is a good performer meet with the supervisor for a brief period. The following six guidelines should be helpful.

1. At random, pick an employee who has not had to be counseled for a negative occurrence within the past three months and whose last performance evaluation was at or above the standard. This allows an equal opportunity to select from people on all shifts, part-time and full-time employees, and employees in various job categories.

2. Ask the employee to schedule a conference with the supervisor at one of three times the supervisor has set aside for such conferences. Tell the employee that the purpose of the conference is to ask the employee to discuss particularly satisfying aspects of the job and to discuss career or job-related goals.

3. Permit no complaints during the conference either by the supervisor or by the employee. To assist employees to communicate in a totally positive way, the supervisor may need to provide open-ended comments such as, "Tell me about the most satisfying aspect of your job"; "As you can recall, what is the best example of excellent patient care on our unit within the past month?"; "Would you share

your most recent observation of cooperation between our unit and another unit or department?"; or "What goals have you set for yourself to accomplish within the next year?"

4. Establish a time frame for this conference and stay within that limit. Ten minutes is usually satisfactory.

5. Restate the purpose of the conference at the beginning. Despite the fact that employees are told the nature of the conference, many of them are so conditioned to only having discussions of negative events with the supervisor that they may arrive believing they have done something wrong. Reassure them that this is a positive conference.

6. Record the major items discussed and summarize the employee's responses immediately after the conference. This record might be an especially useful resource when reviewing reports for trends and when trying to match interested employees with new opportunities.

It takes less than 30 minutes per week to conduct, record, and evaluate a positive employee conference. The benefits of time spent in this manner are numerous. Staff members discuss with other staff what they should say when they are selected to attend such conferences, and if staff spend time thinking about the positive aspects of the unit, their morale should be enhanced.

*Too often nursing contacts are filled with social conversation rather than professional, goal-specific interactions. A totally professional conversation consumes no more time than a superficial social exchange.*

## TIME MANAGEMENT

Better use of time is something that many people strive for. Time management experts unfailingly talk about the need to set goals, prioritize actions, and evaluate results. The supervisor must help the nursing staff become expert in these three activities. Mastering these skills will allow the nurse to identify accomplishments and enjoy some flexible time. One of the greatest misuses of time over which nurses have full control is their failure to maximize the therapeutic value of their contacts with patients. Too often nursing contacts are filled with social conversation rather than professional, goal-specific interactions. A totally professional conversation consumes no more time than a superficial social exchange. It does require thought, however, and nurses may need assistance in polishing their skills in professional interactions. The supervisor may wish to consider role playing during inservice education programs for this purpose. If a full-scale inservice program is not possible, a structured role-playing exercise might be constructed and enacted at the shift change. This assumes, of course, that the exchange of information at report time is already being handled in an adequate but expeditious manner. As an alternative, the supervisor may simply choose to give a demonstration by role modeling professional interaction with a patient on the unit. With quality interactions, one is practically assured of generating valuable content to place in the record.

## SELF-ANALYSIS

Supervisors might often say that they long for bedside contact, that they felt satisfied in the clinical role but now feel less satisfied since moving from the clinical to the administrative arena. In such situations, a thorough examination of one's periods of greatest satisfaction is required. The supervisor must determine whether satisfaction was derived solely from the clinical practice of nursing per se or whether happiness was coming primarily from other things. For example, was happiness most pronounced in instances when there was excitement related to redecorating a unit; when a new or different nursing care modality was initiated; when there was a periodic infusion of new activities brought by new groups of students; when new equipment was being introduced; or when exciting clinical research was being conducted? That supervisor must also examine what was going on

in her or his personal life. Was there a wedding; a new baby; admission to an important social group; selection as an officer in a professional organization? If, after examination, the nursing supervisor decides that the actual clinical performance of direct patient care provided the most enjoyment, that nurse should hurry back to the bedside. Some nurses are reluctant to return to the bedside after entering supervisory roles; they often fear loss of face. It is important for them to recognize that supervision and administration exist for the purpose of enhancing clinical practice and that each role is equally valuable. If the nurse is self-contented with the decision to return to the care-giving role for professional fulfillment, the questions of others will be of lesser importance. Certainly the nurse will not feel deprived by the absence of administrative responsibility.

•   •   •

Supervisors in nursing have been important in facilitating the delivery of health care for many years. Nursing supervisors will be successful in these stressful times if they adopt a common-sense survival strategy. They must learn to face the facts, document essential activities, be good to themselves, manage time wisely, and conduct a self-examination to be sure that supervision is indeed what they want.

# Confrontation: An underused nursing management technique

**Ruth Davidhizar**
*Director of Nursing*

**Margaret Bowen**
*Assistant Director of Nursing*
*Logansport State Hospital*
*Logansport, Indiana*

CONFRONTATION is the application of a direct approach by which feelings are communicated forthrightly and clearly. When confrontation is used by the nurse manager, others encountered in the job situation are made aware of the manager's ideas or ways of thinking without covert or mystifying approaches or other indirect methods.

For most nurses, confrontation does not come naturally and is not viewed as a desirable communication technique. In normal development, many children are socialized to avoid saying what they truly think and feel. Nurses are likewise socialized in subservience and passive listening techniques rather than in direct approaches that may appear hostile and aggressive.[1] Nurses commonly elect to take no action rather than face an issue head on and risk conflict. The technique of confrontation is seen as uncomfortable and risky.

*Health Care Superv*, 1988, 7(1), 29–34
© 1988 Aspen Publishers, Inc.

However, for a person in a management position, conflict is a common occurrence, and dealing with issues rather than avoiding them becomes essential for a healthy organization and for the well-being of the manager. Interpersonal risks must be taken, and problems cannot be avoided if growth is to occur. Nurse managers who do not question what they are told, or who do not ask about the discrepancies between what others are doing and what they should do, will not be strong managers. Confrontation can be a significant technique for facilitating self-growth, resolving conflict, and prompting problem solving. Open and honest confrontation is frequently a low-risk approach to conflict resolution.[2] Expertise in confrontation skills should be part of the repertoire of interpersonal techniques of a manager. This article presents guidelines for the successful use of confrontation by the nurse manager.

## DYNAMICS OF CONFRONTATION

Nurse managers are frequently appointed because they have certain kinds of ideas and exhibit particular ways of thinking, that is left brain skills of deduction and analysis, that will contribute to the effective operation of a health care organization. Also, nurse managers have some perception of how and when to share these ideas, for example, the right brain skills of intuition, inductive thinking, and empathy.[3] Although both deductive and inductive skills are among the basic abilities required of a nurse manager, the technique of confrontation requires an integration of both left and right brain functions. Effective confrontation requires both ideas worth sharing and an intuitive sense of

timing in regard to when and with whom to share these ideas.

## GUIDELINES

Successful confrontation must be both a technique and a process. Confrontation begins with identification of the need for confrontation, preplanning, and an astute sense of timing. During the confrontation, both the problem and the desired behavioral change must be clearly identified. Finally, the confronting individual must have credibility and empathy. Use of humor can add to the effectiveness of confrontation.

### Identify need for confrontation

Often the most difficult task is to determine whether or not confrontation is appropriate and will be useful. Because resolution of problems is usually an objective of confrontation, confrontation may be contraindicated if there are no options available. A helpless manager who sees no options will not improve the situation with confrontation.

Once the need for and benefits of confrontation have been established, preplanning is necessary. Preplanning includes a thorough assessment of the situation and identification of available options. It is necessary for the nurse manager to understand the issues involved and be able to speak knowledgeably about the specific behaviors that are being addressed.

Usually, confrontation is less effective and is contraindicated if the person's psychological or physical defenses are down or the person has no ability to tolerate criticism. An awareness of the strengths and weaknesses of the person confronted will be significant for the successful outcome of confrontation. Knowledge of the individual should influence not only whether confrontation should be used but also when, and how, it will be most effective.

### Timing

Optimal timing for confrontation is crucial. The physical environment should be considered, that is, privacy. Confrontation should occur in private or with carefully selected individuals. If actions are required after the confrontation, can they in fact be taken? For example, if the personnel director must be consulted, is the confrontation timed when that person is available? Will there be support persons for the individual to talk with after the interaction if necessary? The timing of confrontation should be evaluated in terms of the work day. In some cases it will be more effective if the confrontation occurs before the work day has begun, but in other cases it will be most effective at the end of the day. When will the person be most receptive—before or after going on vacation?

### Clearly identify the problem

It is essential that the problem to be confronted is clearly identified by the nurse manager. Also, when the confrontation occurs it is essential that the issues under contention be stated in simple concrete terms so both persons understand the focus. A common mistake in utilizing confrontation is vague or ambiguous knowledge about the problem or the desired change. Unless behavioral problems or goals are clearly stated, confrontation will be ineffective; for example, "Your supervisor told me you have made three medication errors in

the past week, and more than three medication errors in a year is unsatisfactory clinical performance in this hospital" is far more effective than "I hear you've been doing bad work."

The confrontation should involve facts rather than opinions and focus on behavior rather than the person: "Your written assessments have not been satisfactory" rather than "You have not been satisfactory."

One of the most effective ways of confrontation is to gather information from an outside source and have that individual present the employee with the testimony in person—the director of nursing may call in a supervisor who has witnessed the unsatisfactory performance of an employee to describe this behavior in front of the employee. If employee and supervisor are to continue in a working relationship, this kind of confrontation can help mend broken communication and facilitate supervisor–employee communication.

In confrontation the message should be worded carefully. Caution must be exercised in making absolute statements. Maneuverability is important when the technique of confrontation is used. A manager must avoid becoming boxed into corners or drawing lines over which others are not supposed to step. The manager must be ready to use action to back up a statement such as "If you do this one more time you will be terminated." A contingency plan that anticipates the worst must always be available.

### Identify the behavior change required

A confrontation should include not only the identification of what is wrong but also an indication of what must be done to correct the situation: "Your clothes are dirty and it is an expectation of the nursing department that employees appear neat and clean." Discrepancies must be identified in the confrontation. It is important for employees to know and understand the supervisor's expectations. Once the employee has perceived the discrepancy between the immediate situation and certain facts, the nurse manager can go about helping to solve the problem. For example, if attendance is poor and better attendance is a requirement of the job, the necessity to decrease the discrepancy between the employee's attendance record and the requirement can be identified. Confrontation usefully demonstrates discrepancies between intent and effect, between word and action, and between stated rules and actual practices.[4]

In situations involving conflict over resources, procedures, or turf, compromise is a most useful tactic. It provides a solution that can be perceived as "win-win," a solution through which both or all sides gain something. The other side of the coin is a trade off, the giving of something of value for something in return.[5] Both options can apply in the resolution of a confrontation.

## Credibility

Experience within the organization may not only assist in increasing the nurse manager's understanding of the issues but may also provide the added benefit of enhancing the manager's credibility. Confrontation will be more effective if the manager has a track record of consistency and reliability. If a person was fired for the same offense last year and this is common knowledge at the hospital, a statement such as "Employees

*Because confrontation is a power technique, the credibility of the confrontation must be supported by a tone and posture of authority*

who commit this infraction are terminated" will have credibility. If the employee is aware that someone committed the same act last week and nothing happened, the confrontation will be ineffective. Credible managers have developed trust and respect by maintaining a manner of openness and honesty in interpersonal relations over a period of time. A trusted manager delivers no mixed messages and can be depended on to share feelings of approval as well as indications of disapproval. Because both knowledge of the issues and a development of trust are necessary, one can rarely step into an ongoing situation and gain maximum benefit from confrontation.

Credibility is also established by consistency between verbal and nonverbal messages. Because confrontation is a power technique, the credibility of the confrontation must be supported by a tone and posture of authority and self-confidence. Effective confrontation is not achieved by a manager who comes across as meek and insecure.

## Empathy

Confrontation is most effective if the employee feels empathy from the nurse manager. "I know how hard you've worked to improve your reporting, and the effort shows. Now you need only give some attention to penmanship" will be a more effective statement than simply "Your writing is still dreadful!" If an empathetic relationship exists between the nurse manager and the person confronted, this positive relationship will balance off the negative effects of the confronting statement and will be more likely to facilitate a positive behavioral change.

As well as being a technique in its own right, confrontation occurs in the context of a relationship as part of an interpersonal process. When confrontation is used too early in a relationship, it may hinder the development of a positive relationship, because confrontation by a stranger will be perceived in a different context than in an established relationship.

### Verbal confrontation

Inexperienced managers sometimes try to apply a confronting approach with a memo or letter. This is usually ineffective. One benefit of confrontation is that it sets the stage for resolution of a problem. Without a face-to-face encounter, a major advantage of confrontation, the prompting of immediate negotiation, is lost. A face-to-face encounter also gives the nurse manager the opportunity to back down or to modify what has been said. On the other hand, a written confrontation presents the additional problem of potential misinterpretation. Confrontation in memo form is the coward's way out.

A written confrontation may be appropriate when one believes that time is needed before a solution can be found. In this case it should be followed up with a face-to-face contact so that resolution can be sought.

### Humor

Because most persons are immediately threatened when confronted by others about their faults, tempering one's statements with humor often makes a confrontation more acceptable. The personal acceptance experienced in sharing laughter occurs simultaneously with the criticism of the confrontation, diluting its negative effect. Humor can also take the edge off a tense situation, allowing both persons to rally their resources for negotiations.

•    •    •

Confrontation is a powerful time-saving technique that can move an interaction quickly toward resolution and problem solving. When a confrontational style is used, individuals are more likely to know where they stand and what the manager thinks of them under the circumstances. Confrontation can promote open and honest interaction.

However, a confrontational approach can be damaging to the self-esteem and ego of a fragile personality. This is especially true if the person utilizing the technique is held in high regard, when options are not readily available, or when support is not present. If the confronting approach is not seen in the context of a supportive relationship, it may appear threatening and negative. Confrontation can be overused; thus it should be only one of the variety of interpersonal techniques used by the nurse manager.

## REFERENCES

1. Smoyak, S. "The Confrontation Process." *American Journal of Nursing* 74 (September 1974): 1632–35.
2. Citron, B. "Facing Up to Conflict." *Nursing Life* 4 (July/August 1985): 47–49.
3. Agor, W. "Intuition: The New Management Tool." *Nursing Success* (1984): 23–24.
4. Ruesch, J. *Therapeutic Communication.* New York: Norton, 1961.
5. Brooten, D. *Management in Nursing.* Philadelphia: Lippincott, 1984.

# Intuition, ethical decision making, and the nurse manager

**Sharon Cranendonk Gearhart**
*Inservice Instructor*
*Virginia Beach, Virginia*

**Sue W. Young**
*Associate Professor*
*School of Nursing*
*Old Dominion University*
*Norfolk, Virginia*

E THICAL DILEMMAS are not new to nursing, but recent changes in the health care delivery system have spawned ethical controversies that have created new and perplexing moral issues. Ethical decision making enables a nurse to arrive at a carefully derived decision, thus resolving the ethical conflict before taking action. Ethical decision making also allows a nurse to become more aware of conflicting issues, examine the roles and responsibilities of each participant, and arrive at a more reasoned decision through the use of an established rationale.[1] Ethical decision making uses ethical theories to initiate decisions that are rationally justified, as opposed to decisions based strictly on intuition and preference.[2]

Intuition cannot function as a consistent base for nursing judgments, but neither can a systematic, rational approach. Both lack the ability to provide the all-encompassing database needed for ethical decision mak-

*Health Care Superv,* 1990, 8(3), 45–52
© 1990 Aspen Publishers, Inc.

ing. This article assumes that intuition enhances the systematic, rational approach to the decision-making process used by nurses. The article analyzes a recent study by the authors that supported the necessity for providing nurses with increased depth and understanding of the appropriate decision-making process to be used in resolving ethical dilemmas in nursing practice.

## RESEARCH FINDINGS

The focus of this study was on identifying the reasoning process used by nurses to resolve ethical dilemmas. Curtin's model for ethical decision making supported by decision-making theory served as the theoretical framework.[3] Ethical decision making was defined as a systematic, rational approach that can lead to critical ethical reasoning and analysis to rationally determine a course of action.[3] The decision-making process used by nurse participants was measured using the Ethical Theory and Decision Making Tool, which consists of 11 scenarios representing typical ethical dilemmas. Respondents were requested to sequentially identify the steps of the decision-making process for each scenario. Curtin's model was used to formulate the item choices.

Statistical analysis of the data showed the steps of the decision-making process to be internally consistent, with statistical reliabilities of between .81 and .90 (see Table 1). These ∝ levels represent a high degree of test variance in the ordering of decision-

**Table 1.** Steps and reliabilities of the decision-making process

| | Steps | ∝ levels |
|---|---|---|
| Step 1: | Background information | .81 |
| Step 2: | Identification of ethical components | .82 |
| Step 3: | Ethical agents | .85 |
| Step 4: | Identification of options and courses of action | .90 |
| Step 5: | Reconciliation of the facts and applying principles | .81 |
| Step 6: | Resolution of problem | .86 |

making process steps by the 63 nurses participating in the study.

To compare differences between sample respondents' decision-making processes and Curtin's decision-making model, schematic representations were developed. First, a schematic representation of Curtin's decision-making model was developed (see Figure 1). Data were then sorted according to the ethical frame of reference—deontologism or utilitarianism—used by the nurses.

*Deontologism* is an ethical theory that emphasizes the rules and principles that guide actions. An action is right if it accords with a moral principle or rule and wrong if it violates that principle or rule. Therefore, deontologists determine outcomes by the rightness or wrongness of an act in accordance with a moral principle. *Utilitarianism* is a consequential theory of ethical reasoning. Utilitarians base their actions on the

**Figure 1.** Curtin's ethical decision-making process.

**Figure 2.** Ethical decision-making process for nurses with a deontologic preference.

consequences that will result from those actions and hold that any action that produces more harm than good is wrong and should be avoided.

Ethical frame of reference was determined by the sum score, a summary statistic that represented the sum scores of ethical theories, either deontologic or utilitarian, chosen by the nurse respondents, and the number of times each value was obtained. A sum score more than or equal to 6 indicated a respondent's preference for either a deontologic or a utilitarian position from which to resolve ethical dilemmas. Based on this process, participants were placed in a deontologic ($n = 44$) or utilitarian ($n = 16$) frame of reference for decision making (problem resolution). The mode occurring most frequently for the hypothetical situations was used to represent the steps of the decision-making process for the respondents, with a deontologic and utilitarian preference for problem resolution. Schematic representations were then developed for the decision-making process used by those respondents in the deontologic group (Figure 2) and those in the utilitarian group (Figure 3).

Nurses with a deontologic frame of reference approached ethical decision making by choosing step 4, assessing options and alternatives, as the second phase in the process. Nurses with a utilitarian frame of reference

approached ethical decision making by choosing step 3 (persons involved) before step 2 (ethical components), and step 5 (applying principles) before step 4 (options and alternatives). Background information (step 1) and resolution (step 6) were identified in the same sequence as Curtin's model. Data analysis revealed an unsystematic approach to ethical decision making by nurses in both groups.

Qualitative data provided further information. An open-ended question requested respondents to list any other comments they had in reference to the questionnaire, providing the qualitative data source. Responses for this question were grouped into five categories. The categories, from largest to smallest, were: (1) inadequate number of solutions, (2) decision-making steps produced forced choice, (3) issues relevant and thought provoking, (4) questionnaire too long, and (5) ethical dilemmas more problematic for physicians than nurses. Responses indicating that the steps of the decision-making process produced forced choices revealed that the tool design prevented them from expressing "gut" feelings that help in making a decision. This forced-choice format was described by participants as misrepresenting the decision-making process actually used in practice. Further comments revealed that participants per-

**Figure 3.** Ethical decision-making process for nurses with a utilitarian preference.

ceive practicing nurses as "not having the time" to use a rational process for each ethical dilemma that occurs.

Findings of a nonsystematic approach and a lack of consistency in the ethical decision-making process combined with the qualitative data suggest that there is a need to design a more dynamic measurement process that accurately portrays the reflective or critical thinking involved in ethical decision making. The systematic evaluation approach used in this study was insufficient by itself for measuring ethical decision making used by nurses in practice. The researchers concluded that ethical decision making is a multidimensional process, and recommended that further exploration measure both the analytic and intuitive processes.

## INTUITION

Nursing has long stressed a systematic, analytic approach to decision making. Scientific, rational thinking dominates the teaching and learning process emphasized by nursing educational programs. Ethical decision making encompasses both reasoning and decision making and is focused on objective data collection. Historically, intuition has been renounced because it was thought to be unscientific, feminine, and incongruent with the philosophy of logic.[4]

### The use of intuition in decision making

Intuition, as defined by Westcott, is the "reaching of a conclusion on the basis of less explicit information than is ordinarily required to reach that conclusion."[5(p.71)] Webster defines intuition as "revelation by insight or innate knowledge."[6(p.445)] Gerrity reports that "intuition permits perception

---

*The use of intuition in the decision-making process is a relatively new concept in nursing practice, but has finally been acknowledged in the nursing literature.*

---

beyond what is visible to the senses, including possible future events."[7(p.65)]

The use of intuition in the decision-making process is a relatively new concept in nursing practice, but has finally been acknowledged in the nursing literature.[7] Agor reports that intuition has gained acceptance and respectability as a management decision-making tool in the 1980s.[8] Managers who use an intuitive approach often see new possibilities in a situation and generate new ideas, and this results in ingenious solutions to old problems.[9]

Several factors have contributed to the acceptance of intuition as a viable component of decision making. Research has indicated that analytic, systematic techniques are not always useful in guiding decisions that need to be made in a climate of rapid change. Also, systematic reasoning that is based solely on past trends can be misleading and inaccurate.[8]

Another factor that supports this use of intuition, identified by both Agor and Crossett, is quantitative physiologic evidence.[8,10] The brain has two potentially independent mental systems: the left brain (the center for intellect) and the right brain (the center for intuition). These two hemispheres are connected by a bundle of nerve fibers that have the potential to work in harmony. Integration of these hemispheres allows for an increase in the total productive capacity of the brain. According to Crossett, the highest achievements of individuals have been as a result of this integration. Therefore, exclusively fostering analytic, rational decision making may not result in the highest achievements or the best outcomes.

Schraeder and Fischer have identified four factors that influence intuitive thinking in clinical decision making: (1) characteristics of the nurse; (2) feelings of relatedness to the patient; (3) perception of the physiologic individual cues that are not easy to quantify; and (4) linking of past experiences to present perceptions. Those nurses with more experience and technical proficiency used more intuitive decision-making skills.[11]

Gerrity reported that only 21% of 3,103 nurses used intuition in making judgments. This finding, when compared to results indicating that individuals with high levels of intuitive ability make more effective decisions than individuals with low levels of intuitive ability,[7,12] reveals that current decision-making processes are not as effective as they could be.

Experience and previous solutions derived from the decision-making process are keys to intuition. Caution in the use of intuition alone must be exercised, however, since overlooking facts can result in serious mistakes.[7,9] Learning to use intuition could increase the perceptive abilities of nurses. Perhaps, then, intuition is simply another dimension of reasoning.

### Implications for research

Few data exist to substantiate intuition.[7] Development of empirical data to describe, explain, predict, and control intuition should be a concern of the nursing community.

Westcott identifies three criteria that must be met before intuition can be measured.
1. Individuals must be in a problem-solving situation that includes varying amounts of information.
2. There must be an appraisal system for determining how much information an individual requires to resolve the problem in relation to how much is usually required.
3. The solution must be consensually valid.[5]

These three criteria help to operationally define intuition for empirical testing.

Gerrity reports that the Myers-Briggs Type Indicator (MBTI), a psychometric instrument, provides a simple and reliable method for measuring the presence of intuition.[7] This instrument provides information regarding a person's preferences for certain types of behavior, thereby allowing for easy and quick evaluation of an individual's tendency to use intuitive processes in daily interaction. Knowledge of one's preference or nonpreference for intuitive behavioral responses would be useful to any nurse who has responsibility for decision making.

### STRATEGIES FOR DEVELOPING INTUITION

Nurse managers are in a pivotal role for the nurturing of intuitive abilities and systematic reasoning to enhance the decision-making abilities of nurses. Because nurse managers are held accountable for decision making that results in effective and efficient managements outcomes (i.e., improved productivity for the nursing organization), nurse managers must develop skills that foster intuitive abilities.

> *An individual must be receptive and have the ability to focus attention, relax, and quiet the mind.*

Agor reports that all individuals have intuitive abilities, and identifies three steps that are necessary in order for managers to unlock, develop, and apply intuition. The first is identification of methods that allow an individual to learn cognitively who he or she is. This entails becoming fully aware of the types of tasks and skills that are performed by the individual. The second is identification of methods to assist an individual to believe in intuitive abilities. An individual must be receptive and have the ability to focus attention, relax, and quiet the mind. The last step is the cultivation and practice of intuitive abilities. This involves risk taking on the part of the nurse manager in the decision-making process and requires continual evaluation of the process for further refinement of intuitive abilities.[8]

The nurse manager can also enhance intuitive abilities by being aware of the cues and feelings that make a decision seem right or wrong.[9] It is of prime importance that the nurse manager follow those cues and feelings instead of ignoring them. Intuition leads to true knowledge and conviction.[5]

Another strategy is the development of a portfolio of techniques that assist the nurse manager in focusing the brain to guide the decision. Such techniques include mental, analytic, and relaxation exercises.[9] The nurse manager can incorporate the mental and analytic exercises necessary to activate intuition for ethical decision making through the use of regularly scheduled practice sessions. Abdominal breathing, pro-gressive relaxation by contraction and relaxation of muscles, and visual imagery are several relaxation techniques that help activate intuition. Stress inoculation is a cognitive-oriented coping skills program that can be used to train staff to manage potential stressful situations such as ethical dilemmas. This three-phase process allows for reduction of stress by providing individuals with a sense of greater control over reactions to ethical dilemmas in practice.[13]

The last strategy identified by Agor is the development of a support group by the nurse manager that allows for strengthening and sharing of intuitive skills. Groups have a greater capacity to find innovative solutions for resolving ethical dilemmas.[9] The groups should be composed of individuals who complement each other with different levels of intuitive abilities. Diversity of experience also facilitates creative thinking and communication among members and provides the means by which intuition can be incorporated into the ethical decision-making process.

Brainstorming is a useful group technique that can be used by the nurse manager to assess all the variables in an ethical dilemma. This provides the group with an extensive list of options and allows for grouping of ideas and examination of the questions most relevant to the ethical dilemma.[14]

## MANAGING ETHICAL DECISION MAKING

Agor also identifies three types of management styles for the ethical decision-making process. The left-brain management style thrives on intellect and employs analytic thinking and deductive reasoning.[8]

Ethical reasoning is a form of deductive reasoning.[15] This style involves using a structured decision-making process that is organized, follows specific logical and rational steps, and emphasizes facts and details. Decision trees, Program Evaluation and Review Technique (PERT) models, and probability theory are techniques used by nurse managers with this management style to minimize the uncertainty of and provide structure for those decisions.

The right-brain management style is dominated by intuition and employs intuitive thinking and inductive reasoning.[8] With inductive reasoning, the conclusion is the known phenomenon and the parts that comprise the whole are unknown.[15] The nurse manager who employs right-brain reasoning would resolve ethical dilemmas using life experiences, formal and informal educational experiences, and religious and cultural influences to guide the decision-making process. The right-brain management style emphasizes creative thinking and the interpersonal nature of information and uses pictures and visual images to present the decision-making process.[15]

The integrated management style interchanges the left-brain and right-brain styles depending on the demands of the situation.[8] This may be the ideal style for ensuring the high quality of decisions that resolve ethical dilemmas. In ethical decision making, the decision chosen is considered the best or only choice for a particular situation. Therefore, the best ethical decision must be of the highest possible quality, and an integrated style would logically be the appropriate choice.

Examination of two key components of ethical decision making, intuition and analytic ability, can assist the nurse manager in dealing with complex ethical dilemmas that are present in practice. Nurse managers need to be familiar with intuitive abilities in order to enhance productivity. A more effective, creative, and enlightened decision-making process will result in more effective and efficient decisions and will optimize the nursing organization's productivity.

•    •    •

Analysis of recent research data revealed the necessity to increase the breadth and depth of the systematic ethical decision-making process used by nurses. Intuition, defined as an extension of reasoning, was identified as a key element that enhances the analytic approach.

Ethical dilemmas will continue to increase with the advancing technology used in delivery of health care services. It is the responsibility of the nurse manager to develop ethical decision-making abilities for the entire nursing staff and to encourage the recognition of intuitive abilities as a component of the ethical and management decision-making process. Managers must accept this challenge so that these processes will positively influence professional nursing practice.

## REFERENCES

1. Aroskar, M. "Nurses as Decision Makers: Ethical Dimensions." *Imprint* 32, no. 4 (1985): 28–31.
2. Kieffer, G. *Bioethics: A Textbook of Issues.* Reading,

Mass.: Addison-Wesley, 1979.
3. Curtin, L., and Flaherty, M. *Nursing Ethics: Theories and Pragmatics.* Bowie, Md.: Robert J. Brady, 1982.

4. Rew, L. "Intuition in Decision Making." *Image* 20, no. 3 (1988): 150–54.

5. Westcott, M. *Toward a Contemporary Psychology of Intuition.* New York: Holt, Rinehart & Winston, 1968.

6. *Webster's Seventh New Collegiate Dictionary.* Springfield, Mass.: G & C Merriam, 1972.

7. Gerrity, P. "Perception in Nursing: The Value of Intuition." *Holistic Nursing Practice* 1, no. 3 (1987): 63–71.

8. Agor, W. *Intuitive Management: Integrating Left and Right Brain Management Skills.* Englewood Cliffs, N.J.: Prentice Hall, 1984.

9. Agor, W. "How Top Executives Use Their Intuition To Make Important Decisions." *Business Horizons* 29, no. 1 (1986): 49–53.

10. Crossett, B. "Using Both Halves of the Brain To Teach the Whole Child." *Social Education* 47 (1983): 266–88.

11. Schraeder, B., and Fischer, D. "Using Intuitive Knowledge in the Neonatal Intensive Care Nursery." *Holistic Nursing Practice* 1, no. 3 (1987): 45–51.

12. Cosier, R., and Aplin, J. "Intuition and Decision Making: Some Empirical Evidence." *Psychological Reports* 51, no. 1 (1982): 275–81.

13. Manderino, M., and Yonkman, C. "Stress Inoculations: A Method of Helping Students Cope with Anxiety Related to Clinical Performance." *Journal of Nursing Education* 24, no. 3 (1985): 115–18.

14. Young, S. "The Nurse Manager: Clarifying Ethical Issues in Professional Role Responsibility." *Pediatric Nursing* 13, no. 6 (1987): 430–42.

15. Young, L., and Hayne, A. *Nursing Administrations: From Concepts to Practice.* Philadelphia: W.B. Saunders, 1988.

# Intuition and the nurse manager

*Ruth Davidhizar, R.N., D.N.S., C.S.*
*Assistant Dean*
*Chairperson for Nursing*
*Bethel College*
*Mishawaka, Indiana*

INTUITION IS MUCH more than a hunch, a guess, an instinct, or a gut feeling. Intuition sometimes appears to be a perception outside of traditional channels of sight, smell, taste, touch, or hearing.[1] In other cases, intuition appears to be a process of arriving at knowledge without conscious awareness of rational thinking. In still other situations, intuition describes the ability to integrate and synthesize diverse and complex information.[2] In spite of the varying definitions there is growing fascination with the concept of intuition and with its relevance to certain professions. A recent proliferation of literature on the benefits of intuition to nursing and to management suggests that intuition is a noteworthy concept for the nurse manager.[3–7]

What value does intuition have for nurses and managers? Can intuition benefit the nurse manager? How can intuition be developed? This article answers these questions and also provides guidelines for the manager for maximizing personal intuitive potential.

*Health Care Superv,* 1991, 10(2), 13–19
©1991 Aspen Publishers, Inc.

## INTUITION IN NURSING AND MANAGEMENT

Historically, intuition was attributed only to women, children, and certain cultural groups. Gradually, intuition was introduced and became acceptable to the professions of philosophy and psychology. Today, intuition is not only acknowledged as a phenomenon found in a few individuals but it is also recognized as a creative and powerful individual attribute that often lies dormant, waiting to be developed.[4(p.21)] Recent reports in the nursing and business literature document use of intuition.

### Nursing

Nurses have traditionally considered intuition to be mystical, accidental, or irrational. Nurses have attempted to rely on factual knowledge that could be subjected to logical evaluation. Nurses have capitulated to the scientific and have assumed that only the objective mind could generate significant questions and answers. Only recently have nurses begun to suggest intuition may have legitimacy as an approach to clinical judgments. Benner and Tanner postulate intuition to be present in at least four nursing situations:[8]

1. the nurse who has had previous experience with the problem or situation and has an in-depth knowledge of it;
2. the nurse who grasps the situation as a whole and integrates fragmented bits of information in a meaningful way or is able to grasp a situation that cannot be understood by using available knowledge or by the rules and formulas of linear thinking;
3. the nurse who knows the patient in an empathetic sense, is truly involved with the patient, is able to experience the patient on many levels, and is able to invest self and energy in the patient's well-being; and
4. the nurse who is sensitive to the patient's subtle physiologic cues and whose interpretation goes beyond the cues available.

Whether intuition facilitates the nurse's awareness of physiologic signs and symptoms or psychologic distress, or whether intuition assists in the process of synthesizing information to arrive at a logical conclusion, intuition is being increasingly shown as a powerful nursing tool. The results of intuition for the nurse can be accurate diagnosis, vigilant monitoring, and better patient care.[8(p.12),9,10] Research in nursing shows that, while intuition should be verified with investigation, intuition should be welcomed as an addition to logical reasoning and as a phenomenon that nurses should cultivate.[11]

### Management

Research on intuition began appearing in the business literature in the 1970s. A study by Dean, Milhalasky, Ostrander, and Schroeder found that, of 25 men selected, 12 had doubled their companies' profits in 5 years, and 12 scored above chance on the precognition test.[12] Their average score was 12.8 compared with 8.3 for those who had not doubled their profits. While the study lacked statistical rigor, a study involving 111 business students found that decision makers who qualified as highly intuitive made better subjective decisions in a simulated management environment.[1(p.280)] Testing over 2,000 managers across the country, Agor showed that intuition is a particularly useful brain skill for a health professional.[6(p.23)] Agor described intuition as useful in both handling emergencies and motivating patients.

Intuition encompasses both right-brain skills of perception and understanding raw information and left-brain skills of deductive synthesizing, logic, and application. Since intuitive perception enables a person to sense the possibilities while deductive synthesizing enables the person to foresee intuitively the outcome of potential decisions, intuition involves both right- and left-brain functions. Effective managers combine right-brain sensing, intuitive, and affective abilities with left-brain intellectual and cognitive skills to lead and manage subordinates and to relate with peers and supervisors. Managerial use of intuition involves an exquisite sensitivity to patterns and minimal cues, storing them for future use and then acting on these observations. A manager who states, "My hypothesis is...," "Based on my experience, my prediction is...," or "All the evidence seems to indicate that..." is actively using intuition.

## BENEFITS OF INTUITION FOR THE NURSE MANAGER

The benefits of intuition to nursing and management are compounded for the nurse in a management role. Effective use of intuition is not only useful but essential to expert nursing management. Intuition has both cognitive and interpersonal components and benefits. Not only does intuition facilitate the manager's understanding and grasp of situations, decision making, and actions, but also intuition enables the manager to empathetically sense others and to have increased sensitivity in interpersonal relationships.

### Intuition facilitates understanding

Recognizing patterns and similarities and grasping and understanding situations are aspects of intuitive judgment described by Dreyfus and Dreyfus.[7(p.10)] Recognizing patterns is a perceptual ability to recognize relationships without prespecifying components of the situation. Configurations, relationships, and connections are recognized and understood. Present situations may be related to similar situations in the past.

Recognition of similarities and dissimilarities can assist in problem identification and planning intervention. Employee and patient situations present patterns unrecognizable to the novice but understandable to the experienced nurse manager. For example, an employee who acts suspiciously may prompt an expert manager to assume a less confronting and therefore less threatening manner since a manager experienced in using confrontation will know a direct approach can precipitate and increase paranoid feelings.

Intuitive judgment also involves having a deep grasp of the culture and language so that flexible understanding in diverse situations is possible. Expert managers know to appreciate more than the information they are given but to sense and understand the context of behavior and the consequences of taking certain actions. For example, an expert nurse manager may anticipate an angry employee's appeal of a disciplinary action just as the action the manager must take in response can be anticipated.

### Intuition facilitates decision making

Decision making is facilitated by a sense of salience and deliberative rationality.[7(p.10)] A sense of salience is the ability to respond to situations with differentiation for which pieces of information require a response. Not all tasks are equally important, and not all observations are equally important. Flexibility in application of background information and flexibility in interpretation are necessary to allow certain perceptions to leap out as most important.

Deliberative rationality is the ability to view present situations in terms of past situations so that certain events can be focused on with selective attention. This does not mean that tunnel vision operates but rather that tentative suppositions are made based on previous experience. For example, a prospective nurse employee's inability to relate positively in an interview situation may be given more priority than a high grade point average on a transcript. The nurse manager with a sense of salience and deliberative rationality may be able to "outguess" others when making decisions and may do better at strategic planning.

### Intuition facilitates appropriate action

Intuition also involves the ability to adapt skill and knowledge to individual situations and to take appropriate action. Intuition can prompt the nurse manager to recognize a teachable moment with subordinates or peers and, conversely, to recognize when the situation will not be conducive to learning.

### Intuition facilitates empathy

Intuition provides a bridge between the manager and others. The intuitive manager has greater perception for verbal and nonverbal messages provided in interpersonal situations and thus is able to appear more sensitive to others. Intuitive perception may enable the nurse manager to feel something is wrong or to know when action is inappropriate and listening is best. Without intuitive perception the manager may physically touch others who do not want to be touched or may use humor when a serious

*Intuition provides a bridge between the manager and others. The intuitive manager has greater perception for verbal and nonverbal messages provided in interpersonal situations and thus is able to appear more sensitive to others.*

response is indicated. Since intuitive behavior facilitates effective relating to others, it can have the serendipitous effect of increasing the respect and appreciation others feel for the manager. The ability to relate to others has the additional benefit of positively validating the manager's feelings of interpersonal competency. The manager's increased sensitivity to others and positive self-image free the manager to take the interpersonal risks necessary to connect and keep on connecting with others in a meaningful way.

## DEVELOPING AND MAXIMIZING PERSONAL INTUITIVE POTENTIAL

In spite of the general neglect of the topic of intuition in education and training programs in health care management, some nursing managers are becoming motivated to develop and maximize their own personal intuitive potential. The growing appreciation of the value of intuition is prompted by a variety of factors. Articles and books on intuition have increased the credibility of intuition as a reputable job skill. On-the-job experience has shown some managers that intuition is useful. Some managers who used to admire the intuitive ability of others but thought it was a gift are seeking more complete understanding in order to develop and expand personal intuitive skills. Nurse managers who formerly preferred to discuss only objective management skills are now questioning the value of also using their dormant intuitive skills.

For the nurse seeking to develop intuition the following six guidelines are offered:

1. Intuition must be respected.
2. Intuition requires self-confidence.
3. Intuition requires experience.
4. Intuition involves risk.
5. Intuition requires consideration for the whole.
6. Intuition can be learned from a mentor.

### Intuition must be respected

An important step in the nurse manager's development of intuition is respect for the value of intuition as a management technique. A manager must appreciate not only rational calculation but intuitive perception and judgment. Unless the nurse manager is consciously willing to allow intuition to operate, intuitive ability will be stifled.

### Intuition requires self-confidence

In addition to appreciation of intuition as a management technique, use of intuition requires self-confidence. Self-respect and trust in one's own intuitive judgment is necessary to rely on feelings in decision making. Managers who are insecure or preoccupied will not be able to reach outside of themselves with the interpersonal sensitivity necessary for intuitive perception. Managers who are preoccupied with personal problems will lack intuitive skills since their focus may be narrowed and it will be difficult for them to see situations comprehensively.

There must also be an appreciation of one's own intuitive potential. Formal models are helpful for learning about management principles and the interpersonal situations encountered in a management role. Assessment tools for evaluation of prospective employees, management conflicts, and unit problems are helpful. However, if the manager maintains a checklist orientation rather than a style of active inquiry with attention to instincts, intuitive knowledge is stifled and will not be allowed to blossom. Personal permission must be granted to let intuitive potential develop.

### Intuition requires experience

Intuition is a management technique most effectively used by experienced and expert managers. Nurse managers who are knowledgeable about nursing and management principles and who have a broad base of management experience are able to synthesize in a manner that raises intuition to a level of credibility.[5,13(p.161)] Nevertheless, while intuition is a managerial technique used more effectively by the expert manager, it should be a technique cultivated by the novice. Just as in other areas of practice, a novice nurse manager will be able to become an experienced and intuitive expert nurse with practice.

### Intuition involves risk

An intuitive decision is often made in the absence of knowledge. Making a decision in the face of incomplete information requires risk. However, in nursing management, there is rarely enough information to guarantee that a decision will be correct. A good manager makes a decision based on careful evaluation of the facts and logic available and reliance on personal instincts. The manager's experience decreases the risk involved since experience enables the manager to select situations when intuition will likely be more effectively used.

## Intuition requires consideration for the whole

A manager who wishes to use intuition must have a style that fosters evaluation of the whole rather than segments of a problem or phenomenon. A style that looks at the whole involves seeing the past as well as the present, considering verbal as well as nonverbal components of a message, understanding what is emphasized as well as what is not, seeing patterns of behavior, recognizing priorities, and applying a conceptual understanding to behavior that is seen. Pattern recognition is not taught in lectures or procedural rules but is developed by practice, self-analysis, expert feedback on performance, and ongoing integration of what is learned. Information-processing theories are of some value in learning intuition since they may assist the nurse manager in establishing priorities. They are of little value, however, in developing the intuitive qualities necessary to attend to information that appears unimportant but through intuition takes on significance.

## Intuition can be learned from a mentor

Intuition can be cultivated by close affiliation with a role model who demonstrates intuitive qualities. Careful observation of an expert nurse manager who actively relies on intuition can assist the nurse in developing a comprehensive assessment style that attends to small bits of information and that synthesizes appropriately. A mentoring relationship in which a less experienced manager is guided and directed by a more experienced manager can be an appropriate method of transmitting the skills necessary to effectively use intuition.

• • •

In spite of the present move in health care into the computer age, there is increasing awareness that intuition is an important nursing management technique and that it is linked to success as a manager. Intuition is most effectively implemented by the self-confident manager with experience and expertise as a manager. Nevertheless, a novice manager who values and seeks intuition will find it a technique that will assist in the development of excellence as a manager.

Managers who perceive themselves as having limited skills in intuition and yet are sensitive to the need for intuition can compensate for this deficiency by close association with a coworker who can provide intuitive perceptions and evaluations. For example, a head nurse who is primarily analytical may discuss assignment of nurses with an assistant who is highly intuitive. Managers who are able to compensate for intuitive deficiencies by surrounding themselves with competent and trusted subordinates who have intuitive qualities may be able to effectively use both analytic and nonanalytic managerial techniques.

REFERENCES

1. Cosier, R., and Alpin, J. "Intuition and Decision Making: Some Empirical Evidence." *Psychological Reports* 51, no. 8 (1982): 275–281.

2. Isaack, T.A. "Intuition: An Ignored Dimension of Management." *Advances of Management Review* 3 (1978): 917–922.

3. Benner, P., and Tanner, C. "How Expert Nurses Use Intuition." *American Journal of Nursing* 87, no. 1 (1987): 23–31.

4. Rew, L. "Intuition: Concept Analysis of a Group Phenomenon." *Advances in Nursing Science* 8, no. 2 (1986): 21–28.

5. Schraeder, R., and Fischer, D. "Using Intuitive Knowledge to Make Clinical Decisions." *Maternal Child Health* 11, no. 3 (1986): 161–162.

6. Agor, E. "Intuition: The New Management Tool." *Nursing Success Today* 1, no. 3 (1984): 23–24.

7. Dreyfus, H., and Dreyfus, S. *Mind Over Machine: The Power of Human Intuition and Expertise in the Era of the Computer.* New York, N.Y.: The Free Press, 1985.

8. Benner, P., and Tanner, C. "Skilled Clinical Knowledge: The Value of Perceptual Awareness." *Nurse Educator* 7, no. 3 (1982): 11–17.

9. Blomquist, K. "Evaluation of Students." *Nurse Educator* 10, no. 6 (1985): 8–11.

10. Price, J. and Cordell, B. "Patient Education Evaluation: Beyond Intuition." *Nursing Forum* 21, no. 3 (1984):117–122.

11. Rew, L. "Nursing Intuition." *Nursing 87* no. 7 (1987): 43–45.

12. Dean, D., Milhalasky, J., Ostrander, S., and Schroeder, L. *Executive ESP.* Englewood Cliffs, N.J.: Prentice Hall, 1974.

13. Josefowitz, N. "In Your Heart You Know You're Right; Intuition as a Job Skill. *Ms,* 13, no. 11 (1984): 12–17.

# Intimidation and the nurse manager

*Ruth Davidhizar*
*Director of Nursing*

*Margaret Bowen*
*Assistant Director of Nursing*
*Logansport State Hospital*
*Logansport, Indiana*

I NTIMIDATION, defined by Webster as the act of "compelling or deterring by or as if by threats," is considered by most to be a negative interpersonal behavior.[1(p.600)] A person who gains control or power over another by creating fear may, at first glance, appear to be browbeating the other with little consideration for feelings. Such a bulldozing style of relating may appear to be a primitive interpersonal technique that is unworthy of the professional manager; however, quite the opposite is true. Although discussion of intimidation as a managerial technique is ignored in management and nursing literature, scrutiny of the behavior of expert managers may prove intimidation to be a useful and powerfully positive management tool. A manager's use of intimidation can improve employee performance. When used with sensitivity and selectivity, intimidation will not destroy—and in fact, can increase—an employee's positive feelings about the manager. A manager who uses intimidation

*Health Care Superv*, 1990, 9(1), 27–32
©1990 Aspen Publishers, Inc.

skillfully may even be viewed as highly empathetic.

A successful manager must not only master the art of intimidation, but also learn to respond effectively to comments that are meant to be intimidating. Since intimidation is a subjective experience, a manager can choose not to be intimidated. This article addresses intimidation by discussing the intimidating approach, identifying situations in which the use of intimidation may be appropriate for the manager, describing the controversy that surrounds intimidation as a management technique, and outlining responses a manager may use when confronted with a comment meant to intimidate.

## THE INTIMIDATING APPROACH

Of all the components of the management process—planning, organizing, coordinating, staffing, directing, and controlling—aspects of controlling have received the least attention in the nursing literature. This may be due in part to the nurse's belief that control should be an internal process rather than an external process instituted and maintained by nurse managers.[2] However, while accountability for behavior rests on all members of the nursing department, responsibility for maintaining standards of performance rests in the hands of managers.[3] If nurse managers are to be effective, supervisory skills for controlling the performance of others must be acquired. Levenstein says "at the heart of management lies the concept of control."[4(p.25)] Intimidation is one of a variety of controlling techniques that managers have at their disposal.

Intimidation is difficult to define because it is an abstraction that does not lend itself to quantitative measurement. It exists in the person who perceives that intimidation has occurred, and it is a subjective experience. Intimidation is additionally complex since what may successfully intimidate one individual may not be considered intimidating by another. Generally, however, intimidation occurs when words, nonverbal actions, or certain other phenomena are perceived as threatening and compel or deter certain actions.

The most common type of intimidation is verbal. For example, saying, "Knock it off, you got caught" to an employee who is trying to deny errors can help the employee realize that denial is useless. Intimidation may also be nonverbal; for example, direct and intense eye contact with a tight, unresponsive expression or a harsh tone of voice. Finally certain other phenomena may be found intimidating. For example, when a nurse is told by a physician, "I'm the doctor and I expect you to give this medication at once," the nurse may feel compelled to action by the physician's title and position, even though the dosage exceeds recommended guidelines.

An approach is more likely to be perceived as intimidating when one or more of the following occurs:

- A negative evaluation is rendered, such as "We are not going to have that behavior in this department."
- A high degree of self-confidence is communicated, such as when an assertive and confident tone of voice is used.
- A limit-setting statement is delivered quickly, with no explanation or opportunity for debate, such as when a manager says, "I am not going to see you now," and turns his back on the employee, cutting off discussion.
- The recipient's anxiety level is raised, such as when a call is received from your manager, who says in an abrupt tone of voice, "I want to meet with you in 10 minutes in my office."

- A threat is present, such as when a coworker says, "I'll report you to administration if you don't do what I'm asking."

While the presence of certain characteristics can create the impression that an action or comment is intimidating, intimidation is subjective and is not present unless it is felt. This may result in a manager being perceived as intimidating when there was no intent to intimidate. A manager may be perceived as intimidating simply because of supervisory status. In other cases, a comment meant as neutral may be taken as highly critical and therefore intimidating. For example, a manager's statement, "That training session really was a fiasco," although not directed at the employee, may be taken as personal criticism if the employee feels some responsibility for the session.

The manager who confronts employees with behavior for which they do not accept responsibility must be prepared for personal attack. The employee may try to blame the manager, make the manager feel guilty, or make the manager feel incompetent. However, one of the characteristics of the intimidating approach and also a major advantage of this technique is that it requires quick managerial action and allows little opportunity for response or discussion about the behavior that is being criticized. While the employee who is criticized may have negative feelings about the manager, the manager is not put in a position of necessarily having to deal with the behavior.

## WHEN INTIMIDATION IS APPROPRIATE

Since intimidation may be considered an aggressive approach, it is used by many managers after other less confrontational approaches—such as ensuring the employee understands what is required and how to comply, confronting the employee with performance deficits and discussing these deficits in a concerned and problem-solving manner, and allowing time for improvement and reevaluation after deficits have been confronted—have failed to correct behavior. However, intimidation need not be limited to a last-resort approach. The technique of intimidation may be indicated any time the manager's standards of behavior have not been followed and the manager desires a positive change.

The use of intimidation can set boundaries or limits on others by interrupting manipulative and intrusive behavior. By forthrightly making others aware of the manager's ideas or ways of thinking, intimidation can assist employees toward success on the job. Intimidation can be useful with persons who need direction. Finally, a manager's use of intimidation with employees can encourage acceptable behavior by clarifying expectations. The most common factor underlying unsatisfactory performance is the employee's belief that he or she is performing satisfactorily.[5] In other words, the employee does not know there is a problem. Direct disclosure of unsatisfactory behavior, as may be accomplished when the manager uses an intimidating comment, quickly ameliorates this problem.

Regardless of when intimidation is used, it is essential that it be applied with sensitivity. While sensitivity may not be an obvious aspect of this managerial style, this approach as much as any other demands that managers focus on employees' human needs.[6] Communication of respect is crucial to the manager's approach if positive interpersonal relations with employees are to be developed. The limit setting involved in a confrontational, intimidating approach cannot disregard consideration for the employee as a person.

Finally, to maintain the effectiveness of this managerial approach, it is important that intimidation not be overused. When used too frequently, intimidation tends to lose its effectiveness as a positive technique and thus promote a focus on the negative. Intimidation may cause a positive relationship to deteriorate or may inhibit the development of positive employee–manager relationships, since the manager may be seen as moralistic and condemning. The manager who uses intimidation expertly is selective and limits its use in order to allow for maximum effect.

## INTIMIDATION AS A CONTROVERSIAL MANAGERIAL TECHNIQUE

There is considerable controversy over the use of intimidation as a managerial technique. Intimidation may be seen as a dehumanizing approach that oversteps the boundaries of professional and courteous management. As an autocratic approach, it does not encourage employees to be self-directed, and they are thus less likely to follow through. Such an approach may be seen as unduly hurting an employee's feelings and therefore to be avoided. Part of the bias against an intimidating approach stems from the objection of some managers to using criticism, which is seen as painful and disruptive to the employee's psychological equilibrium. While criticism is viewed by most managers as a necessary management technique, many see the negative evaluation inherent in intimidation and the critic role as

unpleasant and would avoid most negative approaches to employees if given the choice.[7]

However, the process of improving employee performance does not have to be considered negative or painful. Criticism can improve performance; it can increase self-esteem and maintain and improve employee morale.

The use of an intimidating approach can be an effective way to set limits on another's

*Criticism can improve performance; it can increase self-esteem and maintain and improve employee morale.*

behavior quickly, and consequently may result in improved performance. In some cases, an empathetic and problem-solving approach provides the employee with less clarity about the manager's expectations. The directive manner used in intimidation may prove a quicker way to change actions.

While intimidation may be effectively used with supervisors or colleagues, it is a technique more likely to be found useful with those who are supervised and whose actions must be evaluated and guided by the manager. A concise statement of the limit can provide clear information about the manager's standards and can expedite the administrative process by leaving no doubt as to the manager's expectations. Some employees have a genuine desire to do what is acceptable, but at times lack knowledge of the required behavior. For example, an employee may intrude on a private meeting not realizing it is private or may carry out a procedure incorrectly due to lack of understanding of the rationale behind the procedure. In other cases, employees may need assistance in setting limits on their own behavior, such as when an employee is talking to a companion during a meeting rather than listening attentively to the speaker.

As an assertive approach, intimidation is a legitimate technique that may be learned. However, if such an assertive technique causes personal frustration for a manager who ordinarily uses more passive techniques, it may not be appropriate.[8]

## RESPONDING TO COMMENTS INTENDED TO BE INTIMIDATING

From time to time all managers will be the target of attempts at intimidation. When confronted with a negative critical evaluation, it is important to react deliberatively and to assess the truth of the comments that are being made. A manager who can choose a neutral emotion rather than reacting with anxiety and anger will not be intimidated. A manager who is aware that intimidation is not a reality, but simply a subjective experience that can be brought under personal control, can choose not to be intimidated.

A feeling of intimidation results from personal vulnerability and perceived threat to self-worth. For example, an employee may attempt to intimidate a manager by threatening to go to the union about a disciplinary action. If the manager fears the disciplinary action will not hold up under scrutiny a feeling of vulnerability may precipitate feelings of intimidation. On the other hand, if the manager is confident of the action taken, then he or she will be able to say, "You are welcome to do that" without sounding angry or anxious. Managers' personal feelings of security and self-confidence concerning

their actions influence their levels of vulnerability to intimidation. A manager who is easily threatened and vulnerable in the managerial role should investigate ways to improve self-confidence and personal feelings of power. A manager may gain feelings of self-confidence through constructive self-analysis and seeking feedback from colleagues and supervisors. Vulnerability may also result from unrealistic and grandiose self-expectations. A manager who expects never to fail may easily feel threatened when that expectation is not realized. A person already threatened by unmet self-expectations will be easily intimidated. Since personal vulnerability fluctuates with time and in relation to both internal and external factors, vulnerability to intimidation also fluctuates.

A manager may find that humor is useful in neutralizing feelings of threat. For example, if a colleague describes a comical behavior of a person whom the manager finds threatening, the threat may be reduced. It is also helpful to consider the human aspects of persons who might be considered threatening: "He puts his legs in his pants just like everyone else." Talking with colleagues about the behavior of persons who try to intimidate others can enable a manager to gain perspective on that behavior.

•  •  •

In the role of professional, a nurse manager constantly communicates with colleagues, superiors, and subordinates. Effective communication can improve the quality of patient care and work relationships and will ultimately lead to greater job satisfaction.[9] Effective communication skills are essential for the nurse manager. In fact, communication is frequently cited as the most important management skill.[10]

When judiciously applied, intimidation can improve employee performance and facilitate employee success on the job. This article has discussed the intimidation approach and provided suggestions for its appropriate use. Additionally, the controversy surrounding the use of intimidation as a management technique has been discussed. Finally, responses have been suggested for the manager who is the focus of behavior intended to intimidate.

## REFERENCES

1. *Webster's New Collegiate Dictionary,* 1st ed., s.v. "intimidate."
2. Johnson, J., and Luciano, K. "Managing by Behavior and Results—Linking Supervisory Accountability to Effective Organizational Control." In Blancett, S. *Classics from JONA.* Philadelphia, Pa.: Lippincott, 1988.
3. Sherwin, D. "The Meaning of Control." In *Management: A Book of Readings,* edited by H. Koontz and D. Sherwin. New York, N.Y.: McGraw-Hill, 1964.
4. Levenstein, A. "The Art and Science of Supervision." *Supervisor Nurse,* 9, no. 7 (1978): 25–28.
5. Young, L., and Hayne, A. *Nursing Administration: From Concepts to Practice.* Philadelphia, Pa.: W.B. Saunders, 1988.
6. Peters, J., and Waterman, R. *In Search of Excellence.* New York, N.Y.: Warner Books, 1984.
7. Davidhizar, R., and Bowen, M. "The Art of Giving Criticism." *RN* 11 (November 1988): 14–15.
8. Eliopoulos, C., *Nursing Administration of Long-Term Care.* Rockville, Md.: Aspen Publishers, 1983.
9. Warfel, W. "Communication in Complex Organizations." In *Management Concepts for the Nurse,* edited by K. Vestal. Philadelphia, Pa.: Lippincott, 1987.
10. Sheridan, D., Bronstein, J., and Walker, D. *The New Nurse Manager.* Rockville, Md.: Aspen Publishers, 1984.

# Humor: A research and practice tool for nurse scholar–supervisors, practitioners, and educators

*Helen Yura-Petro, Ph.D., FAAN*
*Eminent Professor Emeritus*
*School of Nursing*
*Old Dominion University*
*Norfolk, Virginia*

PROVERBS 17:22 says, "A cheerful heart is a good medicine but a downcast spirit dries up the bones." The human need for humor is part of the theoretic framework titled Nursing's Human Need Theory but has been virtually untouched by nurse supervisors administering nursing services and by nurse scholars engaged in research.[1] Collegial collaboration using humor effectively in nursing practice could benefit not only the nurse supervisor, but the nursing staff, clients, nursing students, nurse educators, and members of the interdisciplinary health care team.

The human need for humor encompasses the perception, the frame of mind to enjoy and express a sense of the clever, the funny, the comical. Associated descriptive phrases for

This article is adapted from a paper presented at the Second Annual Helen Yura Research Symposium, April 6, 1989— A symposium jointly sponsored by Epsilon Chi Chapter, Sigma Theta Tau, International Honor Society of Nursing and the School of Nursing, Old Dominion University, Norfolk, Virginia.

*Health Care Superv,* 1991, 9(4), 1–8

humor include amusement, lightheartedness, wit, recognition of the incongruencies and peculiarities in a situation, looking on the "bright side," laughter, comedy, and mood elevation.[1] The nurse supervisor and nurse scholar can begin research effort by validating this definition within the theoretic framework and then proceeding with descriptive research into the physiological, psychological, emotional, cultural, growth and developmental, and gender elements evident when this need is satisfied or met. The literature reflects an initial collection of ideas describing humor, including the positive and negative impacts of its use.

## CAUSES AND EFFECTS OF HUMOR

Peter and Dana describe laughter as:
1. producing beneficial physiological results;
2. exercising the lungs and stimulating the circulatory system;
3. causing full action of the diaphragm, the main muscle of respiration, situated between the chest and abdomen;
4. benefiting the entire cardiovascular system from robust laughter because the deep respiration that accompanies it increases the oxygen in the blood.

These activities are of particular benefit to persons who have been inactive due to long-term or seriously debilitating illnesses.[2]

Norman Cousins calls laughter a form of internal jogging.

In responding to the initial phase of a typical joke, comedy routine or story, muscle tension increases in anticipation of the climax of the story or punchline. Immediately following the story climax, the thorax (chest), abdomen and face get a vigorous workout. In convulsive laughter, where the individual really breaks up, even the legs and arms are involved. During this phase, heart rate, breathing and circulation are speeded

up. When the spasm of laughter subsides, the pulse rate drops below normal and the skeletal muscles become deeply relaxed. During the laughter response, the body is revitalized by what sometimes is called internal massage.[2(p.7)]

Sir Francis Bacon gives a succinct and lively description:

"…laughter causeth a dilation of the mouth and lips; a continued expulsion of the breath with a loud noise, which maketh the interjection of laughing, shaking of the breasts and sides; running of the eyes with water, if it be violent and continued."[3(p.2)]

Laughter creates a decrease in tone of skeletal muscles of the body, making it difficult to grasp an object while laughing vigorously. Humor theorists believe that laughter involves a release of tension or surplus energy.[3]

Laughter may occur from causes other than humorous material—being tickled, for example. This is a reflexive response apparently free of a cognitive element. Hearty laughter can be followed by episodes of hiccoughing or coughing. Research has pointed out that infants more often respond with laughter to tickling by a familiar and loving person (mother or father) than by an unknown person—then the response is usually crying.[3]

Psychologically, humor and laughter generate regressive human behavior in that one reverts to an earlier level of mental and emotional functioning. This also explains why, when staying up past customary bedtime or overtired, we become exceedingly giggly. Remarks that wouldn't seem amusing at 3:00 P.M. may be viewed as hilarious at 1:00 A.M. Moody believes that a partial regression of early development levels accompanies the gradual onset on sleep. "Perhaps, as in yawning, the body is making an attempt by allowing more laughter to bring in more oxygen."[3(p.9)]

Socially, laughter is contagious. If one or two people start giggling, soon the entire group will do the same. Recall your experiences in elementary school. "It is interesting to ponder why some other apparently automatic responses of the diaphragm or respiratory apparatus share this contagious quality of laughter while others as hiccoughing do not."[3(p.13)] Coughing and yawning are contagious. Laughter is mobilized by ridicule or satire and has cultural implications. In Japan the primary mode of disciplining children is to warn them that, if they behave in certain ways, other people will laugh at them.[3] Humor and laughter enhance interpersonal communication and serve as social lubricants. Peters and Dana tell us that humor contributes to the buoyant spirit that energizes our total being.[2]

---

*Socially, laughter is contagious. If one or two people start giggling, soon the entire group will do the same.*

---

There are many positive aspects of humor:
- It acts as a pain reliever, releasing endorphins and breaking the vicious circle of pain and tension.
- It contributes to health and enhances the body's immune system and reparative ability.
- It positively affects the muscular, cardiovascular, and pulmonary systems through the act of laughing.
- It helps us out of the embarrassing social situations in which we find ourselves at times.
- It makes terrible events bearable and helps give dignity and grace to those who suffer them; life's difficult or painful situations are often eased by humor.
- It is used to poke fun at things over which we are powerless.

- It can be a major factor in overcoming depression.
- It is an aid to the expression of emotions such as love and hope
- It is an aid to transmitting important messages of a spiritual, political, commercial, and educational nature.
- It is linked to longevity—almost all very healthy elderly persons have a good sense of humor.[3-5]

Negative dimensions of humor—which reflect the nursing diagnoses of a lack of humor, disturbance of humor, or excessive inappropriate humor—are seen in diseased states of the brain and nervous system, such as Alzheimer's disease and mental illness. Moody tells us that deviations in laughter and the sense of humor play a profound role in mental illness, and that the understanding of humor and laughter plays a correspondingly significant role in understanding clients with mental illness.[3]

A mode of laughter-making that has been perverted to detrimental social ends is ridicule. In some instances, ridicule has been utilized in forms that may be harmless, as the "roasts" of a person where friends insult and poke fun at the appointed person. The victim's voluntary complicity is secured, and tolerance earns one the label of a good sport. Professional comedians may be granted license to belittle others in a funny way with social convention being established that no offense be taken. But ridicule can sometimes be taken to extremes with unfortunate circumstances. Humor can be cruel and sadistic, such as derisive laughter at those with deformities or physical and mental defects.[3] Some forms of humor in our time may be deplorable, vulgar, psychologically unhealthy, and socially destructive: Vulgarity, obscenity, and general disrespect are generally not considered funny.[5]

## TOPICS FOR HUMOR RESEARCH

With this brief description of the human need for humor and a selection of some of its deviations or alterations, the author will suggest areas of research for the nurse educator, practitioners of nursing, and the nurse supervisor.

### Improved learning ability

Humor can be used to teach dry and difficult subjects. It is speculated that students relax and are better able to absorb material when the teacher takes a humorous approach to teaching. Thus, researchable questions for the nurse scholar educator may be:

- Do students (nursing students, staff, clients, health care team members) have a higher level of comprehension when humor is incorporated in teaching strategies by the nurse educator? Settings for this study may be an academic institution in which students pursue formal preparation for professional nursing practice, or a health care agency involving staff development, inservice education, and client teaching.
- What teaching strategies are most likely to be effective in increasing the learning ability of nursing students, practitioners of nursing, and clients of nursing? This study could involve assessing the variables of gender, growth and development, age, culture, and socioeconomic background and their influence on the use and success of humor by nurse educators and cadre of students taught.

### Creativity

Nurse educators can strive to create an environment conducive to creativity, laughter,

and individuality rather than one of discipline, regimentation, and control.

- Is the student more likely to respond toward more effective and positive behavioral change when humor is an adjunct of evaluation, academic advising, and counseling? I have collected interesting and unusual statements I found as answers by students to examination questions. For example, in response to an essay question about how to facilitate the admission of client to a hospital, one student wrote, "Be congenital—talk to the patient." In response to a question about how to teach a client to give himself insulin, one student wrote, "Tell the patient to rotate his legs." Using these statements anonymously can effectively fill in gaps or clarify content and its expression in the examinations.
- Do students who study and learn in an environment in which humor and wit are valued and utilized derive higher satisfaction from the learning experience? This study could investigate whether these students rate the teacher, the program, the health care clinical settings, and the academic institution higher than those in an environment in which humor and wit are viewed as nonprofessional.
- Do nurse educators and students who nurture and draw on their sense of humor experience higher levels of problem-solving ability, more effective social interactions, and less depression that those who do not?
- Do those who create laughter in the nonacademic, nonbusiness components of their lives experience higher levels of success in teaching and learning?
- Is the ability to laugh and appreciate funny material a valuable and valued indicator

of the state of health of the teacher or student?

- How is humor integrated into the curriculum? Consider whether students are taught to obtain assessment data about the human need for humor; what nursing strategies are designed for what kind of client outcomes; what priority level is assigned to the human need for humor in contrast to other human needs in developing nursing care plans, in collaboration with clients, and reviewed by nurse educators.
- What humor strategies do students use to promote peer relationships?
- What humor strategies do nurse-scholars as nurse educators use to promote peer relationships?

### Perspective

In classroom, laboratory, and clinical settings and meetings, how do nurse educators and nursing students distinguish between laughing "with" and laughing "at" someone? Moody tells us that when we laugh *at* someone we exclude them from the network of love, understanding, and support while in laughing *with* them we enfold the person in the network.[3]

---

*Humor and wit are useful in helping to achieve a broader perspective on life for the client and the nurse.*

---

For the nurse-scholar practitioners of nursing, enormous possibilities exist to research the human need for humor. Research opportunities abound in the client setting. Research questions pertain to every element of the nursing process and almost every human condition encountered in the practice setting. Different practice settings contribute additional variables

to the research efforts. Humor and wit and nursing strategies can diminish recognition of pain, enhance tolerance of discomfort, and diminish sensitivity. Most readers are familiar with the story of Norman Cousins, who cured himself of a fatal disease using large doses of humor with the blessing of his physician. A firsthand account of his experience is found in the book *Anatomy of an Illness*.

Humor and wit are useful in helping to achieve a broader perspective on life for the client and the nurse. Researchable questions are:

- What client assessment data do nurses use to verify that the human need for humor has been met? How do the variables of age, gender, health state, and level of growth and development affect the assessment database?
- What nursing strategies do nurses prescribe to bring about a humor experience for the client? How do these prescriptions accommodate the variables of age and gender? What are the similarities or differences?
- Does the ability of the nurse to assess the level of fulfillment of the client's need for humor require that the nurse's need for humor be satisfied?
- What are the characteristics of the nurses most likely to use humor effectively with clients, colleagues, and co-workers? Are these nurses more likely to use humor to improve staff relationships, resolve client complaints, and improve their own work life?

Patty Wooten, who runs humor seminars for colleagues in Davis, California, tells about a nurse working in a hospital unit at the end of a hectic day. At the worst possible time, a troublesome client buzzed for the umpteenth time. "What's wrong?" the nurse asked as she tried to be cheerful approaching his bedside. "It's my dinner," snarled the client. "This is a *bad* potato." The nurse picked up the potato in one hand and spanked it soundly with the other. "Bad potato!" she reprimanded. "Bad! Bad! Bad!" The client burst into laughter; so did the nurse.[6] The client's perception of his experience improved thereafter.

### Stress release

The nurse practitioner deals with profound emotional and physical stress on a daily basis.

- When do humor and comedy provide relief? What kinds of humor, wit, and comedy are most effective? Laughing at something frightening is believed to give a luxurious moment of distance. Is this true?
- How can the practitioner of nursing affect the practice environment to maximize the use and benefit of humor for the client, the client's family, and the nurse? A "laugh break" would be more beneficial in the work day than a coffee break. The nurse may have access to humorous material for self-use or with and for clients. A woman who had suffered a stroke and was reconnected with her humor said, "It is so good to laugh again. I haven't laughed for a long time."[7]
- What humor strategies are effective in helping the client and the nurse cope with embarrassing, debilitating, and painful occurrences? It has been theorized that the use of selectively placed wit and comedy can improve the client's ability to be anesthetized and diminish the amount of analgesia required during and after surgery.
- Do practitioners of nursing who incorporate humor as a significant dimension in their practice receive improved perfor-

mance evaluations and achieve a higher level of client outcomes than those who do not?
- Do practitioners of nursing who create laughter in the nonworking components of their lives experience higher levels of success in the practice of nursing?

### Supervisory applications

The nurse scholar supervisor is in a strategic position to focus attention on the human need for humor of self, clients, the nursing staff, and members of the health care team. Again, the research possibilities for the nurse supervisor are enormous. Settings for research include acute and chronic care facilities, long term care settings, ambulatory and home care services. For example:

- What is the impact on staff morale and productivity when the nurse supervisor incorporates humor in administrative problem solving?
- If the nurse supervisor designs a "laughmobile" or "humor resource room" on the nursing unit, what benefits accrue to the clients and their families, the nursing staff, health team members, and the nurse supervisor?
- How effective are the nurse supervisor's wit and humor in reducing tension, fear, and anxiety in the work setting?
- Is there a difference in outcomes for clients and nursing staff when a unit is administered by a nurse supervisor who incorporates humor in interactions in contrast to one who does not?
- Is the nurse supervisor who facilitates the staff's and client's need for humor more likely to be evaluated as effective than one who does not?
- What is the impact of the use of humor by the nurse supervisor in acquiring the

needed human and material resources to achieve the purpose of the nursing unit?

- Do nursing staff have a lower incidence of burnout on units in which the nurse supervisor attends to the human need for humor of self, clients, and staff?
- Is the nurse supervisor who influences the health care complex to attend to humor and invest in humor resources rated as more effective than unit administrators generally?

Negotiating space for opportunity to view humorous videotapes (e.g., "Candid Camera," Phyllis Diller, Erma Bombeck, the Marx Brothers, and Bill Cosby) and generating resources to replenish funny material shows consideration by the nurse supervisor for the human condition. I know of no health care facility designed and built to accommodate a place and time to nurture the human need for humor. Modern facilities have refashioned a space for humor therapy. The nurse supervisor's membership on a construction or a building committee can be used to influence architects to include "humor space" in the design of health care facilities. This experience may serve to raise the humor-value consciousness of architects in their future design efforts.

Clowning as a communication form has extended beyond the circus and into academic and health care facilities. Nurse-scholars—as supervisors, practitioners, and educators—have downed baggy costumes, orange hair, and floppy shoes to send a message. This message may be one of hope, perseverance, behavioral change. Clowning can bring moments of healthy diversion, laughter, and well-being to those who are tired, stressed, noncommunicative, lonely, in pain, fearful, or feeling abandoned or overwhelmed with responsibility. For the clown, the benefits include giving of self, optimism, affecting the human condition in a positive way, helping to break the pain-fear-tension cycle, smoothing the rough spots on life's journey. The young and the old are particularly vulnerable to the antics of the clown. It is believed that the more difficult the times, the more necessary is the need for humor and laughter. Research should be generated to validate clowning as an art form benefiting the human experience.

Even in the darkest moments, a person's sense of hope may be rekindled. Steve Allen tells of the classic cartoon by Shel Silverstein that amused him so much that he made the sketch a national favorite on his weekly television talk show:

- The scene is a medieval prison chamber—a deep shaft.
- Against one wall, two unfortunates are spread-eagled several feet in the air, their wrists, ankles, necks, and waists secured by heavy metal clips.
- Escape is hopelessly beyond their reach at the top of the shaft, which is covered by heavy iron bars.
- The two look emaciated, as if pinned to the wall for a long time.
- One unfortunate turns to the other and whispers, "Now here's my plan."[5(p.2)]

Allen suggests that the reason this cartoon has become a classic has to do with the mystery of life itself. Humor in all its aspects is of enormous importance.

---

*Even in the darkest moments, a person's sense of hope may be rekindled.*

---

Personal benefits for the nurse scholar, whether in the supervisory, practice, or educator role, include the experience of exquisite pleasure, and reinforcement that no human is perfect. Humor fortifies the ability to smile, laugh and perceive the inherently humorous dimensions in human experience.

What physiological data support the influences of humor on the body? Reading the works of Robert Benchley, S.J. Perelman, James Thurber, and Woody Allen and viewing classic film comedies (many available in videotapes) can create funny moments and reinforce the idea that humor should be taken seriously by nurse scholars, particularly the nurse supervisor. Laughter can be especially useful in the human communication process; as an aid to expressing emotions such as love, tenderness, and forgiveness; and as an aid to the transmission of important spiritual, political, educational, and commercial messages. "It is a crucial component of psychological well-being, indeed of sanity itself."[5(p.2)]

The nurse scholar is aware of destructive communications labeled humor/comedy. Some are vulgar, deplorable, psychologically harmful, and socially destructive. Those forms dominated by vulgarity, obscenity, and general disrespect have limited value in healing the human condition. The nurse scholar as supervisor, practitioner, or educator should be alert to the negative impact of these forms, including the impact of ridicule and sarcasm, which deter the pursuit of well-

being and create interpersonal and intrapersonal turmoil. Research data should be accumulated to verify the negative impact of these forms of humor.

Alison Crane, founder and executive director of the American Association for Therapeutic Humor (9040 Forestview Road, Skokie, IL 60203-1913) suggests the concept of "unit-dose comedy." "A portable unit-dose dossier for the nurse scholar incorporates 'Herman' and 'The Far Side'—books which can be opened to any page to enjoy a cartoon and feel cheered."[7(p.42)] What humor forms have the most profound positive effect for the nurse supervisor, practitioners of nursing, nurse educators, clients of nursing, colleagues, and students? Inherent in this question is a font of researchable ideas.

• • •

The nurse scholar, whether a supervisor, an educator, or a practitioner, has a lifetime of research opportunities as well as personal experiences related to the human need for humor. We need to develop the means to assess the individual's and group's response to humor. Nurse scholars, particularly the nurse supervisor, can make a significant contribution in the search to harness some of the energy we use in laughing and direct it toward helping us heal our human conditions.[3]

## REFERENCES

1. Yura, H., and Walsh, M.B. *The Nursing Process.* 5th ed. East Norwalk, Conn.: Appleton & Lange, 1988.
2. Peter L. and Dana, B. *The Laughter Prescription.* New York, N.Y.: Ballantine Books, 1982.
3. Moody, R. *Laugh after Laugh.* Jacksonville, Fla.: Headwaters Press, 1978.
4. Harayda, J. "What Makes Us Laugh?" *Glamour* 76 (December 1978): 190–91, 262–66.
5. Allen, Steve. "Humor Me." *Creative Living* 17, no. 4 (1988): 2–5.
6. Hock, N., and Hock, D. "Take Time to Laugh." *Reader's Digest* 132, no. 790 (February 1988): 59–64.
7. Perlmutter, C. "Comic Relief." *Prevention* 40, no. 3 (1988): 39–42, 106–108.

# An approach to nurse managerial reporting: An essential task

*Frankie C. Nail*
*Consultant*
*Private Practice*
*Picayune, Mississippi*

*Enrica K. Singleton*
*Professor and Coordinator*
*Nursing Service Administration—*
 *Graduate Program*
*Louisiana State University Medical*
 *Center School of Nursing*
*New Orleans, Louisiana*

NURSES HAVE long recognized the importance of documentation as it relates to their clinical practice. Documentation of patient care is a part of the basic nursing curricula and good clinical nurses master this skill. Often, nurses' clinical expertise is recognized and rewarded by promotion to managerial positions. Without the advantage of either role models who highly value the managerial aspects of nursing or educational preparation for management, these nurses often fail to recognize the importance of transferring their documentation skills to the reporting of significant events related to managerial tasks and responsibilities.

## FUNCTION OF REPORTS

Certainly, reports in a health care organization are a routine means of communication. They may be simple or complex and

*Health Care Superv*, 1990, 8(2), 12–17
© 1990 Aspen Publishers, Inc.

may cover daily, weekly, monthly, quarterly, or annual periods. They include data on finances, number of employees, and materials; information on accidents, transfers, and leaves of absence; interviews of applicants for positions; results of performance appraisals; and quality assurance reports. Reports specific to nursing include admission data on patients; charges for services and supplies; medication, treatment, and dietary requirements; staffing; scheduling; patient classification by acuity; and patient census. Also, there are reports by supervisors, middle managers, and head nurses; change-of-shift reports; and other reports as necessary.

## ADVANTAGES OF MANAGERIAL REPORTS

One important report is a monthly summary of managerial activities. This reporting activity is recommended for middle managers and upper-level managers. A monthly managerial summary provides a historical database for reference purposes, a format for objectively examining time spent on various projects and results achieved, and a record of issues and problems that either recur in a cyclic pattern or that are resolved after one occurrence. The monthly summary also provides a quick reference from which the nurse manager can prepare a quarterly or annual summary of unit or departmental activities.

Additionally, a monthly summary provides a communication tool by which the nurse manager can let the supervisor know what he or she has achieved. Many nurse managers, novices in particular, seem to believe that everyone knows what nurse managers do and that appropriate credit will be given. This is not always the case. However, a good monthly summary allows the nurse manager to assess his or her contribution toward the accomplishment of the overall goals of the organization. A review of 6 to 12 consecutive monthly summaries will allow the nurse manager to discern whether his or her goals are synchronous with those of the supervisor and the organization as a whole. These reports can also be useful to the manager in preparing for annual self-evaluations and performance evaluation conferences with the supervisor. Given the current popularity of the matrix-type organization, it is doubly important for the nurse manager to be sensitive to the need to document achievements. As temporary project teams with specific objectives develop and disband, functional managers may have to share authority, control, and credit for the accomplishment of certain tasks. Without systematic documentation of achievements, the nurse manager may lose sight of his or her contributions. Furthermore, with the current climate of economic constraints within organizations, supervisors are responsible for larger areas. This often reduces the amount of time available to "chat with the boss." In this situation, communicating in writing becomes essential.

Reporting accomplishments is certainly not an unusual expectation in the business world. According to Drucker, a manager must know and understand the ultimate business goals and how he or she is expected to contribute to these.[1] He states that some of the most effective managers write a "manager's letter" twice a year. In it, the manager relates a personal view of the superior's job, of the manager's own job, and of the performance standards that appear to be applied to the manager. The letter includes the things the manager must do to attain these goals and outlines the major obstacles encountered in the unit, things the superior and the company can do to help, and an outline of what the manager proposes to do during the next year to reach his or her goals. If the manager's superior accepts this letter, it "becomes the charter under which the manager operates."[1(p.439)] The letter identifies inconsistencies in the demands made of the manager, areas where compromises should be made, objectives that should be thought through, considerations for establishing priorities, and behaviors that should be changed. Drucker further states that mutual understanding results only from upward communications and requires "a tool especially designed to make lower managers heard."[1(p.439)] The present authors are not at this time suggesting anything as extensive as the tool proposed by Drucker, but they do advocate an approach that sends a definitive message to the next level of management.

> *Though managers may think that nursing is difficult to quantify, they must also realize the imperative of having persons outside the discipline of nursing recognize managerial achievements.*

## GUIDELINES FOR MANAGERIAL REPORTING

The following guidelines are important in managerial reporting:

*1. Managerial reporting should focus on achievements (outcomes) rather than on activities (processes).* The monthly managerial summary, therefore, should never be used as a log for recording the manager's use of time in various activities (e.g., brainstorming about new ideas, policies, or program changes). After all, the organization is not necessarily interested in knowing the logistics of accomplishing a task (e.g., necessary steps, level of difficulty, time requirement). Rather, its primary interest is in whether goals are being achieved. The nurse manager may include issues encountered that are related to the goals of the organization, to the need for (or implementation of) major policy changes, and to new programs or methods initiated at the unit or departmental level that will contribute to the accomplishment of organizational goals.

*2. Quantifiable data should be used whenever possible.* Most administrators are concerned about the bottom line and are therefore accustomed to dealing with numbers. Though managers may think that nursing is difficult to quantify, they must also realize the imperative of having persons outside the discipline of nursing recognize managerial achievements. Therefore, nurse managers must quantify whenever possible. For example, a manager's report may read as follows:

> The census is lower, but the patients who are admitted are sicker and must be prepared for discharge in shorter periods. Therefore, we need the same amount of staff that we normally retain with a higher census.

Instead, this information would be more objective and readily understood if the report were to read,

> Given the patient acuity system accepted and implemented by this organization in 1985 and

reevaluated in 1987, this quarter's record shows patient days for patients at level IV increased by an average of 5% over the last quarter. Nursing hours per patient day remain at 5.21 (the accepted standard in this organization). Therefore, we should retain our existing complement of nurses.

*3. Reports should be concise.* Limit the report to one page, if possible. A two-page report should be necessary only when a month has been truly exceptional. Estimates from the authors' experience indicate that a one-page report is twice as likely to be read as a two-page report, and three times as likely to be read as a three-page report. If details are essential for clarification of segments of the report, the information should be included in an addendum.

*4. Managerial reports highlight accomplishments of the manager as achieved through his or her staff.* Positions rather than individuals should be the frame of reference, unless an individual commendation is in order. For example, it is acceptable to state, using names, that a particular nurse was instrumental in recruiting five of the last six nurses hired in the department, or that specific nurses received their B.S.N. degrees. However, a report should not be used to list names of persons who have experienced circumstances that could be conceived as negative. For example, a report might state that three clinical specialists resigned last month. It is unnecessary to say that all three nurses had been assigned to the unit of one particular nurse. However, the manager may schedule a conference with that unit head. Also, a report might state that one employee was referred to the employee counseling center for personal assistance, but that person's name should be withheld.

*5. Reports should include any follow-up information that was promised in a previous*

*report.* For example, suppose the nurse manager initiated a new medication administration record in response to physician complaints and indicated that a six-month evaluation would be conducted. Six months later, the results of that evaluation should be reported. It might be noted that an informal poll of physicians on the medical and surgical units was conducted, and only two indicated that the new medication administration record was not an improvement over the previous system. Furthermore, pharmacists and a sample of nurses from all-nursing units using the system were questioned, and 100% made favorable comments about the new record.

*6. The report should be submitted at about the same time each month, even in unusual circumstances.* For example, if a nurse supervisor elects to report on the tenth of each month for the previous month and plans to be on vacation on the tenth of next month, he or she should prepare the report early.

*7. Select and use a consistent report format.* This will facilitate review in a short period of time.

## ADDITIONAL CONSIDERATIONS

Rowland and Rowland have made several suggestions about writing reports, which include identifying the purpose of the report, the primary person to whom the report is being made, how the report is to be used, the significance of the content, and whether chronological reporting is desirable or necessary.[2] The present authors propose this tool as a means of upward communication to the hospital administrator or nurse executive who provides an overview of the state of nursing service, in whole or in part. It is an internal document that can be used to:

- establish a framework for improving nursing service,
- make a case for action or change within nursing service,
- reveal information that is important for better patient care or more efficient management,
- provide information on how nursing is contributing to the achievement of goals of the organization, and
- pinpoint selected specific actions or achievements of the nurse manager.

If a nurse manager is not asked by the supervisor for a monthly summary, it is acceptable to prepare the summary and title it "Memo for File" indicating that it is for the writer's reference or "For Your Information" until the supervisor becomes accustomed to receiving this report. The supervisor will probably come to expect the report and will become aware of the importance of having information about the nursing organization or a particular unit available for assistance in decision making and organizational assessment.

A sample managerial summary (see the Appendix) was prepared by an area director for the nurse executive. Numbers, dates, and names have been changed to ensure anonymity. At the time of the report, morale, productivity, turnover, quality assurance, student affiliations, and staff development were major nursing concerns.

Though a short managerial report is recommended, a specific amount of time must be allocated to its preparation. According to Drucker, most of the tasks of an executive "require a fair quantum of time."[3(p.29)] He suggests that writing a report may require six to eight hours for the first draft and that this cannot be accomplished in small units of time over several weeks. Rather, five or six hours of uninterrupted time are needed to complete the "zero draft—the one before the first draft." Then one can rewrite, correct, and edit in small installments of time. The Appendix certainly did not require five hours of preparation. However, nurse managers must assess their situations and determine the amounts and levels of activity in their areas of responsibility. Then they can estimate the time needed for report writing and schedule that time.

•  •  •

Managerial reporting is an essential task for managers. It can become a useful tool for upward communication. If each nurse manager keeps the nurse administrator well informed about his or her unit, communication to the hospital chief executive officer regarding the nursing department as a whole will be enhanced.

## REFERENCES

1. Drucker, P.F. *Management: Tasks, Responsibilities, Practices.* New York: Harper & Row, 1974.
2. Rowland, H.S., and Rowland, B.L. *Nursing Administra-* *tion Handbook.* Rockville, Md.: Aspen Publishers, 1985.
3. Drucker, P.F. *The Effective Executive.* New York: Harper & Row, 1967.

# Appendix

## Sample monthly managerial summary for a nursing unit: June 10, 1988

1. *Morale:* Nursing supervisors made a concerted effort to boost morale through activities designed to provide information on anticipated changes and elicit their input. Following six small unit meetings on the night shift, an ad hoc committee of part-time nurses from the in-house pool was established to recommend approaches to assigning staff. Recommendations are due in July 1988.
2. *Productivity:* After downsizing (through implementation of efficiency measures suggested by employees or management), budgeted hours per patient day were met, resulting in an 8% decrease in total combined wages, salaries, and benefits for the unit.
3. *Turnover:* Departmental turnover was less than 1% this month, as compared to 6.2% for the same month last year.
4. *Quality assurance (QA) checks:* All criteria were met except 7a (please refer to the area QA plan), indicating that nursing care plans need to be improved. A plan is being developed to assist staff to meet these standards. Also, medication variances increased by 2% this month as compared to last month and 1.1% as compared to the same month last year. No serious patient responses to these variances were observed. An investigation is underway. All staff are involved.
5. *Affiliations:* Students from West University will begin their clinical experience on this unit in August 1988.
6. *Staff development:* Revisions of the orientation program for permanent and temporary staff have been finalized, and the program has been implemented. (Details are in the addendum, "Minutes of Head Nurse–Supervisor Meeting," January 1988.)

# A proactive approach to computerizing nursing process: A management perspective

**Marcia Shannon**
*Clinical Nurse Specialist in*
  *Psychiatric–Mental Health Nursing*

**Nancy Dextrom**
*Associate Chief*
*Nursing Service for Education*

**Marcia Fuhrhop**
*Assistant Chief*
*Nursing Service*
*Saginaw Veterans'*
  *Administration Medical Center*
*Saginaw, Michigan*

**E**VER SINCE computers were introduced into the health care industry, nursing managers have speculated about the computer's potential to facilitate nursing care delivery. While it is clear that computers cannot substitute for quality nursing care nor magically provide an effective system of care delivery, they can definitely impact nursing service. Nursing administrators at a 150-bed midwestern hospital discovered that computers can be a valuable tool in enhancing the use of the nursing process, promoting independent nursing, building in quality control, improving communication, and providing significant time savings in planning and documenting nursing care.

*Mary Kellogg, M.S.N., Senior Specialist in Client Services, McDonnell Douglas, assisted with development of the computer questionnaire.*

*Health Care Superv*, 1989, 7(3), 71–81
© 1989 Aspen Publishers, Inc.

## BACKGROUND

In 1985, it became evident that the Integrated Hospital System (IHS) selected for this medical center would include a nursing module. Determined to influence the design of the basic system to meet the specific needs of the nursing department, nursing took a proactive approach. An ad hoc computer committee of nursing managers and staff nurses was formed to explore potential applications to nursing practice, design the actual module, and provide direction and support throughout the implementation process. The committee began by contacting area health care facilities that were using computers. Committee members found that although most hospitals had some degree of automation, computers were not being utilized for independent nursing functions.

A review of the literature indicated that most computer applications currently used by nursing focused on administration and management information or involved sophisticated patient monitoring systems.[1-4] Several authors referred to nursing practice applications coming on the market, including care planning, on-line documentation, calculation of patient acuity, and staff scheduling procedures.[5-7] Happ identified some advantages of computers in nursing practice, one being a potential increase in nursing productivity through a decrease in indirect activities such as care plan development, charting, and ordering supplies and medications.[8] Lombard and Light reported that use of a computerized care planning system had a positive impact on the efficiency and quality of the care planning process.[9] Many authors agreed that nursing practice would be affected by computer technology. The impact would depend to some degree on the nurses' understanding of computer technology, their visions and imagination, and their ability to influence the change.[10-12]

In 1983, nursing administration implemented a manual system of patient care management designed to improve nursing practice and documentation of patient care.[13] The system was based on a modified form of primary nursing and emphasized use of nursing diagnoses and nursing process. Nursing autonomy and accountability were built into the system and were consistently reinforced through a quality assurance monitor that measured adherence to nursing process and documentation standards. This project succeeded in its purpose. The ad hoc computer committee decided that major goals of automation would be to preserve or further improve the quality that had been achieved thus far and to decrease manual paperwork with the goal of providing time savings that could be diverted to direct patient care.

## NURSING MODULE DESIGN

The nursing module was developed to replace manual nursing care plans, traditional Kardex-type patient care data forms, and a manual patient classification system.

Initial efforts were devoted to the computerization of nursing care plans. Attempts were made to preserve the same format that Nursing Service had implemented several years earlier. The assessment tool was modified to organize assessment information into Marjorie Gordon's 11 functional categories.[14] After assessment, the admitting nurse utilizes data to generate a nursing care plan by going to the computer and selecting a nursing care plan function. A list

CN3C1R-X4                          PATIENT NURSING CARE PLAN

VA MEDICAL CENTER
SAGINAW                MI 48602
Patient: JOLL, CRIS

Location: 510  1  W5A    Sex: M    Age: 27  Y    Birthdate: 12/12/1960
SSN: 969-69-6969   Account #: 0-44099-0
Ht 5 Ft 10 In   Wt: 158 Lbs  0 Oz   Primary nurse: AMB   Associate nurse: BJC

| | |
|---|---|
| Admitted date:  10/01/87 | Attending Dr: RORA, LARRY |
| Chief complaint: Scheduled ABD surgery | Consulting Dr: |
| Drug allergies: NKA | Visually impaired? Glasses/not legally blind |
| Food allergies: NKA | Hearing impaired? |
| Other allergies: NKA | Care plan discussed with pt [   ] |

Diabetic? N          Telemetry? N               Isolation?
Primary diagnosis: Bowel obstruction
DRG: 0

| | | Start | Eval/Stp | Sts | Init |
|---|---|---|---|---|---|
| NSG DX: | ACTUAL INFECTION: WOUND/SKIN | 05/04/88 | / / | ACTIVE/IN PROG | JEV |
| ETIOLOGIES: | Surgical incision | 05/04/88 | / / | ACTIVE/IN PROG | |
| | AEB REDNESS AROUND INCISION, PURULENT DRAINAGE | 05/04/88 | / / | ACTIVE/IN PROG | |
| GOALS: | Have his infection resolved | 05/04/88 | 05/07/88 | ACTIVE/IN PROG | |
| | Have no cross-infection to other body sites/individuals | 05/04/88 | 05/07/88 | ACTIVE/IN PROG | |
| INTERVEN- | | | | | |
| TIONS: | Inspect for odor, purulence, erythema, inflammation, and pain | 05/04/88 | / / | ACTIVE/IN PROG | |
| | Enclose soiled dressings in bag to dispose | 05/04/88 | / / | ACTIVE/IN PROG | |
| | Strict aseptic dressing change | 05/04/88 | / / | ACTIVE/IN PROG | |
| | Promote healing by positioning off wound site/elevate | 05/04/88 | / / | ACTIVE/IN PROG | |
| | INSTRUCT PT. IN PROPER HAND WASHING, CARE OF WOUND | 05/04/88 | / / | ACTIVE/IN PROG | |
| | | | | | |
| NSG DX: | BODY IMAGE DISTURBANCE | 05/04/88 | / / | ACTIVE/IN PROG | JEV |
| ETIOLOGIES: | Nonintegration of changes in his body | 05/04/88 | / / | ACTIVE/IN PROG | |
| | AEB | 05/04/88 | / / | ACTIVE/IN PROG | |
| | STATED INABILITY TO ACCEPT AND CARE FOR COLOSTOMY | 05/04/88 | / / | ACTIVE/IN PROG | |
| GOALS: | Manage his own bodily care | 05/04/88 | 05/08/88 | ACTIVE/IN PROG | |
| INTERVEN- | | | | | |
| TIONS: | Help patient verbalize changes in his body | 05/04/88 | / / | ACTIVE/IN PROG | |
| | Encourage expression of neg. feelings: dirty, unsightly | 05/04/88 | / / | ACTIVE/IN PROG | |
| | Encourage patient to look at/touch body parts | 05/04/88 | / / | ACTIVE/IN PROG | |
| | Allow patient to verbalize fears of rejection by others | 05/04/88 | / / | ACTIVE/IN PROG | |
| | Assess changes in lifestyle because of bodily changes | 05/04/88 | / / | ACTIVE/IN PROG | |
| | Teach pt. to manage a change in function of body part | 05/04/88 | / / | ACTIVE/IN PROG | |
| | TEACH PT. TO CARE FOR COLOSTOMY | 05/04/88 | / / | ACTIVE/IN PROG | |
| | | | | | |
| NSG DX: | GRIEVING: DYSFUNCTIONAL | 05/04/88 | / / | ACTIVE/IN PROG | JEV |
| ETIOLOGIES: | Loss or perceived loss/change | 05/04/88 | / / | ACTIVE/IN PROG | |
| | AEB | 05/04/88 | / / | ACTIVE/IN PROG | |
| | DEATH OF WIFE 1 YEAR AGO; CRYING SPELLS; STATED | 05/04/88 | / / | ACTIVE/IN PROG | |
| | DEPRESSION | 05/04/88 | / / | ACTIVE/IN PROG | |
| GOALS: | State 3 positive coping behaviors | 05/04/88 | 05/07/88 | ACTIVE/IN PROG | |
| INTERVEN- | | | | | |
| TIONS: | Assess previous successful coping behaviors | 05/04/88 | / / | ACTIVE/IN PROG | |
| | Encourage verbalization of feelings | 05/04/88 | / / | ACTIVE/IN PROG | |
| | ID stage of grief: denial, anger, bargaining, dependency, acceptance | 05/04/88 | / / | ACTIVE/IN PROG | |
| | Discuss healthy ways of dealing with grief | 05/04/88 | / / | ACTIVE/IN PROG | |
| | Give info about normal feelings during grief | 05/04/88 | / / | ACTIVE/IN PROG | |

**Figure 1.** Patient nursing care plan. Reprinted with permission from Saginaw Veterans' Administration Medical Center, Saginaw, Michigan. 5/5/88.

of the 11 functional categories of nursing diagnoses appears. The nurse selects one of the functional categories and all of the nursing diagnoses under that specific category are displayed.

In the example (Figure 1), the registered nurse (RN) has selected the functional category, "Health Perception–Health Management Pattern," and under it the nursing diagnosis, "Actual Infection: Wound/Skin." Each nursing diagnosis consists of three components:

1. the problem, or nursing diagnosis stem;
2. the etiology; and
3. the signs and symptoms manifested.

The etiology "Surgical Incision" has been selected from a list of three possible etiologies. The signs and symptoms underneath these statements are described as "AEB (as evidenced by) redness around incision; purulent drainage." The RN can select from preentered information or elect to type in her or his own data. Further screens offer the RN preentered lists of goals and interventions that can be chosen by simply entering "Y" for "yes" in front of the selection. In all cases, the nurse can opt to create any part of the nursing care plan or use any of the prefilled data. After completing one nursing diagnosis, the nurse returns to the original list to review the remaining functional categories. The RN can then select other nursing diagnoses and elements until the care plan is complete.

After all nursing diagnoses, goals, and interventions are recorded, the nurse enters evaluation dates into the right-hand column across from the appropriate diagnosis. Evaluation dates may be short- or long-term (varying from a few hours to three weeks or longer) depending upon the severity of the problem. Throughout the patient's stay, progress toward nursing goals is reevaluated and dates may be extended as needed. Elements of the nursing care plan may be completed as problems are resolved. For the duration of the patient's hospital stay, an "In Progress" nursing care plan is printed that addresses unresolved problems. At discharge, a more complete version is printed including not only the nursing diagnoses in progress but also those that have previously been resolved. This complete, chronological copy is included as a permanent part of the patient's medical record.

The second major form to be computerized was one that had previously served as a Kardex reporting tool. Most of the demographic information from the Kardex was incorporated by using the same computer heading utilized for the nursing care plan. This Kardex form was additionally redesigned to incorporate several new ideas:

- to show current physicians' orders,
- to show current nursing orders,
- to serve as a reporting tool,
- to serve as an instruction sheet at the bedside for the caregivers, and
- to serve as a documentation tool at the bedside.

The final form was entitled the DR/NSE Order Treatment Sheet (Figure 2).

After the computerized nursing care plan is produced, the nurse initiates the DR/NSE Order Treatment Sheet. The first screen lists 15 categories from which physician/nurse order treatments can be selected. The nurse must minimally identify orders under four categories: Basic Hygiene, Activity/Exercise, Vital Signs/Weight, and Nutrition/Metabolic, to provide specific directions to the caregiver about bathing, activity, diet, and vital signs. Many nursing orders supple-

CN4CTN1R-X4                                    DR/NSE ORDERS
VA MEDICAL CENTER
SAGINAW    MI 48602

Patient: JOLL, CRIS
Location: 510  1  W5A    Sex: M    Age: 27  Y    Birthdate: 12/12/1960
SSN: 969-69-6969    Account#: 0-44099-0            Primary nurse: AMB   Associate nurse: BJC

DIETETIC SERVICE
LC        LOW CHOLESTEROL
PT. EDUCATION
WR        WT REDUCTION, MON (1&3) 1:00 L

                                                                    Nurse charting

BASIC HYGIENE                              _____

    Shower QOD even  Init: _____          _____

    Set up assistance for bath only        _____

ACTIVITY/EXERCISE                          _____

    Up ad lib                              _____

    Use cane while ambulating              _____

NUTRITIONAL/METABOLIC PATTERN              _____

    Patient independent in feeding         _____

    1 can ensure if pt. eats <50% of meal tray   _____

    I&O                                    _____

ELIMINATION/DRAINAGE TUBES                 _____

    COLOSTOMY CARE QD AND PRN; INSTRUCT PT. WHEN READY   _____

TEACHING/LEARNING                          _____

    TEACHING FLOW SHEET OUTLINES PROGRESS ON COLOSTOMY CARE   _____

    INSTRUCT IN HAND WASHING, WOUND CARE   _____

COPING/STRESS TOLERANCE                    _____

    Relaxation exercises 3X Day #1_____ #2_____ #3____   _____

    Encourage participation in all ward activities   _____

    CLINICAL SPECIALIST TO SEE 2X WEEK     _____

    SPEND 5MIN/SHIFT TO ALLOW VENTILATION 1:   2:   3:   _____

SURGICAL PROCEDURES/WOUND CARE             _____

    Irrigate with H2 O2 and saline QD  Init:   _____

    Change dressing Q shift  Init: N _____ D _____ E _____   _____

| TIME: | BP | P/R | T | 24 HR | INTAKE 24 HR | OUTPUT circle: | DIET | SPECIMEN | _____ |
|---|---|---|---|---|---|---|---|---|---|
| ___ | ___ | ___ | ___ | TUBE ___ | URINE ___ | B: P F W | ___ | ___ | ___ |
| ___ | ___ | ___ | ___ | ORAL ___ | STOOL ___ | L: P F W | ___ | ___ | ___ |
| ___ | ___ | ___ | ___ | IV ___ | TUBE ___ | D: P F W | ___ | ___ | ___ |
| ___ | ___ | ___ | ___ | | EMESIS ___ | SLEEP | ___ | ___ | ___ |
| ___ | ___ | ___ | ___ | TOTAL ___ | TOTAL ___ | P F W | ___ | ___ | ___ |

Sig/init:      D    _____ ___,_____ ___,_____ ___
               E    _____ ___,_____ ___,_____ ___
               N    _____ ___,_____ ___,_____ ___
Ancillary:          _____ ___,_____ ___,_____ ___

**Figure 2.** DR/NSE Order Treatment Sheet. Reprinted with permission from Saginaw Veterans'
Administration Medical Center, Saginaw, Michigan. 5/5/88.

ment physician's orders (see box, "Orders").

Other orders can be specified from the remaining 11 categories depending on patient needs. The intensive care and surgical nurses have tailored specific steps of complex procedures into the computer for printing onto the DR/NSE Order Treatment Sheet for detailed instructions.

*Each Order Treatment Sheet serves as a documentation tool at the bedside for the immediate 24-hour period.*

Once the RN completes a DR/NSE Order Treatment Sheet on a new admission, two copies are printed. One is placed at the bedside on a clipboard and the other is kept at the nurses' station with the nursing care plan. All future changes are entered into the computer. Verification slips are automatically printed at the nurses' station and are given to the caregiver for communication purposes. Changes affecting today's care are manually added to the DR/NSE Order Treatment Sheet at the bedside. All changes will automatically be printed on the next day's sheet.

Each DR/NSE Order Treatment Sheet serves as a documentation tool at the bedside

| Orders | |
|---|---|
| **Physician** | **Nurse** |
| NPO | Oral care q 4 hr. while NPO |
| Weigh QOD | Even numbered day at 6 A.M. |
| 1,800 cal ADA | Set up meal trays |

for the immediate 24-hour period. Space at the bottom of the form is provided for data previously filed on two separate manual forms (the Graphic Sheet and the Treatment Record). All vital signs, intake and output summaries, sleep patterns, food intake, and specimen collections are entered on this form. Previously necessary transcription has been eliminated.

The last step of the admission process is patient classification. The RN selects the appropriate computer function and then places a "Y" in front of the applicable patient care criteria. The computer automatically calculates the acuity. Census and acuity data are transferred to the automated staffing and scheduling systems and are reflected in productivity and other management reports.

## OUTCOMES OF AUTOMATION

Since nursing administration had such a large investment in the nursing module, multiple evaluation methods were selected to evaluate the outcomes of automation. A private consulting firm performed time-and-motion studies to evaluate changes in direct patient care activities. A pre- and postcomputer questionnaire was designed to assess general staff satisfaction with the system. A nursing practice monitor that measured progress toward nursing service goals was used. Lastly, nursing management comments were consistently monitored through ongoing "wrap-up" computer meetings.

### Time-and-motion studies

A private consulting firm was hired to evaluate the entire IHS computer project. As

**Table 1.** Direction of nursing activities pre- to post-IHS

| Percent direct patient care (Treatments, patient education, patient communication, etc.) | | | |
| --- | --- | --- | --- |
| | Pre | Post | % change |
| HN | 10 | 11 | 1 |
| RN | 40 | 45 | 5 |
| LPN | 45 | 53 | 8 |
| NA | 40 | 49 | 9 |
| Percent indirect care (Reporting, telephone, computer functions, noting, orders, etc.) | | | |
| | Pre | Post | % change |
| HN | 40 | 36 | −4 |
| RN | 38 | 42 | 4 |
| LPN | 22 | 25 | 3 |
| NA | 20 | 22 | 2 |
| Percent administrative (Paperwork, staffing, supply activities, etc.) | | | |
| | Pre | Post | % change |
| HN | 50 | 53 | 3 |
| RN | 22 | 13 | −9 |
| LPN | 34 | 22 | −12 |
| NA | 40 | 29 | −11 |

part of the evaluation, time-and-motion studies were done pre- and postimplementation to monitor the impact of automation on nursing activities. Results showed a significant increase in direct and indirect patient care activities, with a corresponding decrease in caregiver time devoted to administrative duties (Table 1). The consultants also commented that quality of nursing documentation improved thus: "Nursing care plans and up-to-date treatment sheets were available on every patient. The documentation is legible, comprehensive, and current. Nurses and physicians expressed strong acceptance of the patient data being recorded by nursing personnel."[15]

### Pre- and postcomputer questionnaire

Prior to implementation of the nursing module, a 13-item questionnaire was developed to gather staff perceptions on the time required to plan nursing care, ease of use of the computer, staff attitudes about the computer system, and data about the documentation of nursing care.

In comparing pre/post data, staff indicated that the computer saved them time in developing and updating care plans and in documentation of the nursing process. They stated that documentation of nursing interventions improved, as did patient progress toward goals. Staff perceived that computerization significantly improved care planning and aided in utilizing the nursing process. When five questions were repeated two months later, an even higher positive response rate resulted. This growth is attributed to increased familiarity with the module and continued satisfaction with its design. Pre- and postquestionnaire results, as well as the May survey results, are summarized in Table 2.

### Nursing practice monitors

As previously discussed, a nursing practice monitor was developed in 1983 to evaluate progress toward nursing service goals. This same tool was used to evaluate progress following the automation project. The monitor addressed nine criteria including: a complete admission note written in

**Table 2.** Nursing computer questionnaire

| Question | Dec. 1986 pre | Percent positive Mar. 1987 post | May ADP survey |
|---|---|---|---|
| 1.  The computerized NCP really guides my care delivery. | 75 | 76 | |
| 2.  Computerization has improved instructions given to caregivers. | Not given | 84 | 91 |
| 3.  The average NCP takes fewer than 15 minutes to initially develop. | 35 | 63 | |
| 4.  The average NCP takes more than 45 minutes to initially develop. | 25 | 25 | |
| 5.  Our nursing charting system is efficient and easy. | 53 | 67 | 82 |
| 6.  Nursing Care Plans are completed on at least 90% of all patients (with the exception of STAs). | 80 | 98 | |
| 7.  Nursing process is currently used fluently by most RNs. | 66 | 89 | |
| 8.  At least 75% of all nursing actions are documented. | 43 | 68 | |
| 9.  Most charts (75%) have progress toward goals documented. | 58 | 65 | |
| 10.  NCPs are easy to write and update. | 62 | 81 | 94 |
| 11.  The average NCP takes fewer than 15 minutes to update. | 81 | 86 | |
| 12.  The computer system currently helps me utilize the nursing process. | 19 | 78 | 93 |
| 13.  Computerization has improved nursing care planning. | 60 | 79 | 90 |

SOAPIE (*S*ubjective Data, *O*bjective Data, *A*ssessment, *P*lan, *I*ntervention, *E*valuation) format; a complete nursing database; a comprehensive nursing care plan; patient-centered measurable goals; realistic and specific nursing interventions; interim progress notes on a timely basis; evidence of discharge planning; patient/family teaching and patient involvement in his or her care (Table 3).

Eight criteria remained at acceptable levels. Only interim progress notes (No. 6) fell

**Table 3.** Nursing practice monitor results

| Criteria | Percent compliance | | | |
| --- | --- | --- | --- | --- |
| | Before manual project 1983 | After manual project 1984 | 1985–1986 manual average | Postautomation 1987 average |
| Admission note is complete and reflects identified problems. | 80.7 | 84.6 | 87 | 92 |
| Database is current and complete. | 53.8 | 61.5 | 91 | 92 |
| NCP is current and reflects problems addressed in progress notes. | 42.3 | 61.5 | 80 | 88 |
| Goals are patient-centered, realistic, and measurable. | | 15.3 | 80 | 100 |
| Nursing interventions are specific. | 38.6 | 42.3 | 81 | 100 |
| Interim progress notes reflect evaluation of nursing interventions congruent with expected or projected goals. | 34.6 | 38.6 | 80 | 55 |
| Evidence of discharge planning exists, including significant other. | 7.6 | 7.6 | 62 | 58 |
| Evidence exists of patient/family teaching. | 38.6 | 38.6 | 44 | 65 |
| Evidence exists of patient and significant other being involved in his or her plan of care. | 3.8 | 11.5 | 52 | 51 |

below the standard. It was concluded that part of the reason this area dropped was that more charting was now being done at the bedside on the DR/NSE Order Treatment Sheet and less in the actual progress notes. Also, it was recognized that specific guidelines setting documentation expectations of the Treatment Sheet versus the progress notes were not yet established or published.

This lack of structure caused some confusion about what was required.

## Management satisfaction

In addition to data collected by the consulting firm, the computer questionnaire, and the nursing practice monitor, reaction to the system was gauged at weekly wrap-up problem-solving sessions held with key users. Comments were, and remain, tremendously positive and included statements such as: "Automation has decreased paperwork"; "It's nice to see standardized nursing language"; "It's more efficient—I don't have to re-invent the wheel on each NCP"; "My nursing care plans are more complete. The standard orders prompt me to do patient care I might have forgotten before"; and "Charting is easier to do at the bedside." The users are obviously pleased with the system.

### Additional benefits

Nursing administration found other benefits to automation. A goal of nursing over the preceding five years was to encourage independent nursing practice. One way this was emphasized was that nurses were encouraged to add nursing orders to the patient treatment sheet. In reality, this seldom happened using the manual system. However, with automation, the number of nursing orders for each patient increased dramatically. In fact, on the average automated DR/NSE Order Treatment Sheet, 70% of the orders are initiated by nursing.

Nursing care plans became more comprehensive. Seasoned and novice nurses found the automated system combined a wealth of information from a variety of sources. This information made it easy to formulate effective care strategies on-line in a comprehensive manner.

The Nursing Quality Management Committee (NQMC) found that the automated system assisted in its monitoring functions. By design, the nursing module helped reinforce concepts of nursing process defined by the administration on the nursing practice monitor. The NQMC chairperson can access any patient's NCP and DR/NSE Order Treatment Sheet from the Nursing Office to assess for completeness and quality. Patient classification can also be monitored. A list can be printed to alert supervisors as to which classifications have not been updated in at least the preceding eight hours. Individual classification screens can also be viewed and assessed for interrater reliability within the system. Our interrater reliability has risen to an average of 90% thus ensuring accuracy of data being used to make staffing decisions.

Communication has improved among all hospital departments because of IHS. Patients have benefited because plans are complete and legible. Since patients have access to their orders for the day, they now feel more involved in their care. Communication is also more concise since duplication of various entries has been virtually eliminated.

## CHALLENGES OF AUTOMATION

Although the benefits outweigh the disadvantages, automation does present a few challenges. Patient information is more accessible in the system and care must be taken to limit department access to only pertinent information. This is accomplished by limiting base-page functionality on a "need to know" basis and by periodically changing entry passwords.

Training for automation is a challenge and requires careful planning. Each person has a different level of computer knowledge. This necessitates planning for highly individualized training sessions to ensure learning. We also discovered that all levels of personnel need educational sessions, regardless of the number of functions performed on the computer. The educational offerings not only ease implementation, but also build "ownership" of the system among all staff. It was also decided that the process of education and follow-through by the staff would be facilitated by having complete written nursing documentation guidelines in place prior to implementation.

•   •   •

Overall, the computer experience has been positive. Goals set at the beginning of the project have been exceeded. Satisfaction with the system has been extremely positive. Current efforts are being focused on reinforcing procedures, refining the system, and exploring its potential to support quality management and research endeavors. The experience has clearly shown that the degree of success of automation is directly related to the level of commitment of staff and administration, and to the efforts of the people who will be using the system. The technology is available to facilitate the delivery of nursing services. However, it is clear that a software package cannot be taken from the vendor's shelf, plugged in, and provide the benefits for which nursing management is looking. Rather, nurses must be actively involved in the process. They must become knowledgeable about the capability of computerization, clearly define what is needed, and then put forth the effort necessary to make it happen.

## REFERENCES

1.  Amdreoli, K., and Mussen, L. "Computers in Nursing Care: The State of the Art." *Nursing Outlook* 33, no. 1 (January/February 1985): 16–21.
2.  Smith, M. "Computers in Nursing." *Journal of the Operating Room Research Institute* 2, no. 9 (1982): 4–12.
3.  Clark, D., and Lombard, H. "Computers: A New Tool for Nursing." *Computers in Hospitals* 2, no. 4 (March/April 1982): 42–48.
4.  Adams, A. "Computer Technology: Its Impact on Nursing Practice." *Nursing Administration Quarterly* 10, no. 2 (Winter 1986): 21–22.
5.  Amdreoli and Mussen, "Computers in Nursing Care."
6.  Adams, "Computer Technology."
7.  Edmunds, L. "Computers for Inpatient Nursing Care." *Computers in Nursing* 2, no. 4 (1984): 102–08.
8.  Happ, B. "Should Computers Be Used in the Nursing Care of Patients?" *Nursing Management* 14, no. 7 (1983): 31–34.
9.  Lombard, N., and Light, N. "On-Line Nursing Care Plans by Nursing Diagnosis." *Computers in Health Care* 4, no. 13 (November 1983): 22–23.
10. Adams, "Computer Technology."
11. Edmunds, "Computers for Inpatient Nursing Care."
12. Fairless, P. "Nine Ways a Computer Can Make Your Work Easier." *Nursing 86* 16, no. 9 (September 1986): 54–56.
13. Shannon, M., Dextrom, N., and Fuhrhop, M. "The Impact of a Patient Care Management System on Independent Nursing Care Functions and Nursing Process." *Health Care Supervisor* 5, no. 3 (1987): 61–67.
14. Gordon, M. *Manual of Nursing Diagnoses.* New York: McGraw-Hill, 1982.
15. Arthur Andersen and Company. *IHS Evaluation for the Site Summary Project Report for the Veterans' Administration.* Washington, D.C.: Medical Information Resources Management Office, October 1987.

# Part IV
# Other Nursing Mangement Concerns

# Enhancing the image of the nurse: The role of the nurse supervisor, Part 1

*Helen Yura*
*Eminent Professor Emeritus of Nursing*
*School of Nursing*
*Old Dominion University*
*Norfolk, Virginia*

T HE IMAGE OF THE NURSE may be defined as the mental representation of oneself as nurse as well as the mental representation of the nurse held by other health professionals and the consumers of nursing services.[1] The image is an ever-changing amalgam of conscious and unconscious information, perceptions, and feelings about the self as person and as nurse. The image of the nurse is a social creation that incorporates elements of value, identity, and behavior.[2]

Many diverse messages about nurses are fed into the personal, social, and organizational system—messages that can be accepted (i.e., integrated with the self), revised, or rejected.[3] Intuitively, individuals are aware that the nurse's level of functioning and placement within the formal work organization convey a strong message about how nurses feel about themselves and how significant persons in the organization feel about them.[4]

*Health Care Superv*, 1989, 7(2), 1–11
© 1989 Aspen Publishers, Inc.

An important factor in considering the image of the nurse is the traditional view of women within the health care system.

Women have had to confront the medical care system, in particular, because medicine for more than a century has contributed substantially to defining women. Women were defined as incomplete in body, unwell when menstruating, sick when pregnant, nonwomen after hysterectomy, mentally disturbed during or after the menopause, often hypochondriacal and at times slaves to the cyclical nature of their physiology.... Women have worked hard with physicians to have their complaints investigated seriously and to remove the psychogenic labels of their symptoms.[5]

Because women constitute the majority of nurses in the country today, and because most nurses function in hospital settings, it can be assumed that these societal and medical attitudes will affect the image of the nurse, if not overtly, then covertly.

Image involves the concept of a person or institution held by the general public, often one deliberately created or modified by publicity, advertising, and propaganda.

Image making is the key to revolutionize the nursing profession. Nurses have long had a survival orientation. The perspective is to save the rest of the world, even at the expense of one's own well-being. This view leads to professional disenchantment and a low ebb in the nursing image. Lack of energy and enthusiasm, displays of anger and professional sabotage are seen in this rescuer-victim role. Self-worth is the foundation for building positive images.... Polishing the professional image will enable nursing to gain respect and autonomy. When nurses go to the media to tell the public of their plight, the negative aspects of nursing are usually emphasized. No one seems to remember the positive aspects of nursing.[6]

## NURSING PUBLIC IMAGE: AN HISTORIC OVERVIEW

In view of such prominent current issues as changes in national health care policy, rapidly expanding nurse roles and responsibility, the worsening national shortage of nurses, a continuing decline in nursing school enrollments, and drastic proposed cutbacks in federal support of nursing education, it is important to look at nursing's public image over time.[7] Current images and outcomes for nursing are rooted in the past. Kalisch and Kalisch pioneered strategies to determine the public image of nursing. Using three media—novels (written 1843–1970), motion pictures (1930–1970), and television (1950–1980)—the Kalisches researched popular attitudes and assumptions about nurses and their contributions to consumer welfare. They contend that some opinions of nurses held today by the public have been drawn directly from the images projected by the media.[8]

In reviewing a three-decade span of television portrayals of nurses, the Kalisches concluded that "the reality of contemporary nursing practice over the past 30 years has found little or no echo in the largely fictional world of television broadcasting. Over the past 15 years, the popular image of the nurse not only has failed to reflect changing professional conditions, but it has also assumed strongly derogatory traits that undermine public confidence in and respect for the professional nurse."[9]

With few notable exceptions television entertainment creators have paid insufficient attention to the depiction of nursing, using nursing far too often as background scenery for hospital based drama. When nurse characters have been singled out for attention, this attention has usually taken the form of delving into personal problems rather than professional concerns. Moreover, the nurse characters have served and continue to serve as handmaidens to the medical profession. Much of the current image of nursing on television derives from the exaggerated idealism and heroism ascribed to physicians' characters—with the TV physician looming so large that the TV nurse cannot help but pale by comparison.[10]

The Kalisches drew the above conclusions from content analysis of a 20% random sample of programs from 28 series with a regular nurse character. Three content analysis tools were applied by coders whose intrarater reliability was 88.4% and whose interrater reliability was 90.2%. Validity testing was done.[11]

When content analysis was performed for personal attributes of television physicians and nurses, the following were the results: (1) Physicians exhibited higher levels of ambition, intelligence, risk taking, rationality, adeptness, aggression, self-confidence, and sophistication; (2) physicians demonstrated more sincere, altruistic, honest, and perceptive qualities; (3) nurses scored higher only on obedience, permissiveness, conformity, serenity, and flexibility; (4) physicians and nurses did not differ in efficiency, organization, and discipline; (5) physicians scored higher for their values regarding achievement, integrity, intelligence, power, self-sacrifice, duty, humanism, and family; (6) nurses ranked equally with physicians in virtue and love. Notice that nurses scored lower than physicians even on traits that have been traditionally ascribed to nurses.[12]

What is the impact of television's portrayal on the nurse supervisor and the staff nurse in today's health care institutions? Television is ranked as the second most powerful influence on Americans and absorbs about seven hours of the average American's time daily.[13]

Another powerful medium affecting the public image of the nurse is film. The impact of movies has more than doubled since they became available on videotapes for private showing. Millions of people still attend movies and spend billions of dollars on movie tickets. Add to these the millions who rent and/or buy videotapes of movies for home viewing, and the medium's influence on the public's attitudes and values is staggering.

The Kalisches applied their research methodology to the quantitative and qualitative analysis of 204 motion pictures released between 1930 and 1979.[14] They saw a rise and fall in the image of nursing on the screen, with the best image in the 1940s and the poorest in the 1970s.

This should be of concern to nurses since the current negative image of the nurse in motion pictures is undoubtedly adversely influencing the attitudes of patients and policymakers alike and, perhaps, is also subtly inhibiting nurses' own aspirations. Certainly such views are having an impact on the attitudes of prospective nurses, since the largest proportion of the more than one billion motion picture admission tickets that are sold each year are purchased by adolescents. How nurses are being portrayed to a group that is in the process of making career decisions ought to be a concern of all nurses.[15]

Kalisch and Kalisch found that most nurse characters in films chose nursing for the purpose of caring for others, engaging in altruistic and worthwhile activity, or for patriotic motives. "Although 55.3% of nurse characters viewed a career in nursing positively, 3.4% showed a clear dislike for nursing, and 41.3% demonstrated an ambiguous attitude."[16] In contrast, movie physicians were judged to attach far greater value to their career than did movie nurses. "Physicians used their own judgment in patient care situations more than nurses, and they were also commended more than were nurses."[17]

The strong and positive image of the nurse peaked at the height of World War II. This image has been steadily eroded, with a dramatic decline beginning in the 1960s, intensifying throughout the 1970s and continuing into the 1980s, as the nursing profession was denigrated and satirized in many important and influential films. "During the past two decades, the contribution of nurses to society has been greatly undervalued in motion pictures. While some films have shown the nurse to be competent, the scope of that competence has been limited. Nursing has largely been presented as a self-subordinating, quintessentially feminine profession."[18]

*The strong and positive image of the nurse peaked at the height of World War II. This image has been steadily eroded.*

Nurses in novels are almost always women, which reinforces the traditional biological role of women in relation to nursing. Thus the nurse was depicted as wife, mistress, mother. "Nurse stereotypes usually fall into three general categories: the nurse as man's companion, the nurse as man's destroyer, and the nurse as man's mother or the mother of his children. Very frequently the 'man' in these novels is a physician."[19] In the 207 novels analyzed by the Kalisches, 99% of the nurses were women, most of whom were single, childless, under 35 years of age, and Caucasian. "Over and over again the characteristic image of the nurse in novels has been one of a young woman looking for romance and adventure who is carrying out the often unpleasant but essential job of supporting the magnificent work of physicians."[20]

As in television programs, nurses in novels scored higher than physicians only in obedience and kindness, whereas physicians were more confident, sophisticated, ambitious, intelligent, aggressive, and rational. Physicians and nurses were judged to demonstrate comparable altruism, sincerity, warmth, sympathy, and nurturance. "Physicians were also portrayed to value achievements, power, science, intellect, and scholarliness more than nurses. Thus, physicians have maintained a stronghold on traditionally masculine traits while also exhibiting the nurturant and caring qualities that typify the nursing role."[21]

The Kalisches traced the novelistic image of the nurse from the nineteenth century to the present. Their findings can be summarized as follows:

- The nineteenth century image of an untrained lower class woman, often alcoholic, prevailed through the latter part of the century, when Florence Nightingale brought respectability due to good breeding and social class, though not due to education.
- The time period from 1900 to 1919 reflected nurse heroines searching for meaning in nursing and fulfillment through love and marriage, resulting in a mixed image—competence, intelligence, and determination (success in nursing) versus passivity, dependence,

and submissiveness (success in marriage). "The image of the nurse in novels was given a major boost in 1914 by the emergence of nurse-author Mary Roberts Rinehart...."[22] Nursing's image also improved with the outbreak of World War I.

- The 1920s and 1930s involved two steps backward for the image of the nurse. Novels written just after World War I depicted nurses as less important than they had been during the war, serving mainly to tend the emotional scars left by the war (invisible wounds). A marked decline came with the publication of Hemingway's *Farewell to Arms*. Novels in the 1930s reflected the nurse's conflict between self-interest and the "duty owed to the medical profession and patients."[23]

- During the 1940s and 1950s (the years of World War II), the nurse received unreserved backing and was favorably regarded by the public. After the war, the nurse was depicted as a social reformer and as a heroine, particularly in the accurate and attractive portrayals of the Sue Barton, Cherry Ames, and Penny Marsh series of books for young readers.[24]

- During the 1960s and 1970s, the image of the nurse fell back to the bottom, with nurses depicted as cold and controlling physician helpers who also provided "a ready form of relief for the interns' sexual tensions."[25] The older, unmarried, and often emotionally warped nursing administrator became a familiar type. Romance novels portrayed the nurse as an ultimately submissive woman, never daring to question the authority of the physician, even when the physician was wrong. Nursing was identified as a technical occupation with little emphasis on education and research.

- Although no definitive research has analyzed the depiction of nurses in novels during the 1980s, a cursory review discovers few improvements in their image.

"All these nurse stereotypes in novels, as well as on television and in motion pictures, have maintained a basic element of continuity despite far-reaching changes occurring in real-life nursing education, practice, and research."[26] The Kalisches point out that novelists have badly maligned the image of the nurse. "Most obvious is the fact that the same rigor, intensity of effort, and originality afforded heroic physician roles has not been given to the development of admirable nurse characters."[27] The professional nurse's motivations and health care perspectives are influenced by the depiction of the nurse in novels as well as other media forms.

Although the nursing literature abounds with exciting presentations of the art and science of nursing, the nursing process, nursing theory development, the nurse as client advocate, the nurse as an independent and interdependent practitioner, the professionalization of nursing, and nurse autonomy, the public (including other health professionals) retains the outdated, stereotypic image of the nurse. Beletz verified this outdated image through interviews of a sample population (*N*=18) of clients in an acute care setting, using a questionnaire with 21 open-ended questions. Responses unfailingly presented an image of a technical, functional doer with very few activities in the cognitive or intellectual range. Beletz formed a composite image of the nurse, based on respondents' answers, as "a female nurturer, medicator, physician's assistant, maid, and administrator."[28] Beletz concluded that clients in the acute care hospital setting "saw no difference between nurses' actual practice and their preconceived expectations.... The nurses in this institution were apparently *not* practicing according to the professional model."[29] What was the educational preparation of nurses in this health care agency?

Unfortunately, in contrast with past characterizations of nurses in the mass media, nurses today are usually portrayed in a derogatory light. Such negative public images affect nursing in several important ways. First, since public opinion is vital to the success of sound political and professional groups in attaining their goals, these images distort the public's concept of nursing and reinforce an outmoded legacy of beliefs, expectations, and myths about nursing. Second, such images affect the quality and number of persons who choose nursing as an occupation, particularly troublesome in a time when young women (and nurses are mostly women) are increasingly choosing to enter traditional men's fields of work. Third, these images affect the decisions of policymakers relative to the allocations of scarce resources for the profession. Fourth, consumers, too, are affected as these portrayals deprive the public of knowledge of the many vital services that nurses provide. Physicians continue to receive credit for virtually all positive health care outcomes—a discrepancy reinforced by the print and electronic media.... And finally, these portrayals affect nurses' self-images and undermine nurses' self-confidence, beliefs, and values. Many nurses, therefore, do not watch or listen to media presentations because they find them too painful.[30]

If one were to survey newspapers, news magazines, popular magazines, radio broadcasts, and other media elements, a similar image of nurses would emerge. For example, it is readily apparent in the news media that women with doctoral degrees, physicians, and nurses are addressed as "Ms." Men with doctoral degrees, particularly physicians, are always addressed as "Doctor." Frequent letters to the editor addressing this issue have made no impact. The editorial style of local papers is justified by their editors as that prescribed by the Associated Press (AP). There is no explanation for the lack of effort to initiate change in the AP style protocol.

Newspapers have featured both positive and negative portrayals of nurses. Among the more positive depictions are those dramatic helicopter rescues of badly injured citizens and their transport to medical centers. The negative far outnumber the positive, however, particularly in the reporting of nurses involved in suspected criminal acts; the fact that the suspect is a nurse is boldly displayed. Even when the newspaper article is meant to arouse the public about an issue such as "the nursing shortage," nonnurses (economists, legal experts, legislators, physicians) who offer opinions and comment on the reasons for the shortage are widely quoted, particularly if they disagree that a shortage exists or believe that it was contrived by nurses and nursing organizations.

The recent decision by the Federal Commission of Fine Arts to deny the request for a statue to commemorate the contributions of Vietnam veteran nurses was well publicized. Although this news item might seem innocuous, the publication of the reason for the negative vote and the comparison of a statue for the nurse corps to a statue for the canine corps generated anger among nurses, if not the public. "It is humiliating and degrading for nurses (of whom a majority are women) to be compared to the Canine Corps. Nurses are not dogs, they are not maids, nor are they physicians' handmaidens. They are underappreciated and undervalued by the federal government and the public.... For nurses to be placed in the same category as the Canine Corps by a federal commission tells the nation that nurses contribute nothing," writes Tarasoff in a letter to the editor.[31]

Does this public image of the nurse portrayed in the print and visual media influence the image nurses hold of themselves as nurses and as persons?

## THE IMAGE NURSES HOLD OF THEMSELVES

The image nurses hold of themselves is significantly influenced by the image held by the public at large and by persons significant to the nurse. For staff nurses, low self-image seems to be the cause of self-depreciating behaviors and for receptivity to others' low opinion of nurses—a primary detractor. Nurses must work on all fronts to let the public know that nursing is an autonomous, legally designated practice in which the nurse is directly responsible for the client. Nurses must let the public know that they are responsible, dedicated person/family centered caretakers in their practice, as well as expected to remain theoretically and technically up-to-date and for obtaining the highest level of education in keeping with their responsibilities.

The limited education of some nursing staff members diminishes their power and authority within the formal organization of the hospital. Those with power in the struc-

ture are well-educated professionals. The larger the proportion of nurses who do not hold the baccalaureate degree in nursing, the less value and professional power available for the nurse. It is difficult to conceptualize a collegial relationship with such health professionals as the physician, the pharmacist, or the dentist for the nurse with one, two, or three years of nursing education. This acceptance of minimal nursing education for vocational and technical practice fortifies the subordinate handmaiden image described so eloquently by the Kalisches and others.

Another factor that reduces nurses' self-image is the practice of depending solely on the nurse supervisor and the physician for approval and validation of nursing competency. If validation and approval are not forthcoming, nurses may view themselves with less esteem. The nurse is directly responsible to the client both legally and professionally. It is primarily through clients—through their comfort, their achieving optimal wellness—that nurses can feel satisfied with the services they provide. This focus does not, of course, negate the need for simultaneous positive reinforcement from the nurse supervisor.

*The limited education of some nursing staff members diminishes their power and authority within the formal organization of the hospital.*

Snyder did a comparative analysis of factors influencing registered nurse retention and turnover below the head nurse level in acute care hospitals. The sample consisted of 109 registered staff nurses categorized as "stayers" or "leavers." Stayers were those staff nurses below the head nurse level who worked continuously in an acute care hospital for two or more years; leavers were staff nurses with more than one year of experience who had voluntarily resigned from another acute care hospital within a 50-mile radius of the hospital in which they were presently employed.[32] Ten acute care hospitals composed the setting for the study. The rank order of *esteem sources*, as rated by leavers was (1) client, (2) self, (3) coworkers, (4) client's family, (5) physician, (6) head nurse. The rank order was the following for stayers: (1) client, (2) self, (3) coworkers, (4) client's family, (5) head nurse, (6) physician. The rank order of quality performance *recognition sources* for leavers was (1) client, (2) coworkers, (3) self and client's family (tie), (5) head nurse, (6) physician. It was the following for stayers: (1) client, (2) coworkers and self (tie), (4) client's family and head nurse (tie), (6) physician. Note that the head nurse and the physician were the *last* sources for both esteem and recognition to be named by the staff nurses.

Expertise, quality performance, in nursing should be reinforced by nurses. In the administrative hierarchy of hospitals, head nurses [nurse supervisors] have the responsibility and the authority to judge the expertise of the staff nurse. The data indicated that the staff nurses look to the client to satisfy their need for status, recognition, and appreciation in place of the deserved respect of their colleagues in the nursing hierarchy.[33]

Snyder discovered that human need satisfaction perceptions and equity perceptions differentiate between staff nurses who stay and those who leave acute care hospitals. The satisfaction of human needs through the

workplace was present in all staff nurses. The fact that the nurse works usually assured satisfaction of human needs in physiological and safety categories. Satisfaction of these categories of human needs focused the staff nurses' need drive to social and self-fulfillment categories.

Unless there were opportunities provided at work to satisfy these higher-level needs, there were perceptions of deprivation, and behavior reflected that state. If the nurse observed the ratio of personal outcomes (rewards) to inputs (effort) and the ratio of others' outcomes (rewards) to inputs (efforts) to be unequal, the work environment was perceived as unjust. The presence of inequity created a drive to reduce inequity perceptions. The strength of the drive to correct the inequity was proportional to the tension created.[34]

Still another factor tending to lower the image nurses hold of themselves concerns the lack of savvy about how to have a voice in affairs and policies affecting nursing. This is a limitation for both the staff nurse and the nurse supervisor. This lack of savvy is not limited to the local level but can be found at the state and national levels as well. It seems incredible that policies related to nursing care and nurse manpower whether inside or outside the hospital structure, would be made with no representation or even token representation of academically and experientially qualified nurses. For example, a patient care committee is a common occurrence in health care settings; its expressed purpose is to delineate medical and nursing territories. A close look at committee outcomes will verify that a major focus is to define the limits of nursing practice and to prevent nursing's encroachment into the field of medicine. Has any committee ever prevented the encroachment of medicine into the field of nursing? Have any physicians been restricted from the practice of nursing, for which they have no license to practice?

The nurse supervisor's failure to assure nurse representation on strategic health care agency committees or to view administrative committee work as an important function of the nurse supervisor detracts from the image of the nurse. Nurse supervisors' failures to be prepared for meetings, to serve in the advocacy role for nursing, and to initiate proactive behaviors pose significant hazards not only to the image of the nurse but also to the very survival of professional nursing in health care agencies. The nurse supervisor's support for and participation in replacing registered nurses with newly trained nurses' aides is an example. What will be the impact for consumers of nursing?

The nurse supervisor is in a key position to monitor public relations materials available within the health care agency as well as materials used to publicize the agency. Is nursing reflected in the materials? If nursing and nurses are included, how are they portrayed? If materials coming into the health care agencies from businesses or industry, particularly those advertising equipment, supplies, and computer software, portray nurses negatively or as caricatures, is a formal complaint made by the nurse supervisor, the staff nurse, and/or the health care agency administration? A good example of caricature was the published computer software advertisement for the VistaCARE Staff Scheduling System.

Another source of harm to the image of the nurse is embedded in the role of the nurse supervisor within the organizational structure of the health care agency. For example, is the nurse supervisor merely a conduit for the transfer of policy from top administration to the staff nurses? Does the nurse supervisor actively participate in policy formation if such policy directly affects the provision of nursing services to consumers or the administration of these services by nurses?

Does the nurse supervisor serve as advocate for the nursing staff? Does the advocacy extend beyond the nursing unit to such other health care units as pharmacy, radiology, and the pathology laboratory? Does the advocacy extend beyond the health care setting to influential politicians, community leaders, and consumer groups? Any limitations in these areas could serve to tarnish rather than enhance the image of the nurse.

Does the nurse supervisor demonstrate excessive loyalty and obedience to the medical staff and the hospital administration at the expense of the nursing staff and the consumers of nursing services? Might such excessive loyalty and obedience result from a low self-concept because the nurse supervisor lacks the minimal academic preparation of the master's degree in nursing for this administrative position? This is a primary target for detractors of the image of the nurse in the health care agency, specifically and collectively.

An effective way to diminish the image of the well educated practitioner of nursing is for a nurse supervisor to fail to distinguish among nurses who are vocational, technical, professional-generalist, and professional-specialist practitioners of nursing in position descriptions, hiring practices, and salary ranges.

Health care providers and administrators who place little value on the nursing staff except as dependent workers diminish the image held by nurses in the health care agency. In anticipation of loss of revenue arising from diagnosis related group (DRG) funding, significant numbers of nurses were relieved of their positions. This phenomenon conveyed the message that nursing is a disposable commodity. Data since DRGs have demonstrated an increase in revenue for health care agencies, but rehiring of the nurses relieved of their positions has become a problem of national proportions due to shortages of prepared nurses.

If the health care administrator is threatened by well educated nursing staff (particularly nurse supervisors and nurse administrators) and hires less prepared nursing personnel, further damage is done to the image of the nurse. In the recent past an employment advertisement appeared in the newspaper of a large metropolitan area for the position of director of nursing for one of the hospitals. The master's-prepared nurse administrator had resigned to take a similar position at another local hospital. The announcement stated "diploma graduate preferred"—a level of preparation lower than the minimal educational preparation stipulated for this position. The medical staff objected strenuously, believing that this announcement reflected negatively on the hospital. The hospital administrator yielded to physician pressure and changed the announcement. Unfortunately, no concerted objection was voiced by the nursing staff and nurse supervisor. The hospital in question also prefers to employ vocationally and technically prepared practitioners of nursing. The impact of this scenario on the image of the nurse at this health care agency and throughout the metropolitan area is obvious.

When health care providers other than nurses in an agency take full credit for the positive health results of clients, the image of the nurse as an effective provider of services that contribute significantly to these positive results is distorted. Rarely is the miraculous recovery of clients attributed to anything but medicine, medical science, and technology. The fact is too often lost that nursing is the largest service in health care agencies and that—before and after medical or surgical intervention—nursing is the dominant service in recovery. Health care agency administrators and consumers alike have come to take nursing services for granted. What is the impact of this attitude on the image of nursing in general and on the self-image of the individual nurse?

Another obstacle to image enhancement for the nurse looms larger as the shortage of nurses becomes more pronounced in some health care settings. The expectation that nurses will work double shifts to offset the shortage compounds the image problem. Nurses are told, and unfortunately accept (with much guilt), that "there will be no one to care for clients" if they refuse to work double shifts. This practice occurs without appropriate compensation but most often by time replacement. The responsibility to provide nursing care is not the responsibility of the staff nurse alone. The nurse's high vulnerability to feeling guilty when misused can have a negative impact on the nurse's self-image. An article in a local newspaper about the shortage of nurses quoted the hospital administrator as saying, "The busier people are, the happier they are."[35] This quote caused a furor among nurses, as was attested by letters to the editor. Sources close to the hospital administrator and those with first-hand information stated that no such statement was made, but the item stands unretracted by the newspaper.

One popular enhancer of the image of the

nurse that health care agencies often do arrange is a celebration and/or recognition during National Nurse Week each May. This commemoration may result in positive media results—for the present and the future. Health care agencies bear significant responsibility for the positive portrayal of the nurse, particularly to adolescent groups grappling with the choice of a life-long career. Eliminating those existing practices and attitudes that negatively affect the image of the nurse—both within and outside the health care agency—should be the first priority.

What could nurses, particularly nurse supervisors do to enhance the largely negative image of the nurse? Enhancing that image, which is the responsibility of the staff nurse as well as the nurse supervisor, will be the focus of a later article, which will suggest strategies of image enhancement for the nurse supervisor and discuss their implications for the future from the point of view of nurses, nursing, and the public.

•　　•　　•

There's a minute of life passing! Paint it in its reality and forget everything to do that! Become it itself ... give the image of what we actually see forgetting everything that has appeared before us.

*from Joachim Gasquet* by Paul Cezanne

## REFERENCES

1. Yura, H., and Walsh, M.B. *The Nursing Process*. 5th ed. E. Norwalk, Conn.: Appleton-Lange, 1988, p. 94.
2. Norris, C. "Body Image: Its Relevance to Professional Nursing." In *Behavioral Concepts and Nursing Intervention*. 2d ed., edited by C. Carlson and B. Blackwell. Philadelphia: Lippincott, 1978, p. 5.
3. Ibid., 9.
4. Ibid., 12.
5. Ibid., 17.
6. Owsley, V. "The Nursing Shortage—Nurses Take Action!" *Healthcare Careers of Tennessee and Kentucky*, p. 10.
7. National League for Nursing. "NLN 15th Biennial Convention." Nursing and Health Care (July 1981): 302.
8. Kalisch, P., and Kalisch, B. "Nurses on Prime Time Television." *American Journal of Nursing* 82 (February 1982): 264.
9. Ibid.
10. Ibid.
11. Ibid.
12. Ibid., 265.
13. Ibid., 264.
14. Kalisch, P., and Kalisch, B. "The Image of the Nurse in Motion Pictures." *American Journal of Nursing* 82 (April 1982): 605.
15. Ibid.
16. Ibid., 605–606.
17. Ibid., 606.
18. Ibid.
19. Kalisch, P., and Kalisch, B. "The Image of Nurses in Novels." American *Journal of Nursing* 82 (August 1982): 1220.
20. Ibid., 1221.
21. Ibid.
22. Ibid., 1222.
23. Ibid., 1222–23.
24. Ibid., 1223.
25. Ibid., 1224.
26. Ibid.
27. Ibid.
28. Beletz, E. "Is Nursing's Public Image Up to Date?" Nursing *Outlook* 22 (July 1974): 432–35.
29. Ibid., 434.
30. Kalisch, B., and Kalisch, P. "Improving the Image of Nursing." *American Journal of Nursing* 83 (January 1983): 48.
31. Tarasoff, S. "Statue Decision Demeans Nurses." *Allentown Morning Call*, 24 December 1987, p. A15.
32. Snyder, J. "A Comparative Analysis of Factors Influencing Registered Nurse Retention and Turnover below the Head Nurse Level in Acute Care Hospitals." Unpublished master's thesis, Department of Nursing, Old Dominion University, Norfolk, Va., 1982, p. 7.
33. Ibid., 25.
34. Ibid., 23.
35. *Virginia Pilot/Ledger Star*, 10 July 1987, p. D1.

# Enhancing the image of the nurse: The role of the nurse supervisor, Part 2

*Helen Yura*
*Eminent Professor Emeritus*
*Norfolk, Virginia*

THERE IS LITTLE DOUBT that the public image of the nurse and the nurse's image of self could be improved. In Part 1 (*HCS* 7:2), an overview of the public image of the nurse was presented, as well as the detractors and enhancers of this image. The focus of this article is on the nurse's own responsibility for image improvement and on enhancement strategies for the nurse supervisor. The payoff for correcting and improving the image of the nurse will be the satisfaction nurses derive from the caring role of nursing and the satisfaction of consumers—recipients of nursing care.

## ENHANCING THE NURSE'S IMAGE: SELF-RESPONSIBILITY

### The staff nurse

Nurses' self-image has an enormous influence on their behavior. Self-image embodies a firm nucleus of impressions that a person holds regarding herself or himself.

*Health Care Superv*, 1989, 7(3), 9–23
© 1989 Aspen Publishers, Inc.

These permanent and unchanging images form the self-concept that—to an incredible degree—determine how much of a person's innate potential is likely ever to be tapped. In addition, through a process of socialization, the nurse incorporates knowledge, ideas, and beliefs about nurses, the nursing role, nursing responsibilities, and the nature of professional nursing to yield images of the nurse and of nursing.[1] These images may be wholesome or unwholesome. The staff nurse has a responsibility to enhance the image of the nurse as well as that of nursing. Staff nurses own their behaviors related to self as nurse and as nurse projected to the public.

Foremost in image enhancement is the realization by the staff nurse that education makes a difference and that knowledge is power. Career options should be carefully planned so that academic preparation is appropriate to positions and responsibilities accepted by the staff nurse. If the staff nurse does not possess the minimal academic preparation for professional nursing—the baccalaureate degree in nursing—every effort should be made to offset this academic deficiency. Enhancement of the nurse's self-image is the outcome.

Supervisory and administrative positions in nursing require the master's degree as minimal educational preparation. Specialization in nursing requires master's and doctoral education in nursing. Pursuing educational goals that are similar to and concomitant with the educational goals of other health professionals will make the most significant positive impact upon the image of the nurse. Similar education among health professionals fosters colleagueship, shared power in health care, and professional autonomy. With comparable

education, the nurse would also be less likely to be "working under" someone.

Image enhancement opportunities abound within health care agencies. The nurse's sensitivity to image making would maximize use of these opportunities. For example, the nurse should monitor public relations material to ensure that nurses and nursing (the largest service in a health care agency) receive sufficient, accurate, appropriate, positive representation free of stereotypes perpetuated in the media. Public relations materials on the health care agency that heavily portray biomedical technology and physician specialists in action pictures send a strong covert message to the public about the value placed on nursing.

It is not unusual to see clients and their significant others watching "General Hospital" on television during visiting hours. Does the nurse take time to ask these clients and significant others how they feel about the portrayal of the nurse? How does their impression relate to reality? How does the nurse respond to these impressions?

While advertisements for employment opportunities for nurses fill the classified section of local and national newspapers, little definitive marketing strategy is undertaken to attract nurses to the staff or to foster an environment where nurses stay. Nurses should seek opportunities to review and participate in a marketing plan that interests professional nurses in joining the nursing staff and that interests prospective nursing students in selecting nursing as a career.

Staff nurses should make concerted efforts to develop liaisons with elementary and high school students. Arranging for students to spend time with the professional nurse in the health care setting can be an exciting and informative experience. Since staff nurses have multiple roles, being parents as well as nurses, image building with elementary and high school advisors could increase the number of students going into a nursing career. School counselors and advisors are in a strategic position to influence the career choices of adolescents. Recently a young woman, valedictorian of her high school class, could not convince the school counselor that *nursing*—and not medicine—was her choice. "You're too bright to go into nursing" was the advisor's response.

---

*The staff nurse should propose 30-second and 60-second prime time vignettes showing the present-day and future roles of nurses to offset the old stereotypes that linger.*

---

When successes in health care are being pronounced, the staff nurse should make certain that due credit is given to nurses and that nursing's share in the success is commensurate with nurse involvement. Kalisch and Kalisch[2] demonstrated in their research on the media image of the nurse that successful client outcomes are almost exclusively attributed to physicians. Nurses are involved daily in client situations in which the nurse is the prime agent in bringing about recovery. These situations abound for the very young and the very old clients. Why not share and propagate the triumphs?

To enhance the image of the nurse, the staff nurse must monitor the image portrayed in the printed and projected media on local, state, and national levels. Colleagues should be urged to do the same. Seeking input from clients and other personnel in the

health care setting would maximize the effort. In addition, the staff nurse should propose 30-second and 60-second prime time vignettes showing present-day and future roles of nurses to offset the old stereotypes that linger.

Caution should be exercised by the staff nurse when referring to one's role and place within the formal organization. Describing one's self as a "floor nurse" connotes to the listener an image of the nurse being "stepped on" or "walked all over." "I'm just a nurse" tells much about the staff nurse's image of self. How much more positive and wholesome to describe one's area as a unit—"I'm a critical care staff nurse on Nursing Unit 3," for example. "A positive nursing image requires personal responsibility. It is not enough to just talk. There needs to be action and personal commitment. The self-sacrificing role must evolve into a choice-maker role. A sense of self well-being leads to a sense of awareness and self-commitment. To provide a quality product, the provider must accept responsibility for self image."[3] Staff nurses have much to value in themselves as persons and as nurses. Valuing their service to others; their willingness to offer their strength, knowledge, and concern to consumers; and their commitment will foster an environment in which the consumer, too, will value these nurse qualities and nursing services.

### The nurse supervisor

In addition to participating in image enhancement as described above, the nurse supervisor can also promote a wholesome environment for the practice of nursing and can make the most of her or his place in the organizational level closest to top administration. An effective working environment, a factor in improving the image of the nurse, can ensure a healthy milieu, free of physical and emotional hazards for self and the staff nurse. Physical hazards include poor placement of equipment, furnishings, and the like that requires undue expenditure of energy to provide nursing care or lack of support services to lift, turn, or transport clients. The nurse is expected to transport clients throughout the health care agency so personnel in support service units can function effectively. Clients on nursing units, however, go unattended and an image of the nurse as service person is conveyed to all but client and self. Support service units in health care agencies should develop and pay for required transport services rather than expect the service from the staff nurse. This type of situation, if carefully monitored by the nurse supervisor, can enhance the nurse's image of self and the overall image of the nurse as direct caregiver for clients.

The nurse supervisor's strategic position allows her or him to suggest ways to the employer to increase interest in nursing. By pointing out infringements of autonomy and lack of input by nurses into policy making that directly affects them and the nursing care of clients, the supervisor can make improvements and enhance the nurse image.

The nurse supervisor should be an active member of professional and community organizations whose agendas include monitoring the existing image of the nurse. Participating with the membership in suggesting ways and means to promote the image of the nurse may be more effective than individual efforts.

A plan of recognition should be developed to enhance the value and self-esteem of staff and administrative nurses within the health care agency structure. Recognition should also be planned for nurse leaders, nurse scholars, and nurses involved in creative problem-solving efforts with clients, particularly since such recognition has a positive impact on nursing in the health care agency. Recognition should be planned throughout the year, rather than just once during National Nurse Week. Publicity about the recognitions should be maximized through all available media channels.

Another important way to enhance the image of the nurse as self and the image of nursing in the agency is through a journal of nursing. Active participation by nurses and invitational articles can set a tone for nursing in the agency and the professional nursing community. Such a journal would serve as an additional avenue for recognition. Great care should be taken that it does not deteriorate into an official organ for administrative pronouncements.

If invited by television, radio, or other media, the nurse supervisor should seek counsel from colleagues and participate in prior role playing so that she or he projects an effective, intelligent, and caring image. The nurse supervisor should be alert to, but refrain from responding to, stereotypes or arguing. Seasoned interviewers, particularly those on national talk shows, may attempt to create agitation to appeal to viewers, to the peril of the image of the nurse. Consumers remember the complaining and griping behaviors of nurses encouraged by talk show hosts. It is important that the nurse supervisor talk positively of self and of the service of nursing.

The nurse supervisor is in an ideal position to prevent injustices to staff nurses and self by being alert to problem situations and applying the problem-solving process. It is easier to practice preventative problem identification and resolution than to handle the fallout from failure to act, especially in situations that negatively affect the nurse's image of self and the image of nursing in the health care agency. The nurse supervisor should be part of the solution rather than the problem.

### Scenario of negative impact of nurse supervisor

The following true scenario illustrates the negative impact of the nurse supervisor upon the self–image of the nurse and the image of nursing in a health care agency.

A client, terminally ill with cancer, was given a narcotic for pain at 11:00 P.M. by the evening nurse. When the night nurse arrived for the shift at 11:00 P.M. and noted this client crying, she again gave the client a prescribed narcotic for pain. The error was made known shortly thereafter when the client developed respiratory distress and was transferred to the intensive care unit. The client's physician was notified of the error and became livid with anger at the nurse who made the error. He contacted the nurse administrator to report the drug accident and demanded to meet with unit nursing staff members at 10:00 A.M. the following day. The nurse administrator concurred with the physician and arranged the meeting.

On the way to the meeting, the client's physician and his two residents boarded an elevator full of varied staff and visitors. The physician spoke to the residents about the incompetent nursing staff and about the overdose. All attention was on the physician as the elevator passed four floors. The physician and residents entered the conference room where the entire day nursing staff of a busy progressive care unit was convened. The nurse administrator was in attendance. No nurses were available to care for clients in the interim. The physician expressed his outrage at the nurses. One nurse made an attempt to state that no nurse at the meeting was involved. She was effectively silenced by the nurse administrator and the physician. The physician "vented his spleen" for 20 minutes, then left. The nurse slowly left the meeting in disbelief, embarrassed and angry at the injustice perpetrated by the physician and nurse administrator.

### Scenario of positive impact of nurse supervisor

The next scenario, in contrast, depicts the positive influence on the image of the nurse and nursing by the supervising nurse.

A dispute was in progress in a hospital's emergency care unit between the members of the emergency medical group staffing the emergency care unit and the staff nurses of the unit. One physician in particular who was new to the medical group required that any clients presenting themselves for treatment following an accident and whom he suspected of being under the influence of alcohol be *required* to accept the prescribed treatment. Clients' views about this treatment or their refusal of treatment were ignored.

A woman was admitted after being involved in a car accident. She was strapped to the stretcher and wanted to be removed from the restraints. No data were available to indicate the woman was under the influence of alcohol; no blood alcohol analysis was done. The physician refused to have the restraints removed. The client was upset and wanted to be released. The nurse intervened and took the client to X-ray to verify that no spinal injury was present. The nurse reasoned that if the client left the premises, at least a selected assessment would have been accomplished. After the client refused any further treatment and insisted upon leaving, the physician wanted the nurse to bring the client back and restrain her in the emergency unit. The nurse facilitated the client's signing of the medical release form prior to her leaving. The physician would not accept the signed release and demanded that the nurse bring back the client and "tie her down." The nurse refused to follow the command. The physician reported the nurse to the emergency physicians.

Rumors were circulated that efforts were under way to meet and confront the nurse and to make certain nurses followed *all* physician *orders*. Hearing the rumor, the head nurse of the unit and nursing staff members developed their database, verified the data, and prepared a plan of action to use to verify their role and responsibilities in the emergency unit and to protect the rights of clients while assuring their safety. Rumors were leaked about the nurses' plan to confront the physicians with not only client rights and the episode described, but also concerns including sexual harassment, poor attitude of physicians toward clients, and physician errors.

A meeting was scheduled. The full nursing staff and the head nurse attended, but only one-third of the physicians were present. The physician involved in the episode and one reported earlier for sexual harassment were absent. The tone of the meeting was subdued, and those attending stated their concerns. A mutual sharing ensued; communication between the nurses and physicians was enhanced. Expert legal ad-

vice was sought on the handling of clients suspected of having alcohol in their bodies and incorporated in a protocol acceptable to physicians and nurses and responsive to the rights of consumers to be involved in decision making about their care and the choices available regarding this care. The nurses, all women, received a formal written apology regarding sexual harassment in the emergency unit. Plans were developed to meet, share, and communicate on an ongoing basis.

A follow-up call was made to the client described in the episode to determine her health status and learn of any complications. The woman, who was in good condition with no complications, complained that the physician had been rude and rough during his examination of her. She appreciated the help she received from the nurses and chided them for "not standing up to the physician more."

### Other nurse supervisor initiatives to enhance the nurse's image

Nurse-initiated interdisciplinary meetings to share role developments in nursing and bring forth the feelings, problems, expectations, and accomplishments of the staff would contribute much to offset stereotypes of nursing held by health personnel. The nurse supervisor, in concert with other nurse supervisors and nurse administrative staff, could initiate the planning of meetings around luncheons or receptions and thereby broaden the agenda for scholarly nursing presentations. Such meetings would be an excellent forum for sharing results of nursing research in progress in the health care agency or discussing research that could be brought to the agency.

*Nurse involvement in research would not only have direct results for nursing services but would also boost the image of the nurse as a professional, a scholar.*

The nurse supervisor's support of nursing research within the health care agency is a direct benefit for the consumers of nursing through improved nursing practice. Nurse involvement in research (not merely as data collectors for the research of other health professionals) would not only have direct results for nursing services but would also boost the image of the nurse as a professional, a scholar. Research can be a means of enhancing communication among colleagues.

Most health care agencies do a follow-up evaluation after a client's stay in the agency. The nurse supervisor should review the questions pertaining to nursing. Do the questions focus on the nurses' ability to assess the client's strengths and problems related to health and nursing? Is the planning of nursing care developed jointly by the nurse and client? Were the health problems designated accurately? Were solutions acceptable to the client and effective in offsetting the problem related to health and nursing? Was an evaluation of goal achievement for the client's health status conducted and were the goals accomplished? Were nursing strategies implemented with care and expertise, and did they accommodate the humanity of the client and his or her significant others? These are but a few questions that should be developed to provide data and indirectly verify the role of the nurse in application of the nursing process. These

very questions promote the image of the nurse and facilitate the client's conception of the nurse and nursing care. Feedback from such questions is likely to validate the value of nursing services, define areas to be strengthened, and be conveyed to prospective consumers.

The nurse supervisor's sense of personal value and professional worth is strategic in the service of clients; in the supervision of nursing staff; and in relationships with nurse administrative officers, health care administrative officers, and health professional colleagues. This sense sets the tone for relationships and conveys a positive, worthwhile image for others to emulate. It is true that the public reflects images of the nurse and nursing that are held by the nurse. "The professional nurse is the client's prime product in the health care industry. A positive self-image enables the nurse to market the nursing product and to produce a favorable public image."[4]

## STRATEGIES FOR IMAGE ENHANCEMENT FOR THE NURSE SUPERVISOR: PROFESSIONAL RESPONSIBILITY

The nurse supervisor enjoys a unique placement within the formal organization— close to the operation of specific services and to the formation of policy at nursing and hospital administrative levels. These services are indispensable in ensuring that detailed performance of nursing service meets the goals and objectives of the health care agencies. The nurse supervisor's behavior incorporates (1) planning the performance of specialized services, (2) delegating authority, (3) providing generalized and specialized instruction, (4) fostering nursing staff performance in accordance with academic preparation, (5) supporting personal and interpersonal relationships, and (6) promoting group cohesiveness and pride.[5] The nurse supervisor needs to be vigilant to protect the nurse's autonomy in decision making related to nursing practice. Furthermore, if self-governance and autonomy for nursing are not realities in the health care agency, energy should be mobilized to ensure that they become so. Autonomy and self-governance are "givens" for a viable image for nurses and nursing in any health care agency.

From supervision's vantage point the nurse supervisor can implement strategies to fulfill the professional responsibility of image enhancement for the nurse and for nursing. Strategies may be grouped into (1) those strategies effective in the internal environments and (2) those effective in the external environments that affect the practice of nursing. These strategies are presented below.

### Internal environment

The nurse supervisor may implement certain strategies to enhance the image of the nurse and the image of nursing within the practice setting.

- Pass on the positive responses from clients and colleagues about quality of nursing care—and not just the complaints. Failure to share positive feedback is a significant source of low self-esteem for nursing staff. This also applies to the nurse supervisor's need to receive positive feedback from nursing and hospital administrative officers.
- Analyze complaints about nursing care and validate these complaints with a database. Unsupported complaints should be analyzed as to their source, and strategies should be developed to eliminate them or the source.
- Expect nursing staff to provide quality care to clients. The nursing supervisor's expectations have a very significant impact on the way the nursing staff actually perform. Expectation of perfection in the nurse's every endeavor is an impossible one, however, and the basis for a diminished self-image for the nurse. Let the nursing staff know they are accepted despite flaws and shortcomings; set the stage for a desire to improve one's service performance.
- Display sensitivity to the impact of supervisory behaviors on the nursing staff. The supervisor cannot damage or degrade the staff nurses' self-image on the one hand and legitimately expect their performance to improve on the other. A nursing staff member's performance is *not* the person.
- Remember: A nursing staff member who comes away from a performance evaluation interview thinking and feeling more highly of herself or himself and aspiring to achieve professional goals, comes away with an improved self-image. This improved self-image translates to improved nursing service.
- Foster peer relationships among nursing staff members. Staff members' need for acceptance and recognition can be met through such relationships. The result is a positive impact on image of self and of nursing. These relationships can defuse stressful experiences and lend support at significant times during the practice experience.

- Be alert to the feelings and concerns of the nursing staff—particularly those related to overwork, sexual harassment, misuse of staff competencies, labeling of persons, and evidence of "put-down" types of communication. Provide a formal vehicle for sharing these concerns and for problem solving.
- Act as advocate for the nursing staff to ensure adequate resources for the practice of nursing—academically and experientially qualified staff, operational equipment, consultation services, professional development, and opportunities and recognition (both monetary and award publication). Aiken points out a concern that nurses are very "versatile" in a hospital.

---

*Failure to respond to blatant detractors to the image of the nurse might be interpreted as agreement.*

---

"Nurses can substitute for all kinds of technicians and other professionals. Nurses in certain circumstances can substitute for physicians. A case can be made that if such versatile workers can be had at nursing's relatively lower wage then the demand of such workings in hospitals will be high."[6] Nurse supervisors and staff nurses should be alert to misuse of nursing talents, misdirection, and overgeneralization—particularly on weekends and evening and night shifts. Negotiate for adequate support services so that the offering of nursing services is not compromised.
- Refrain from perpetuating the myth that "a nurse is a nurse is a nurse."

Failure to recognize academic and experiential differences in staff when assigning responsibilities and promoting autonomy can have disastrous results for those nurses who are well prepared, as well as for those in situations for which they are ill-prepared and lack vision and insight.
- Establish a nursing newsletter within the agency. Collaborate with other nurse supervisors if necessary. The newsletter can serve to (1) promote original ideas developed by nurses; (2) recognize those who have had articles published and who have presented papers; and (3) feature nursing staff members—who they are, what they do, their lives away from the work setting, and their community and professional contributions. The newsletter can effectively enhance the image of nursing.
- Let nursing staff know the effects of advocacy with nursing and hospital administrators. Seeking input from nursing staff prior to administrative meetings and interviews can have a positive impact on the image of the nurse as staff nurse as well as that of the nurse supervisor. The nurse supervisor will likely continue to be viewed positively, even though meeting and interview outcomes might be less than expected. Provide feedback and allow for strategies for continued negotiation. Such action will maintain the positive momentum and likely result in successful goal achievement.
- Be alert to detractors of the image of the nurse and intervene quickly to raise the consciousness of persons involved—be they nurses, other health personnel, or nonhealth personnel. Failure to re-

spond to blatant detractors to the image of the nurse might be interpreted as agreement.

- Arrange forums about professional concerns and attitudes for nursing staff members, physicians, and representatives of significant support service units. The physicians invited to attend should be secure in their professional role and should value and respect relationships with other health professionals. Mutual sharing of concerns and group cohesiveness can result and can significantly enhance the image of the nurse, as well as the image of other health professionals.

- Collaborate with other nurse supervisors to establish a nursing research unit. Demonstrate that nursing makes a difference in clients' pursuit of optimal wellness through testing of nursing strategies, varying staffing patterns, and modalities. Recognize the value of nursing research. Arrange for actual research to occur. Then the image of nursing in the health care agency will be substantially enhanced. An important result of recent research for nursing (though nursing was not the focus) came from Dr. William Kanaus and his colleagues at George Washington University School of Medicine. The researchers calculated clients' risks of death in the intensive care unit (ICU) using the tool, APACHE II. Differences in outcome were directly related to dramatic differences in nursing care—a serendipitous finding. When nurses were able to make adjustments and decisions about client treatment and care and when nurses were respected and were able to operate semi-

autonomously, the client death rate was lower.[7] These findings were an excellent image booster.

- Review public relations materials generated by the health care agency to ensure that coverage of nursing is appropriate and just.

- Control the need to feel guilty or to make nurse staff members feel guilty in the work setting. Develop more savvy about propagating the contribution of nurses and nursing within the health care setting—learn and use the political structure of the health care agency. Mullane states that her natural professional bias leads her to predict that client care can be improved only if nurses become really serious about engaging in institutional politics, and only if their efforts are sustained.[8]

- Arrange for inservice education programs for nursing staff that incorporate political process content.

- Monitor employment contracts for fairness and recognition of advanced education and competencies of nursing staff, including the nurse supervisor.

- Offset any academic deficits by achieving the baccalaureate degree in nursing and the master's degree in nursing as minimal academic preparation for specialization in nursing and administration.

- Look for writing talent among nursing staff; encourage authorship of stories for children and adults that foster positive images of the nurse and the practice of nursing. Collaborate with talented consumers who view their experience with nursing positively and thereby maximize the writing and image enhancement effort.

- Review with nurse supervisor colleagues the administrative structure for nursing and its viability. Are staff nurses supportive of the administrative structure? Do they find it workable? Do staff nurses feel valued within the structure? Do they appeal to the nurse supervisor for assistance on problem solving and resolving dilemmas with the work experience and in the work setting? Or do staff nurses take their problems to non-nurses—physicians, for example? Are nurse peer review and joint decisional authority critical components of the organization?
- Foster nurse–physician colleagueship when possible. Joint planning for client care necessitates and therefore lends itself particularly well to cooperative interventions.
- Convey respect to nurse and non-nurse associates and expect respect in return.
- Analyze the workload and the work environment of the staff nurse (and the nurse supervisor) to ensure time for meals and for "protected time" away from the nursing unit for using the agency library; participate in relaxation exercise; participating in committee activities; doing research; sharing experiences with nursing students, potential nursing students, and consumers. Negotiate for physical space for these activities. Establish support groups as needed.
- Promote the right of academically qualified nursing personnel to self-determination, governance without outside control, and the capacity for professional independence. Aroskar states, "Independence places some immediate limitations on autonomy of

any group of health professionals since health care often requires the technical expertise of several disciplines."[9] Aroskar further indicates that professional autonomy requires that practitioners be self-regulating and have control over their practice in employment settings. "Nurses are confronted daily with the reality that others are (or consider themselves to be) in control of nursing."[10]
- Plan quality time away from the worksetting and expect the nursing staff to do the same. Facilitate time adjustment for staff who wish to avail themselves of professional enhancement and replenishing leisure activities. Seek out overcommitted staff nurses and facilitate their acceptance of and plans for quality time away from the practice setting. Refer these staff nurses for counseling assistance in self-development away from the work setting. These efforts can have a remarkably positive effect on the person of the nurse, which can translate into a positive professional image.

### External environment

The nurse supervisor may engage in the following additional strategies to enhance the images of the nurse and of nursing:

- Convene, with the assistance of nurse supervisor colleagues, an advisory group of prominent citizens and consumers of nursing. Seek advice about and discuss (1) contributions of nursing service; (2) ways to maximize the contribution of nurses; and (3) ways and means to clarify and enhance the image of nurses—practitioners, researchers, teachers, and administrators, for example.

- Support academically and experientially qualified nurses in becoming members of local, state, and national governmental and nongovernmental commissions, committees, and agencies and thus ensure nurse representation and input on deliberations affecting nurses and nursing. The nurse supervisor's name may be among those names submitted.

- Support nursing organizations through active membership. Target improvement of the image of the nurse as a priority. Encourage and reward nurse staff members who actively fulfill a commitment to organizational activities, particularly those that enhance the image of the nurse.

- Establish lines of communication with prominent media figures so that they know where to seek expert nurse input when nurses and nursing are the focus of media efforts. Give compliments when deserved but also point out media portrayals that require improvement. Focus more heavily on philosophical and social impact of the portrayal rather than its technical dimensions. Provide the media with anecdotes from the wealth of nurse experiences. According to Owsley, "A positive image should be the prime message to the media. Focusing on self-image and emphasizing nursing's assets will help to dissipate the negative force [see Part 1, *HCS* 7:2]. Blaming the situation, demographic data, the media, or administration leads to negative results without positive opportunities. When professional nurses work together for a particular purpose, the work is bettered by cooperation."[11]

- Recommend for awards those media producers who present the wholesome, significant service of nurses. The American Academy of Nursing (AAN) and Sigma Theta Tau International, the honor society of nursing, present media awards during annual and biennial meetings of the membership. The Columbia Broadcasting System (CBS) was the recipient of the media award of the AAN for 1986 and 1987.

- Invite a news reporter to spend a day with the professional nurse. Take time to explain the intellectual skills used, the effort of setting priorities, the sensitivity to timing of nursing interventions, the observations, the conclusions, the flexibility of style to accommodate the client condition and mood, the person- and family-centered efforts of planning nursing care, and the creativity and comfort in participating *with* the client rather than *doing to* the client.

- Establish liaison with faculty members, particularly those in baccalaureate and higher-degree programs in nursing. Joint efforts between representatives of nursing education and nursing service increase the credibility of nursing and, therefore, its image. Refrain from any situations that convey divisiveness and lack of consensus about matters of importance.

- Meet regularly with consumer groups such as chapters of the American Association of Retired Persons; with parents of children in elementary, junior, and senior high school (e.g., PTAs); and with school counselors to share what nurses do. Arrange discussions with and observations of staff for interested persons, particularly young students, by planning experiences such as "a day with...." Observing and conversing with a caring nurse can do much to enhance the image participants have of the nurse and reverse the prevailing stereotypes.

- Support sustained advertising or public relations efforts to improve the image of nursing in concert with nurse supervisors in other health care agencies, including ambulatory care, home care, and community health agencies. Identify those characteristics of nurses and the role of nurses for special treatment in advertising.

- Sponsor health fairs, seminars, and workshops that introduce nurses to citizens of the community. Bring in nurse leaders to enhance the image of the nurse. Funding could be shared by several agencies and be a collaborative effort of nursing service personnel from all local health care agencies. Representation should reflect both nursing staff and nurse administrators.

- Contact, with the help of nurse colleagues, legislators to provide updated information about professional nursing practice and the nursing care needs

---

*This consensus leads to the predicted image for the 1980s and 1990s of the "nurse careerist."*

---

of consumers, particularly the elderly. Kalisch and Kalisch ask, "How can legislators make informed decisions about the expansion of nursing practice when they, too, may suffer from me-

dia-induced misconceptions about the profession? The future of nursing requires that voters and politicians understand that nurses do not operate within the restricted sphere of menial duties shown on television."[12]

## IMPLICATIONS FOR THE FUTURE

"You could tell the difference between those who had deep convictions about themselves and those who did not. People who had deep seated beliefs about the meaning of life [and the value of their service], who knew who they were, were simply not afraid anymore," reports E. Fitzgerald.[13] This statement incorporates a significant message for the nurse supervisor and contains a prediction about the future for nursing and its image. Unless nurses propagate their deep convictions about caring about and for consumers and unless nurses fearlessly describe the benefits of this care, image struggles will continue.

Vernice Ferguson, President, Sigma Theta Tau International, reported on the honor society's first national level "think tank" conference: The conference reached a consensus that many widely held beliefs about the nursing shortage were myths, that the current shortage has less to do with an untapped reservoir of nurses than with many new needs brought on by greater demands from a more complicated delivery system, and that fundamental changes need to take place that provide nurses with authority worthy of the responsibility they bear.[14]

This consensus leads to the predicted image for the 1980s and 1990s of the "nurse careerist." This image is one that "emphasizes equality, commitment to career, and renunciation of nursing as a physician-dominated occupation demanding an impossible degree of obedience."[15] Substitution of androgyny for traditional, rigid female imagery in media nurse representations would effectively provide alternative role models that would begin to open nursing up as a strong career option for both sexes.[16] The nurse's incorporation of this careerist image model would significantly enhance the nurse's image in the future. This careerist image would replace the dysfunctional stereotypes that diminish self-identity and self-esteem. As Kalisch and Kalisch point out, "What is needed now is to create a new ideal nurse image for the 1980s and 1990s...an intelligent, logical, progressive, sophisticated, empathetic, and assertive woman or man who is committed to attaining higher and higher standards of health care for the American public."[17]

A significant implication for the future of the image of the nurse lies in efforts to appropriately cost-out nursing. In many instances today, nursing services come with the room, bedsheets, meals, and paper towels. Determining the legitimate cost of nursing would do much to cancel the image of the nurse as a disposable commodity much like meals and paper products. It could even be speculated that, once costs are known, consumers would be impressed with the dollar value of nursing services.

Image improvement will be marked if more men enter nursing. The obliteration of sex stereotypes—particularly the negative image of women's work—would enhance the image of the nurse. Bem believes that the "truly important effects of sex stereotypes occur not at the individual level, but at the institutional level."[18] After delineating sex stereotypes in the hospital work environment (similar to those noted in Part 1, *HCS* 7:2 and in this article), she concludes, "...physicians and hospital administrators thought such a work environment to be appropriate for women or they thought that women would not fight to have a more professional work environment...would have thought it inappropriate for men or they would have thought men would fight it."[19] The message for the nurse supervisor is that nurses cannot wait for attitudes toward them to change but must face a new environment so they rightfully share in the benefits resulting from services rendered by nurses to both the health care agency and to consumers. As Barnard states, "Real success of image development will come with the personal encounters nurses have with each other, their patients, clients, with mayors, city council members, with scholars, congressmen, with labor union leaders, business and professional colleagues—encounters in which they demonstrate and discuss their own practice."[20] It is significant for nurses "to revalue their role, understand their reason for being, and assess the social consequences of their role. If nurses do these things, there will be a change in institutional structures.... Behavior is a strong way to bring about image change."[21]

Lucy Kelly reminds nurses that "regardless of what the public sees on TV, in X-rated movies, in newspapers or magazines, people are not stupid. They know that those are indeed images, and although they may believe some aspect of those images if they choose to, they only choose to if they aren't already influenced by another image of the nurse. And that is the image of what they see in 'real life,' their contact with a real nurse in the various settings in which people seek health care."[22] She offers suggestions to ensure an enhanced image for the future: (1) develop a critical mass of nurses whom nurses and nurse supervisors would like to see as image makers in places where consumers "can see and talk to and be touched" by these nurses; (2) encourage a sense of pride and power in being a nurse, starting with nursing students, and incorporating nurse specialist practitioners, researchers, teachers, and administrators; and (3) take advantage of the positive image nurses *do* have with many of their public.[23]

•    •    •

Thus, the future image of the nurse will be bright if nurses project their own positive image of nursing and if nurses convey collectively and with solidarity their deep belief in nursing and their commitment to provide competent, compassionate nursing to consumers for all their publics to hear.

"The only difference, the very only one, is that they have begun to understand what they really are and have begun to practice it."[24]

## REFERENCES

1. Kalisch, B., and Kalisch, P. "Anatomy of the Image of the Nurse: Dissonant and Ideal Models." In *Image Making in Nursing*, edited by C. Williams. Kansas City, Mo.: American Academy of Nursing, 1983, p. 3.
2. Ibid.
3. Owsley, V. "The Nursing Shortage—Nurses Take Action!" In *Healthcare Careers of Tennessee and Kentucky*, 1987, p. 10.
4. Ibid.
5. Yura, H., Ozimek, D., and Walsh, M. *Nursing Leadership: Theory and Process.* 2d ed. New York: Appleton-Century-Crofts, 1981.
6. Aiken, L. "Nurses for the Future: Breaking the Shortage Cycles." *American Journal of Nursing* 87 (December 1987): 1617.
7. Holzman, D. "Intensive Care Nurses: A Vital Sign." *Insight* Reprint. December 1986.
8. Mullane, M.K. "Nursing Care and the Political Arena." In *Readings in Community Health Nursing*, edited by B.W. Spradley, 2d ed. Boston: Little, Brown, 1982, p. 89.
9. Aroskar, M.A. "Establishing Limits to Professional Autonomy: Whose Responsibility." *Nursing Law and Ethics* 1 (May 1980): 1.
10. Ibid.
11. Owsley, "The Nursing Shortage," 10.
12. Kalisch, P., and Kalisch, B. "Nurses on Prime-Time Television." *American Journal of Nursing* 82 (February 1982): 270.
13. Fitzgerald, E. "What Keeps Us Going?" *Pace* (April 1987): 7.
14. Ferguson, V. "Arista 87: A Focus on the Nursing Shortage." *Sigma Theta Tau Chapter Officers' Newsletter* (September 1987): 8.
15. Kalisch and Kalisch, "Anatomy of the Image of the Nurse," p. 19.
16. Ibid.
17. Ibid., 21
18. Bem, S. "The Making of Images: A Psychological Perspective." In *Image Making in Nursing*, edited by C. Williams. Kansas City, Mo.: American Academy of Nursing, 1983, p. 43.
19. Ibid.
20. Barnard, K. "Discussion of Dr. Hill's Paper." In *Image Making in Nursing*, edited by C. Williams. Kansas City, Mo.: American Academy of Nursing, 1983, p. 59.
21. Ibid.
22. Kelly, L. "Discussion of Dr. Lindeman's Paper." In *Image Making in Nursing*, edited by C. Williams. Kansas City, Mo.: American Academy of Nursing, 1983, p. 67.
23. Ibid.
24. Bach, R. *Jonathan Livingston Seagull.* New York: Macmillan, 1970, p. 83.

# Nursing leadership evaluation

*Helen Yura*
*Professor of Nursing*
*Graduate Program Director*
*Department of Nursing*
*Old Dominion University*
*Norfolk, Virginia*

T HE NURSE LEADER may be found at all organizational levels of the health care system. The leader serving at the supervisor or head nurse level is in the hierarchy of the formal organization that is closest to effecting the detailed nursing care provided to clients of health care. It is the provision of expert nursing care when and where it is needed that fulfills the overall goal and objectives of a health care organization. The nurse supervisor is closest to and most directly involved with the nursing staff; the number of persons with whom the nurse supervisor is involved is larger than that for the nurse manager or for the nurse administrator.

*This article is adapted with permission from Yura, H., Ozimek, D., and Walsh, M.B. Nursing Leadership: Theory and Process 2nd ed. New York: Appleton-Century-Crofts, 1981.*

*Health Care Superv*, 1984,2(3),16–28
© 1984 Aspen Publishers, Inc.

## NURSING LEADERSHIP

Nursing leadership is viewed as a process whereby a person who is a nurse affects the actions of others in goal determination and achievement.[1] Nursing is an encounter with a person and family as clients in which the nurse contributes to the maintenance of optimum health and provides care during illness until the client can resume a normal life. When recovery is not possible, the nurse provides compassionate assistance as long as life is a reality.[2]

The process of nursing leadership comprises the behaviors of deciding, relating, influencing and facilitating. When goals are determined and realized through the use of these four categories of behavior, the participants—the leader and followers—will have participated in a leadership act. Communication permeates the use of the process and nursing leadership evaluation is realized through judgments about the way the leader decides, relates, influences and facilitates goal determination and goal achievement. It is noted that being in a supervisory position does not determine leadership status; rather, the use of the nursing leadership process designates the supervisor as leader. This process framework for nursing leadership evaluation is guided by the following premises.

- Evaluation is viewed as feedback regarding behavioral events comprising acts of leadership inherent in deciding, relating, influencing and facilitating (DRIF).
- Evaluation is an ongoing vital activity in which judgments are made about quality of experiences, goals and outcomes based on predetermined leadership expectations and standards or criteria.
- The nursing leadership process components and related behaviors serve as criteria or standards for evaluation of leadership behaviors.
- Evaluation is mainly an intellectual activity that requires a framework of tools and techniques for data gathering and quantification.
- Quantification of data about leadership behavior results in a judgment that leadership was satisfactory because goal designation and goal achievement were achieved, or leadership was unsatisfactory because goal designation and goal achievement were not achieved.
- Job descriptions for the nurse leader in a supervisory position in a formal health care organization should reflect the type and caliber of decision making expected, the manner of relationships and the persons involved, the expectation of influence, and the range and capability for facilitation of unit goals.
- A formalized plan for evaluation should be specified and implemented for the nurse supervisor. Opportunities for formal and informal evaluation should be reflected in the plan.

• Evaluation (formal and informal) should result in a growth experience for the evaluator and evaluatee.

## EVALUATION OF NURSING LEADERSHIP

To facilitate use of the process framework for nursing leadership evaluation, the situations of two nurse supervisors of critical care nursing units will be used.

### The situation of Ms. Ballister

Ms. Ballister had been appointed critical care supervisor for a large critical care unit in a south side health care agency in the city of Middleton two years ago. Throughout her tenure as supervisor, her major effort was pleading for staff coverage of the unit. Top priority was given to finding critical care nurses to come to work on short notice. When nursing staff members were found, it followed that an inordinate amount of additional work time was devoted to orienting these staff members. Few of the temporary or float staff returned to the unit, which could have lessened some of the orientation time.

The unit had a 40 percent turnover rate and a high sick day use rate by the nursing staff. Ms. Ballister prided herself on the orientation program she developed for new critical care nurses. She expected each critical care nurse to work toward and to achieve certification. Ms. Ballister's

second priority was teaching the critical care preparatory course on an ongoing basis to ensure a continuing supply of prepared staff nurses.

In an effort to ease the workload of the nursing staff, nursing care conferences were kept to a minimum, and an assortment of policies were developed to save time (e.g., limiting family members' visiting time and restricting phone calls to designated times during each shift). Nursing staff members expected Ms. Ballister to help out when staff was short. If she engaged in paperwork, staff commented negatively. In response, Ms. Ballister helped with bathing, lifting and distributing medications. Ms. Ballister was sensitive to the plight of the critical care nursing staff and mindful of the great demands placed on the nursing staff by clients in the unit and their physicians.

Ms. Ballister solicited the aid of the medical staff to plead her case for more help in the critical care unit. Physicians followed through by personally visiting the director of nursing to describe limitations of nursing care due to insufficient staffing and to ask for relief. The director of nursing met with the critical care supervisor and nursing staff to share the imposed budgetary constraints and to state that nursing care costs in the critical care unit were the highest of any department in the hospital. No more monies could be allocated.

During the two-year period that Ms. Ballister served as supervisor, no formal evaluation was provided for her, and she requested none. On occasion the director of nursing suggested to Ms. Ballister that she try some creative approaches to solve the ongoing staff problem since additional staff would not be forthcoming. At the end of her second year, Ms. Ballister requested and was approved for transfer out of the critical care area. She was reassigned as nurse supervisor of a self-care unit and of outpatient services.

## The situation of Ms. Redins

In a similar situation in another health care agency on the north side of Middleton was Ms. Redins, critical care supervisor. She too had responsibility for a large critical care unit. She had been appointed about the same time to head the critical care unit as was Ms. Ballister. Ms. Redins faced a 50 percent turnover rate, a 60 percent absentee and sick leave rate, and complaints of omissions in nursing care from physicians, family members and critical care nurses themselves.

Initially Ms. Redins's efforts were geared to "get coverage," but simultaneously she sought to obtain data that might shed some light on the reasons for the high turnover and absentee rates. On appointment to the position of critical care supervisor, she was provided with a job description, an orientation to the supervisory process and a monthly conference with the director of nursing to explore the goals for the unit and the progress toward goal achievement. The director offered the support Ms. Redins

needed, maintaining an open door policy. In addition, Ms. Redins was scheduled for and received a formal annual evaluation by the director of nursing.

Ms. Redins spent the first three months in her position collecting data about activity and demand levels for services in the unit. She shared her impressions resulting from these data with the critical care nursing staff who seemed surprised that the supervisor did collect data and that these data seemed to point to three high-demand times during which existing nursing staff were particularly vulnerable to high stress levels, errors and exhaustion.

Ms. Redins had developed a tally sheet for more intense data collection and invited the nursing staff to participate in a month-long collection experience on an individual basis. These data would be processed and used for problem identification and resolution. Though participation was voluntary, every critical care nurse decided to participate. Orientation to data collection followed, and the study was formally launched covering the entire 24-hour period of nursing activity. Physicians and family members were oriented to the project; they voiced support with some skepticism that anything could be done to change the situation.

Concurrently, Ms. Redins collected data about the client census and needs, and physician and family members' satisfactions and dissatisfactions. Ms. Redins also needed data about the work patterns of critical care staff members (days and times absent) along with contrasting data from other nursing units in the hospital. Getting these data from personnel services proved to be a major obstacle. Despite a clear explanation of the purpose for the information it was considered too time consuming to retrieve the data; there was an inherent sensitivity to "letting this information out" to a nursing staff member. Anonymity was assured. Ms. Redins solicited the intervention of the director of nursing. Eventually the data were released on a weekly basis. Ms. Redins plotted the data on graphs to increase usability and readability of the dated data.

In addition to orientation to data gathering, critical care staff nurses were encouraged to search the nursing literature for research articles about job satisfaction, staffing patterns (particularly in critical care units), causes for staff shortages and absenteeism, as well as for tested solutions that might be applicable to the current situation. To encourage this exploration, Ms. Redins planned for two hours of library release time

---

*Critical care staff nurses were encouraged to search the nursing literature for research articles about job satisfaction, staffing patterns, causes for staff shortages and absenteeism, as well as for tested solutions that might be applicable to the current situation.*

---

for each staff member on a weekly basis. Members were provided with a list of library resources in the city and were expected to annotate sources most useful for distribution to the critical care nursing staff.

Data were tabulated on a weekly basis with two different critical care nursing staff participating each week. This activity generated much interest and spurred staff on to submit more accurate and more complete data for tabulation. Physicians expressed interest and waited to see results from the weekly tabulations.

As data unfolded, activity demands recurred in regular patterns with significantly increased activity in the early morning when personal care for clients, nursing rounds, medical rounds and orders, laboratory tests, and body weights of patients took place. Early afternoon was a second heavy demand period when admissions and transfers, conferences, preadmission and posttransfer visits, and other high-priority occurrences coincided. The final demand period was noted in late evening when physicians made rounds, when clients were prepared for the evening and night, and when restocking and administrative activities prevailed.

When all data were tabulated and shared, the following questions emerged. How do we handle the three peak periods of nursing activity? And if handled, will job satisfaction increase and staff turnover and absenteeism decrease? To answer these questions, the phase of problem resolution was planned by the critical care nursing staff. Ms. Redins served as chairperson of a committee of the whole since all nursing staff members expressed interest. A physician was included as a voting committee member. The committee's activities were outlined for a three-month period and included activities gleaned by nursing staff from the literature search. These activities included a study of advantages and disadvantages of the use of 8-, 10- and 12-hour shifts; a study of the advantages of an all RN nursing staff for the critical care unit and the optimal educational mix, and continued data collection regarding staff turnover and absenteeism. A task force approach was used to accomplish the tasks.

After data from these activities were assembled by the task forces and analyzed by the committee of the whole, it was decided that a pilot study of the use of variable shifts (8-hour, 10-hour, 12-hour) be used with the heaviest coverage and shift overlaps planned for the three peak nursing activity periods. The pilot study was initiated for a six-month period. Conference time was planned for time overlaps and reaction sheets were submitted by each critical care nurse at the end of each week. Data from these reaction sheets were analyzed. Simultaneously, data were collected on turnover and absenteeism and sick leave use. At the end of the pilot period, data revealed that critical care nurses viewed with satisfaction the variable shift patterns. These patterns met individual work needs and could accommodate the fluctuat-

ing demands by the staff nurse's family or desire to pursue advanced education. The critical care nurse staff voted to continue the variable shift pattern for another six months with a scheduled evaluation of the pattern at the end of the time period.

One year later, data showed that turnover dropped to 20 percent with a significant increase in the number of interdepartmental requests for staff transfer to the critical care unit. In addition, a 50 percent drop in absenteeism and sick leave use was recorded. Within one and one-half years of the initiation of the problem-solving effort, problem resolution was in sight. Throughout this period the director of nursing served as support person, influencer and facilitator for Ms. Redins. Staff voiced satisfaction and requested that the two-hour, library release time be continued. There was increased interest among critical care nurses to pursue advanced nursing education with 25 percent making formal application to baccalaureate and master's programs in nursing.

With this level of success, other problems were identified for problem solving over the next year. Top priority was given to a study of the problems and concerns of family members of clients in the critical care unit and determining the means to solve them.

Formal evaluation of Ms. Redins was based on behavioral data related to decision making—relating to nursing staff, clients and their families, and physicians—influencing and facilitating the goals of the critical care unit. Ms. Redins enjoys her position and wants to continue to develop the position of supervisor of the critical care unit.

Were both Ms. Ballister and Ms. Redins nurse leaders, and to what extent each were they using the components of the nursing leadership process—deciding, relating, influencing and facilitating? As their situations show, it is important that a formalized plan of evaluation be developed and followed for supervisory nursing staff members as well as those in managerial and administrative staff positions.

## EFFECTIVE LEADERSHIP BEHAVIORS

Basing the evaluation of nursing leadership on the components of deciding, relating, influencing and facilitating ensures that significant behavioral areas are reviewed for the nurse supervisor.[3] With the situations of Ms. Ballister and Ms. Redins in mind, the following questions should be considered.

*Deciding:* Does the nurse leader who is supervisor

- know what decisions to make;
- make decisions from a data base;
- recognize problem situations, determine strategies to solve them, implement strategies and evaluate outcomes;
- involve nursing staff members in goal designation;
- consider nursing staff-centered decisions related to goal designation and goal achievement;
- consider cost factors inherent in decisions made;
- establish key result areas;
- know the risks involved in decisions;
- demonstrate willingness to take risks to operationalize results;
- maintain standards of nursing performance, fairly and consistently applied;
- appraise nursing staff performance in accordance with job expectations and accepted standards of nursing practice;
- focus on the immediate and long-range future as well as the here and now when problem solving;
- demonstrate sensitivity to the impact of self on others;
- use knowledge of change theory to influence and determine direction of change in individuals and groups;
- collect and analyze data from multiple sources (clients, nursing staff, administration, records) regarding problem designation and resolution;
- determine challenging goals;
- delegate to the appropriate staff at the appropriate time;
- discriminate between temporary and ongoing problems;
- prepare a budget appropriate to the goals of the unit;
- have a working knowledge of the power, authority and system of communication within the hierarchical structure of the health care agency; and
- serve as a model for expert nursing practice for the nursing staff?

*Relating:* Does the nurse leader who is supervisor

- achieve cooperation with nursing staff, support personnel and interdisciplinary health care team members;
- listen effectively;
- foster positive staff interrelationships;
- remove barriers to effective communication;
- anticipate staff reactions—both positive and negative—in the unit;
- provide constructive feedback to nursing staff and support personnel;
- collaborate effectively with interdisciplinary personnel;
- use knowledge of human behavior in dealing with nursing staff, support personnel, interdisciplinary health care team members, clients and their families;
- determine the direction and mechanism for needed behavioral changes for staff and self;
- have an awareness of impact of the individual staff member on the group and vice versa;
- have mastery in the use and determination of verbal and nonverbal communication; and
- have competency in eliciting needed information?

*Influencing:* Does the nurse leader who is supervisor

- create a climate that produces positive staff motivation;

- give recognition to nursing staff for effective problem solving;
- set challenging work goals for nursing staff and self;
- use counseling and coaching to motivate nursing staff toward realistic goal setting;
- clearly convey ideas, opinions, expectations and goals to nursing staff, support personnel, interdisciplinary health care team members;
- demonstrate a range of strategies for goal achievement;
- deal with the here and now while looking ahead to the future;
- know how to deal with resistance to change;
- prevent circumstances and situations that may lead to future staff grievances and dissatisfactions;
- know when to control a situation and when to share control with staff;
- use supportive discipline and corrective action to enhance productivity and goal-oriented behavior;
- have an appreciation of the individual needs and differences of staff members;
- know the forces and constraints within the unit and the hierarchical structure-at-large that impact on goal achievement; and
- effectively use knowledge of the power structure and power holders within the unit and the health care agency to obtain needed resources and to promote goal-directed change and goal achievement?

*Facilitating:* Does the nurse leader who is supervisor

- effectively reduce common causes of job stress;
- remove specific barriers to effective communication with and among nursing staff, support personnel, interdisciplinary health care team members;
- use positive reinforcement and praise to enhance goal-oriented behaviors;
- provide supportive discipline and corrective action;
- provide coaching and counseling services to staff;
- provide constructive feedback to nursing staff regarding goal designation and strategies to achieve goals;
- develop an effective organizational structure to ensure meeting overall unit goals;
- optimize the use of resources, e.g., time, personnel;
- know what needs of staff are met by working;
- requisition needed resources, such as staff (considering qualifications, competencies and numbers), facilities, supplies;
- demonstrate ability to take the risks involved in operationalizing planned action;
- compromise effectively with unit staff and organizational staff;
- display sensitivity to the need for nursing staff and support personnel to accomplish a task;
- monitor use of resources (staff, facilities, supplies) for effective and economic use; and

- negotiate with appropriate personnel for time, resources and freedom to do what must be done?

## EVALUATING LEADERSHIP BEHAVIORS

When data from responses to the four categories of questions developed for evaluating nursing leadership are analyzed, judgments are made about strengths and limitations in decision making, relating, and influencing and facilitating goal designation and goal achievement. Significant limitations in one or more categories may point out the lack of leadership displayed in the supervisory role. Furthermore, limitations may denote a task-oriented, dependent view of the position of supervisor. These judgments could serve as a basis for the nurse supervisor to learn leadership behaviors and expand the effectiveness of the supervisor role. For the nurse supervisor whose evaluation-affirmed evidence of effective leadership behaviors related to deciding, relating, influencing and facilitating, plans can be made to strengthen and expand these behaviors and provide an opportunity to plan to learn additional leadership behaviors.

From the situations of Ms. Ballister and Ms. Redins, it can be seen from the data provided that Ms. Redins has evidenced significant leadership behaviors in all four categories (DRIF). She knew the decisions that needed to be made in the critical care unit, she developed an effective data base for the top priority problem—excessive nursing staff turnover and absenteeism—and she was cognizant of the tremendous cost in time, effort and resources of the identified problem. Ms. Redins was willing to take the risk inherent in implementing the plan to solve the problem over time. She was supported by the director of nursing and she gleaned the involvement and support of the nursing staff, support staff, physicians and clients' families.

Ms. Redins's particular asset was her ability to handle the present situation while looking to the future for a more permanent resolution. She effectively sought information data from varied sources and energized nursing staff to explore the literature for answers. This very exploration by nursing staff members provided an intellectual respite while opening avenues for solutions that might be possible. Staff involvement in all dimensions of goal determination and effort toward goal achievement gave greater assurance for success since success depended heavily on staff willingness to change. It gave staff a

---

*Staff involvement in all dimensions of goal determination and effort toward goal achievement gave greater assurance for success since success depended heavily on staff willingness to change.*

---

goal-directed purpose for which they could "get fired up about" in contrast to the usual "burnout."

In her actions, Ms. Redins displayed a knowledge of how changes take place and of the power, authority and communication structures within and outside the critical unit. She set up challenging work goals for the nursing staff; she was influential in motivating them to aid in problem resolution. Her arrangement for two hours of library release time improved a setting that had previously allowed few amenities for staff other than a time for meals. She demonstrated that her ideas worked and her strategies worked, and that the outcomes benefited nursing staff, support personnel, clients' families and physicians. She did not use her energies to maintain the status quo. Ms. Redins did not merely function from crisis to crisis. Her ideas and their outcomes more effectively used resources allocated to the critical care unit. Money, time and staff effort were saved.

Ms. Redins was influential in creating a problem-solving environment rather than one that was mainly problem producing. She set reasonable goals. She cleverly dealt with resistance to change by getting affected personnel involved in the biggest problem facing the critical care unit. She was sensitive to the needs of the staff and supported and maximized the reasons and motives behind their selection of the critical care unit for employment. She had first-hand knowledge of the constraints and forces operating within the critical care unit and the larger health care organization. She also was aware of forces that facilitated goal achievement.

Ms. Redins knew the mechanism for obtaining data and was undaunted by refusal (e.g., obtaining data about turnover and absenteeism). The impact of the problem-solving actions in the critical care unit has broader implications. The model used for problem solving can be used in other units. The effective use of data (data that were accumulated for a restricted purpose) for additional purposes could impact the way data are accumulated and handled in the organization at large.

The positive results demonstrated by Ms. Redins's leadership behaviors related to deciding, relating, influencing and facilitating provided personal and professional growth benefits as well as successful outcomes from a staff, client and family, physician and economic viewpoint. Particularly significant were the establishment of future problem-solving efforts as well as continued surveillance over the staffing achievement.

In contrast, the evaluation of nursing leadership behaviors of Ms. Ballister portrays significant limitations. Her actions drew her physical and emotional energy away from goal achievement and away from the experience of professional satisfaction. Ms. Ballister made decisions and demonstrated a high level of sensitivity to the needs of the nursing staff and clients and their families. She op-

erated from a limited data base. Her focus was exclusively "today" without looking ahead to resolution of the severe staffing turnover and absenteeism problem over time. She knew the key result areas, but she tried to problem solve the current situation singlehandedly. All of her efforts were geared to achieving standards of acceptable nursing practice, though this was not realized. She seemed fully aware of the excessive cost in time, effort and effective use of human resources inherent in the continuing effort to replenish and orient nursing staff members.

Staff reaction to Ms. Ballister's involvement in paperwork was accepted as received. She responded by helping with client care as time permitted. In a sense she validated staff's opinion of paperwork. Ms. Ballister's view of the risks involved in problem solving staffing and absenteeism was client centered but spanned only a 24-hour range of coverage. Her major effort was dealing with the results of problems rather than with causes. Her relationships with staff could be considered temporary rather than long term due to frequent staff changes. It is difficult to imagine that much cooperation and positive interpersonal relationships could be achieved with nursing staff with the transiency she encountered.

Ms. Ballister was limited in her ability to create a climate that produced positive staff motivation. She, herself, was not provided with a comparable environment by her superior administrative officer. She had a limited support system for herself. Her major challenge was providing for coverage; little of a challenging nature was evident in work goals for the nursing staff. Coping activities were a high priority. An inordinate amount of acceptance of the prevailing situation by Ms. Ballister without a view that the future could be improved may have been a significant factor in the request for transfer out of the critical care unit. This action might have been reversed had Ms. Ballister been the beneficiary of a scheduled periodic evaluation as well as ongoing informal evaluation by her superiors. Help with planning for future outcomes and reinforcement of productive leadership behaviors may have changed the results of Ms. Ballister's tenure as supervisor.

Ms. Ballister was probably aware of the forces and constraints within the critical care unit and the elements of the total agency, but she was handicapped in her ability to turn forces and constraints into facilitators for problem resolution. One senses the powerlessness in Ms. Ballister's role experiences. Based on data about complaints of omissions and deficiencies in nursing care from the nursing staff, families of clients and physicians, it can be assumed that standards of nursing practice for critical care nursing have not been met. As expert practitioner of care and consultant to the critical care nursing staff, the nurse supervisor must have experienced frustrations in meeting client care goals as well as difficulty in appraising nursing staff perfor-

mance in relation to job expectations. Many more problems were generated in this environment and the nurse supervisor must delineate weaknesses in staff performances, causes and solutions. Little positive input was evidenced from nursing staff, physicians, support staff, clients and their families. Sorting out problems for priority resolution was very difficult for Ms. Ballister. She had limitations in the direction to go and consultative resources available to her in her role as supervisor.

While Ms. Ballister's problems are multifaceted, her coping ability and her endurance must have been great. Her strengths and limitations regarding deciding, relating, influencing and facilitating would support serious deficiencies in her leadership abilities. Ms. Ballister's potential for improvement in her use of the nursing leadership process should be explored with a definite program for career goal achievement designed. A mentor could be selected to provide support and oversee her efforts toward goal achievement. Ms. Ballister's transfer to another unit may be useful to her at this point in time. Failure to provide feedback to her through a formal evaluation in relation to DRIF may thwart her productivity and success in her next supervisory role. She may be a supervisor but not necessarily a leader.

Much more could be said about Ms. Ballister and Ms. Redins, and each question in the four process categories could be answered in detail. However, the objective of this presentation has been accomplished; a workable framework for nursing leadership has been developed and presented.

Questions comprising the component framework can be further refined, expanded or changed to reflect the breadth or specificity needed to accommodate the roles requiring supervisory, managerial and administrative experience of the nurse. Performance in these roles will be enhanced if leadership behavior is an expectation.

Evaluation of nursing leadership, viewed as a growth experience, would contribute to and facilitate the personal and professional goals of the nurse. The nurse leader would be valued in the formal organization in which she functions. She could clearly identify those legitimate personal needs met by her function as nurse leader in a supervisory role. The nurse leader would meet her ongoing educational and inservice requirements to keep up to date. She would require a support system in which professional colleagues, coworkers and superiors would allow space and opportunity for growth, creativity and risk taking inherent in the experience of nursing as supervisor and as leader.

The purpose and focus for nursing leadership evaluation stems from the definition of nursing leadership as the ability to promote goal designation and goal realization. Leadership behaviors of deciding, relating, influencing and facilitating ensure goal designation and goal realization and determine the framework for evaluation of the nurse who is leader.

## REFERENCES

1. Yura, H., Ozimek, D., and Walsh, M.B. *Nursing Leadership: Theory and Process.* 2d ed., New York: Appleton-Century-Crofts, 1981, p. 94.

2. Ibid.

3. Ibid., 188–98.

# The nurse supervisor charged with change

*Helen Yura*
*Professor of Nursing*
*Graduate Program Director*

*Sue Young*
*Associate Professor of Nursing*
*School of Nursing*
*Old Dominion University*
*Norfolk, Virginia*

ALVIN TOFFLER makes a strong point in his discourses about change and its direction toward high technology (information) and service industries. He notes that we are bombarded by stimuli from outside ourselves that affect what we see, hear, taste, smell, and touch. "The way we organize this endless, incoming flow of data is crucial . . . not merely for daily life, but even more so for management decision-making, for education, for political organizing and a thousand other activities."[1] The nurse supervisor can identify with Toffler's words in briefly reviewing each encounter and the myriad of persons with whom he or she communicates. High technology and information and its transfer are very much a part of the nurse supervisor's work place.

Generally, elements of change theory that prevail in the health care service setting and are managed by the

*Health Care Superv*, 1987, 5(3), 12–27

nurse supervisor are those developed by Kurt Lewin, the classical change theorist.[2] The elements describe a process of unfreezing, moving to a new level, and refreezing.[3] As solutions are identified and accepted, the changees begin to acknowledge the change and move to a new level of behavior. At this level, the changees begin to try out the solutions and work toward acceptance. With assistance from the change agent, the solution is verified and validated as it is integrated by the changees. As the changees are changed, refreezing—the final stage of the change process—is initiated. Throughout the entire change process, the changees are supported, nurtured, and positively reinforced by the change agent. During each phase of the change process, forces that are facilitating and forces that are restraining are identified by the change agent. The goal is to enhance and increase the facilitating forces while effectively diminishing the restraining forces.

## ELEMENTS OF CHANGE

The elements that involve change as a process occur over time. Those related to knowledge or information may require less time to assimilate than those that require attitude change or individual and group behavioral changes, which take the longest time by comparison. Occurring simultaneously is the societal sweep toward a different future that will affect the health system gener-

ally and the nurse supervisor particularly. The position of the nurse supervisor on the organizational chart is closest to where the information is needed and the nursing care is given to the client. Supervisors are heavily affected by change, but are also charged to operationalize the changes.

What are the changes (now and in the future) and the issues inherent in these changes that have an impact on the nurse supervisor? What is available to the nurse supervisor to cope with change, to know how much change is needed and when to change? How can the nurse supervisor initiate or support change affecting health care and nursing? How is the decision made to change? What is the direction of and for change?

### The client

A major change for the nurse supervisor has been the higher acuity of clients in health care settings, requiring more intense nursing by astute, well-educated nurses. The acuity level is such that reference is made to acute care settings as oversized intensive care units. This high client acuity demands accurate frequent exchange of information about the health status of the client among nurses and other health professionals. It is this information that involves critical judgments based on data related to impressive changes or minute or hardly noticed changes in the client's condition supported by data from technical monitoring devices.

What do these data mean? Are interventions necessary? What kind? By whom? When? Were these changes expected? Do these changes have a positive or a negative impact on the client? Are the hardly noticed changes harbingers of more serious events to come if not noticed by the nursing staff that is available 24 hours a day? What changes have family members perceived? Where are family members or significant others? If interventions are needed, what is the cost to the client in terms of discomfort, suffering, pain, and disability? What is the cost to delay or withhold intervention? What is the cost to all involved if minute behavioral changes are missed or if the nursing staff fails to respond to "hunches"? How is this information communicated to the nurse supervisor? What does the nurse supervisor do with this information? What is the role and responsibility of the nurse supervisor in this situation? Are these questions about clinical data and role responsibility for the supervisor alone? If not, who else will answer them?

**The nursing staff**

Stemming from, or relating to, change in the clients' acuity is calculation of the number and preparation of professional nurses required to accommodate the care demands of clients who are critically ill. Evidence is mounting to show that it is most cost effective to employ well-educated nurses who also are self-directed, do not need large numbers of supervisory personnel, come prepared to give generalized and specialized nursing service, are not likely to have "dead time" (time in which they wait to be told what to do), and provide high client satisfaction. Another factor to benefit the consumer is the nurses' accuracy and sensitivity matching the acuity level of clients' illnesses.

More hospitals are turning toward an all-professional nursing staff. This type of staff has the leadership and collaborative ability to work with both a broad range of interdisciplinary health personnel as well as with family members and other persons significant to the client. The perspective of nursing care covers the current experience and projects into the clients' homes and neighborhoods before and when clients leave the acute care setting. Does the nurse supervisor recognize the increasing complexity required for delivery of nursing care? Can the supervisor's staff respond to these demands? Is the staff educationally prepared to meet these demands? Does the supervisor believe staff development and education are paramount to effective delivery of client care? Can the nurse supervisor negotiate the staff changes required to meet the needs of both the consumer and the system?

*Nursing requirements*

The Western Interstate Commission for Higher Education was commissioned by the Division of Nursing, Bureau of Health Professions, Health Resources Administration, U.S. Department of Health and Human Services, to design an approach to determining nursing requirements at both the state and the national level. This was accomplished with the following results: criteria were developed for nursing staff based on educational preparation; staffing requirements were projected (as upper-bound and lower-bound projections) for all types of health care agencies including specified units within these agencies; and estimates were made for nurse manpower requirements from now to the year 1990. Projected for general units in acute care settings were 81 (full-time equivalent) registered nurses per 100 clients. The educational preparation would be 50 percent baccalaureate nursing graduates and 50 percent with associate degrees in nursing (upper bound). By contrast, 405.5 (full-time equivalent) registered nurses were projected for critical care units per 100 clients with 60 percent being baccalaureate nursing graduates and 40 percent having associate degrees in nursing (upper bound). These projections affect the nurse supervisor, who will plan to meet these projections. The benefit for the supervisor who can negotiate this change will be a better prepared nursing staff that is more self-directed, more astute, and able to generate greater client satisfaction. Implementing these projections will provide for the client a more educated nurse who delivers person- and family-centered care in an effective manner with cost saving for the client and the acute care agency.[4]

---

*Nonnursing activities diminish time and energy for the direct provision of nursing care to patients and cut into the time spent with patients and their families and significant others.*

---

### Nonnursing activities

Related to the issue of the background and educational preparation of each member of the nursing staff is the issue of whether nurses are doing nursing or are involved in nonnursing activities. Nonnursing activities diminish time and energy for the direct provision of nursing care to clients and cut into the time spent with patients and their families and significant others. Brown, who in 1978 analyzed client outcomes, provider satisfaction, and costs, determined the yearly cost of nonnursing activities performed by nursing units in a 600-bed teaching hospital.[5] She calculated daily and annual costs and found that the annual cost of nonnursing activities was $440,463. This annual total included $43,435 for trips to central supply and the dumbwaiter; $165,953 for checking diet trays, passing and picking up trays, and trips to dietary; $23,178 for pharmacy activities—trips for medications and narcotics and making out pharmacy commission slips; $19,801 for laboratory delivery and pickup activities; $72,148 for public relations activities such as maintaining flowers and directing visitors; $83,463 for housekeeping activities such as cleaning bathrooms and carpets; and $32,485 for transportation activities such as taking patients to other departments.[6] Performing these activities causes the nurse to be unavailable to care for the clients. How does the nurse supervisor face this economic and professional dilemma? How does the nurse supervisor initiate attitude and behavioral change on the part of nurses and other health care and administrative professionals?

## Containing health care costs

Another critical issue is the expectation that nurses, particularly nurse supervisors, cut the economic excesses of other health professionals, especially physicians. Aside from the inappropriate expectation that one professional group is delegated the responsibility to stem the excesses of another professional group, nurse supervisors are not afforded the authority to accompany the delegated responsibility. The result is a very real sense of powerlessness and diminished satisfaction for the nurse supervisor. Furthermore, hostility and rejection are directed toward the nurse supervisor from those physicians who feel their ultimate authority is being threatened and from health care administrators who want evidence of economic results. The nurse supervisor is placed in an extremely difficult, conflicting role. Hospital administration demands assistance in containing health care costs. Nursing sup-

ports that goal but wants to be involved in cost containment activities specific to the practice of nursing and not the management of health care costs resulting from the practice of medicine. How does the nurse supervisor change some of the inappropriate directions and responsibility delegated to nursing in this volatile area of health care management?

Closely related to these economic issues is the issue of budget cuts disproportionately affecting nursing. Because nurses are the largest employee group in a health care agency and provide the largest consumer service, they are also the most vulnerable from a budgetary restriction standpoint. Frequently, limited representation exists for nursing input for budget negotiation, and rarely is the representation proportionate to the size of the nursing staff. Perhaps more related to this issue is the scarcity of data about the direct cost of nursing care as separated from maintenance, upkeep, and other nonnursing elements. While client acuity is up, the number of academically qualified and experienced nurses available to meet the client nursing care demands may have remained the same or even diminished. How does the nurse supervisor negotiate changes in the cost of nursing service?

## Other elements of change

Other issues that prevail for the nurse supervisor are the rise of consumerism; the demand for services such as day care for the children of the staff; policies and services for impaired employees; information and training demands of families whose member returns home for recuperation and care while still very sick; rising fears by consumers that the health care agency is a place to get sick—nosocomial diseases; clients seeking out nurses for information that other health care providers may or may not be available to provide or willing or capable to provide to clients and family members. These are only a few of the issues that directly affect the nurse supervisor and the nursing staff. You as readers are surely aware of others.

Inherent in these issues are changes, changes, and more changes. The nurse supervisor is affected and charged with change from many directions—within the nursing unit, within and outside the health care agency, within and outside the nursing profession, and within and outside other health care professional groups. It is no wonder that the word charge is used when the nurse supervisor considers change and its elements and process. Forceful words are used to define "charge," and a selection of these clearly depict the nurse supervisor's dilemma: "to load," "to make responsible for," "to fill to capacity," "to saturate," "to give a task to," "to command authoritatively," "to accuse of wrongdoing," "to make liable for error," "to ask as a price," "to record as a debt," "to bear down or set upon with force," and "a debt entered."[7]

## HANDLING THE CHARGE OF CHANGE

How can the nurse supervisor handle the charge? How does the nurse supervisor decide what, when, and where changes should occur? How does the nurse supervisor select "the preferable" future for the nursing unit from among the probable futures?[8] Lancaster and Lancaster propose a model for change that can be a useful tool for the nurse supervisor. It includes the following 11 components: idea generation and diagnosis of the problem; assessment of motivation and resources for change; assessment of resources and capability of the change agent; diagnosis of the type of change strategy needed; development of the implementation strategy; pretesting (trial) of the implementation strategy; revision of the strategy as required; implementation of the change project; observation, handling avoidance, or overcoming of resistance to the project; evaluation of the effectiveness of change; formulation of recommendation for future actions or modifications.[9] Table 1 diagrams this model, combined with the elements of the change process proposed by Lewin and ideas from Toffler.

When the nurse supervisor values this model and tries to incorporate it as a way of discharging the charge for change, the supervisor assumes the role of change agent. Lancaster and Lancaster's guidelines for the change-agent role provide the methodology for effective action for

**Table 1.** A model for change

| Unfreezing | Moving | Refreezing | Moving toward a preferred future |
|---|---|---|---|
| Idea generation<br>Assessment of:<br>• motivation and re-sources for change;<br>• resources and capa-bility of change agent;<br>• diagnosis of type of change needed | Development of implementation strategy<br>Pretesting or trial of implementa-tion strategy<br>Revision of strat-egy as required<br>Implementation of change project<br>Observation, handling avoid-ance, or overcom-ing resistance to project | Incorporation of change<br>Evaluation of effec-tiveness of change<br>Reassessing and modifying of strat-egy to maintain effectiveness of change<br>Formulation of recommendation for future action and modification | Achieving a preferred future |

change. They suggest that all persons affected by the change should be involved in the process from the start; that persons are more motivated toward change if they are listened to and if their contributions are considered and respected. In addition, they recommend planning for change by considering (1) where the system is inflexible, (2) the elements of change (what, how, and when), and (3) achieving sanction for any change by controlling members of the health care organization by those negotiating change and by those affected by the change. Reeducation and a balance between leading and shared leadership helps maximize the use of the combined talents of change agent and changee. It is helpful to anticipate an outcome that may differ from the original plan and expect and resist resistance and unforeseen prob-

lems or circumstances and unusual reactions from changees. It is also essential to provide recognition and support for involved persons, noting all positive actions and reactions toward the goal for change. Finally, "the key element in implementing change is developing trust."[10] The element of trust should be demonstrated by both the change agent and those affected by the proposed change.[11]

These guidelines for implementation of change have been supported as a significant dimension in successful management, administration, and leadership in nursing as an outcome of the Magnet Hospitals Study conducted by the Task Force on Nursing Practice in Hospitals of the American Academy of Nursing.[12] The following criteria were used to develop a national sample of 165 hospitals nomi-

---

*The element of trust should be demonstrated by both the change agent and those affected by the proposed change.*

---

nated by the Fellows of the American Academy of Nursing from which the final selection of 41 magnet hospitals was made:

- Nurses considered the hospital a good place to practice nursing and a good place to work.
- The hospital had the ability to recruit and retain professional nurses as evidenced by a relatively low turnover rate.
- The hospital was located in an area where it had competition for staff from other institutions and agencies.

Analysis of the data obtained through a variety of data collection techniques and interviews resulted in the designation of factors as essential for a nursing service department in a magnet hospital. A selection of these factors as perceived by the director included:

- decentralization of decision making to the unit level;
- strong, effective, visible leadership;
- participative management with active involvement of nursing staff in planning and decision making;
- primary nursing as the staffing methodology with recognition of the autonomy, accountability,

and responsibility of the professional nurse for quality client nursing care;

- a staff, predominantly consisting of registered nurses, that is fully supported by the nursing administration;
- open communication with positive feedback to staff;
- adequate staffing and flexible scheduling; and
- a focus on providing quality client care and recognizing and rewarding excellence.[13]

These same areas were perceived as significant by staff nurses for promotion and retention of staff.[14] How can nurse supervisors legitimize these factors in their work setting so they, too, would achieve the magnetism that draws competent staff to their units?

## AN EXPERIENCE IN CHANGE

In an effort to actualize the change model shown in Table 1 and to respond to factors inherent in successful change experiences, Sue Young designed a data-gathering and problem identification and resolution consultation experience with nurse supervisors in a selected health care agency. Additional information about this project is available from the author. This was a first step of many to be initiated eventually. Two premises underpinned the project design: (1) a belief that nurse supervisors should approach the nursing administration with a core of theoretical principles and concepts to facilitate effective management actions, and (2) the project (program) must be institutionally specific for acceptance and perceived usefulness by the target group.

## Description of the project

The project was designed to provide the nurse supervisor with an opportunity to gain the knowledge and skills required to develop a change theory as a framework for nursing administration. It was believed that to be an effective manager in a complex and constantly changing world of health care delivery systems, the nurse supervisor must recognize the concepts and principles of change theory so that nursing service can both respond to and influence the directions of rapidly developing changes. To accomplish the purpose and accommodate this belief an institutionally specific continuing education program (CEP) was developed. Its focus was on change theory as a framework for nursing administrative problem identification, planned intervention, and system outcomes. The CEP was designed as an intervention study in which formal content was developed and presented. The participants for this project were nurse supervisors who were divided into three groups: mid-level managers (group 1), first-line managers (group 2), and potential nurse managers (group 3). Any registered nurse who supervised either nursing personnel or nursing programs or both in

a specific health care agency was eligible. The format for the CEP was 12 hours of program content divided into three formal 4-hour presentations per week every other week until completion. During the weeks when there was no formal content presentation, on-site consultation was provided to participants. This portion of the project protocol covering a five-week period may be summarized as: (1) four hours of formal presentation; (2) consultation; (3) four hours of formal presentation; (4) consultation; and (5) four hours of formal presentation. This format allowed for a formal presentation utilizing the seminar as an adult learner–teaching strategy combined with an opportunity for the participants to discuss their supervisory concerns or change-theory application difficulties with a knowledgeable, experienced, and objective external nurse consultant.

In addition to the CEP portion of this project, three specific parameters related to change theory were to be evaluated: knowledge, application skills, and behavior or performance appraisal. In addition, the demographic variables of age, level and type of nursing education, nursing practice experience, and nursing management experience were to be identified. Three tools were developed that explored relationships among three parameters and demographic data.

Two multiple choice questionnaires were developed. One tested knowledge of specific change theory concepts and the other measured the application of these concepts in nursing management situations. To ascertain current behavior and principles, a 26-item Likert-scale performance assessment form was designed. Each participant's performance (behavior) was evaluated by the immediate supervisor. Data using these tools were to be collected from participants prior to beginning the CEP and then again at two months, six months, and one year after completion of the program to document change over time.

The two questionnaires (a knowledge test and an application test) were pilot tested to establish validity and reliability. A decision was made to use criteria-based evaluation for testing; thus, a score of 80 percent or better was needed on both questionnaires. A score of less than 80 percent on either questionnaire was believed to represent a less than adequate change theory knowledge base and application ability as a framework for nursing administration. Only the pre-implementation data are presented here.

### The setting and the participants

The setting for this project was a 250-bed local acute care facility—approved by the Joint Commission on Accreditation of Hospitals (JCAH)—with the following nursing services: medical–surgical, intensive care, operating and recovery, emergency, outpatient surgery, and home health.

Participation in this project was negotiated and accepted as designed. This acute care setting is typical of its kind in the United States and is affected by an atmosphere of rapid technological and organizational change. Services constantly are being deleted, expanded, or developed. For example, a pediatric unit currently is being opened so this community facility can remain competitive with other local agencies, and an entire obstetrical service will open in several months, when construction is completed. As a result, nurses are being hired, transferred, and oriented at various levels of nursing management. In addition, the problem of ineffective documentation continues.

Producing effective documentation that complies with JCAH requirements is an ever-present goal. Revised charting and recording systems are being implemented; several approaches to a modified form of primary nursing are being considered. All of these changes are occurring within the constraint of cost-containment as available health care dollars continue to shrink.

This acute care facility functions with a traditional nursing service department. The department's organizational structure includes an assistant administrator responsible for nursing, four clinical nursing directors, two assistant nursing directors (evening and night supervisors), a staff development director, and a systems management director for budgeting and staffing. Each of these directors reports to the assistant administrator for nursing. For this project, these directors were identified as mid-level managers and designated as group 1 (N = 9).

Organizationally, the clinical directors of group 1 supervise a group of unit coordinators or head nurses. The number supervised varies according to the service provided. This group of unit coordinators were considered first-line managers and were placed in group 2 (N = 11). The unit coordinators supervise the charge nurses on the evening and night shifts.

The third group of participants were the potential nurse managers. Group 3 (N = 14) was made up of registered staff nurses who occupy the position of either permanent evening or night charge nurse. Those unit coordinators with client care units that provide 24-hour service supervise both evening and night charge nurses.

Analysis of age, nursing education, nursing practice experience, and nursing management experience revealed for the total group an age range of 24 to 56 years with a mean age of 38 years. The mean age by group was: 42 years for group 1, 38 years for group 2, and 35 years for group 3. As expected, the youngest participants were at the lower administrative level of the organization. For nursing education, 45 percent (N = 34) of the total group had a diploma in nursing as the current level of nursing education achieved. Only 31 percent (N = 9) of the participants had a baccalaureate or higher degree in nursing. Analysis of their nursing practice experience also produced predictable results. Participants in group 1 had the most nursing practice experience with the mean number of years worked being 17. The means for groups 2 and 3 were 15 and 11, respectively. Group 1 participants also had the longest nursing management experience—the mean was 11 years. The mean for group 2 was 9 years and for group 3 was 3 years.

## Results

The content areas comprising the questionnaire designed to test knowledge about specific change theory concepts and principles included the definition of planned change; the elements of unfreezing; implementation and refreezing; the steps in change; response to change; group versus individual change; timing; goal evaluation; and the change agent. Table 2 depicts the knowledge scores. For the questionnaire measuring skill in application of change principles and concepts, content areas included the stages of change, resisters, level of change, role identification, force-field analysis, leadership principles, resistance, timing, unfreezing, and response to resistance. These results are also depicted in Table 2.

In analyzing the knowledge tool, four items were given incorrect responses by 50 percent or more of the participants in groups 1, 2, and 3. These items related to concepts about the refreezing phase of change, individual versus group behavior in

**Table 2.** Nurse supervisors' responses to change theory knowledge and application according to group

| Group | Knowledge scores* range | $\bar{X}$ | Application score† range | $\bar{X}$ |
|---|---|---|---|---|
| Mid-level nurse manager | 5–8 | 6.5 | 3–8 | 5.2 |
| First-level nurse managers | 4–9 | 5.4 | 2–5 | 3.4 |
| Potential nurse managers | 3–8 | 5.9 | 4–7 | 5.3 |

\* A score of 8.8 or better from a highest possible score of 11 = 80–100%.
† A score of 8 or better from a highest possible score of 10 = 80–100%.

change, evaluating change, and the change agent role. Only 9 percent of the first-level nurse managers (group 2) responded correctly to the concept concerned with timing as a factor that positively influences successful planned change. For group 3 (potential nurse managers), an additional item—the steps in the change process—received an incorrect response from 58 percent of the group. All participants in groups 1 and 3 correctly responded to the item relating to implementation, and all participants in group 2 answered the item defining planned change correctly.

The analysis of the responses to the tool measuring application of change concepts and principles revealed that all participants in group 1 responded correctly to the item related to stages of change. This was the only instance of 100 percent correct response among the groups. In the items relating to level of change, force-field analysis, leadership principles, and

unfreezing, less than 50 percent of each group responded correctly. Groups 1 and 2 answered incorrectly more than 50 percent of the time for the item role identification. In addition, group 2 was incorrect more than 50 percent of the time in responding to items of resisters to change and response to resistance.

An analysis of variance (ANOVA) was used to test for differences in knowledge between groups. No significant differences for knowledge were found to exist when using 2 degrees of freedom and a $p$ value of .2. Similarly, an ANOVA was used to determine if differences existed between groups according to application ability. Using 2 degrees of freedom and a $p$ value of .00 the ANOVA demonstrated that a significant difference did occur between groups for this variable.

Data from the performance assessment form (completed by the supervisor of each participant) were ana-

Table 3. Nurse supervisors' scores on the performance assessment form according to group

| Group | Range* | $\bar{X}$ |
|---|---|---|
| Group 1—mid-level nurse managers | 30–76 | 56 |
| Group 2—first-line nurse managers | 47–71 | 59 |
| Group 3—potential nurse managers | 58–87 | 69 |

* A score of 26 represented the highest level of performance possible; a score of 104 represented the lowest level of performance possible.

lyzed by using a scoring mechanism with a value of one for an *always* rating, two for the *frequently* rating, three for the *occasional* rating, and four for a *never* rating. Scores could range from 26 to 104 for the 26-item questionnaire. A score of 26 would indicate that the participant always used concepts and principles of change theory in this supervisory behavior as measured by this tool. Among the content items included in the tool were those of initiating organization change, recognizing resistance (sabotage, aggression, forgetting, etc.), using employee involvement as a strategy, considering marketing as a factor influencing successful implementation, identifying evaluation method prior to change, facilitating upsetting the equilibrium to begin change, facilitating selection of change method, and collaborating with appropriate interdisciplinary groups. Scores on the performance assessment form are outlined in Table 3.

Analysis of these data revealed significant differences among the groups in their performance relative to exhibiting behaviors representing use of change theory. This finding was calculated using an ANOVA with 2 and 25 degrees of freedom, an F value of 4.79, and a $p$ value of .017. Through item analyses, selected behaviors were rated as *occasional* or *never* by 50 percent or more of the group. These items were occasionally or never seen for participants in group 3, were less frequently rated occasionally or never for group 1, and least likely to be rated as such by participants in group 2. Only two content items, namely initiating organizational change and identifying the evaluation method prior to change, were either occasionally or never present for 50 percent or more of the time for all three groups.

A critical evaluation of these data implies that nurse supervisors in this sample have knowledge and application ability deficits relating to change theory concepts and principles. Since these are preimplementation data for this project, findings are limited to this project population. Caution must be used in generalizing these findings to a larger population. It is recommended that this project be replicated with a larger sample. Should similar findings result, it would be appropriate to conclude that nurse

> *A critical evaluation of these data implies that nurse supervisors in this sample have knowledge and application ability deficits relating to change theory concepts and principles.*

supervisors need assistance in developing their knowledge and use of change theory as a framework to guide their practice of nursing administration: How can the nurse supervisor take charge of change when there may be significant deficits in know-how?

While this project continues and full findings are incomplete, the project was presented as a model for speculative and illustrative purposes pending more elaborately designed research. It is a beginning solution for determining a group's current abilities relative to knowledge, application, and performance—critical dimensions if one is considering change in a system. This sample reflects a profile of a selected group of nurse supervisors from a typical health care facility in the United States at the present time. It is a first step toward helping the nurse supervisor who is charged with change to learn how to deal with it.

## SOLUTIONS AND FUTURE DIRECTIONS FOR THE NURSE SUPERVISOR

It is clear that the nurse supervisor is coping with enormous change within the organizational unit of nursing, within the health care facility, and within the health care system, with further changes in client and family systems, economic and political systems, and the educational system.

The best solution to this problem is for nurse supervisors to attain advanced academic credentials in nursing. This approach would offer long-term benefits for negotiating and accomplishing preferred changes in contrast to attempts to survive imposed change through the modality of crisis intervention. Concurrent with guiding nurse supervisors to achieve the first professional degree, ongoing leadership development programs could be provided that focus on change theory, decision-making and problem-solving processes, and communication. This additional experience has been provided to the sample population in this described project. It is anticipated that there will be improvement in the areas of knowledge development, application, and positive behavioral change as a result of this continuing education effort. The critical question is: Will the improvement remain constant over time without ongoing academic involvement by the nurse supervisor? National educational standards specify the minimum of the baccalaureate degree in nursing as the expectation for charge nurses and those expecting to be nurse supervisors in the future. For all other nurse administrators, the minimal preparation for this area of specialized practice is a master's degree in nursing.

A second solution for nurse supervisors who are charged with change to consider is the utilization of qualified, on-site, ongoing nursing consultation. Criteria should be established for the academic preparation and experience of the consultant. Contacts with various nursing organizations may be fruitful in developing a list of eligible consultants with records for effective service.

Establishing an advisory committee with consumer input is another solution that will provide the nurse supervisor with critical data about the expectations held by consumers of health and nursing care and problems encountered with these services. Consumers can provide needed support for the nurse supervisor when negotiating for budgetary allocations to increase the number of qualified nursing staff members and for establishing informational programs and additional or alternative services.

An all-professional nursing staff with a high full-time equivalent ratio is a significant solution to the high demand for nursing services required by ill clients and their families. Health promotion is the only viable long-term solution to cost containment for the present and the future. Projections for staffing in the near future reflect a highly professional (full-time equivalent) nursing staff. If this is to be a reality, it is imperative that the nurse supervisor offset academic deficits. There is no greater organization anomaly than a large professional staff nurse population academically and experientially qualified, supervised by a largely unprepared nurse supervisory staff. The nurse supervisor's charge with change will be facilitated when those supervised are goal-directed and accomplished and their service results in high levels of client satisfaction.

Lastly, a strong, sophisticated, and creative staff development program for the nurse supervisor and the nursing staff will ensure readiness to identify areas for change, determine the direction for change, supply the modalities for change, and encourage and support the nurse supervisor and nursing staff to maintain acquired changes.

When the nurse supervisor can "take charge" of the charge for change, change can be a challenge and a reward for professional growth and fulfillment. The nurse supervisor will agree with the words of Alfred North Whitehead when he says, "The Art of Progress is to preserve order amid change and to preserve change amid order." [15]

## REFERENCES

1. Toffler, A. *Previews and Premises*. New York: Bantam Books, 1983, p. 203.
2. Lewin, K. *Field Theory in Social Science*. New York: Harper & Row, 1951.
3. Lancaster, J., and Lancaster, W. "The Nurse as Change Agent." In *Concepts for Advanced Nursing Practice*. St. Louis: Mosby, 1982, pp. 7–8.

4. U.S. Department of Health and Human Services. *Evaluation and Updating of the Criteria Established by the WICHE Panel of Expert Consultants.* DHPA Report No. 81–91. Washington, D.C., USDHHS, Public Health Service, Health Resources Administration, Bureau of Health Professions, 1982, p. 68.
5. Brown, B. "Reorganizing Hospital-based Nursing Practice: An Analysis of Patient Outcomes, Provider Satisfaction, and Costs." In *Health Policy and Nursing Practice,* edited by L. Aikin. New York: McGraw-Hill, 1981, p. 122; pp. 212–39.
6. Brown, "Reorganizing Hospital-based Nursing Practice."
7. Guralnek, D., ed. Webster's *New World Dictio-*

*nary of the American Language.* New York: William Collins and World Publishing, 1978, p. 239.
8. Toffler, *Previews and Premises,* 146.
9. Lancaster and Lancaster, *Concepts for Advanced Nursing Practice,* 22.
10. Ibid., 21–22.
11. Ibid.
12. American Academy of Nursing. *Magnet Hospitals: Attraction and Retention of Professional Nurses.* Kansas City, Mo.: American Nurses' Association, 1983, p. 4.
13. American Academy of Nursing, *Magnet Hospitals,* 81.
14. Ibid., 40.
15. Interview. *Forbes* (December 1, 1957).

# Index

# Notes

# *Notes*

# Notes

# Notes

# Notes

# Notes

# Notes

# Notes

# *Notes*

# *Notes*

# *Notes*

# *Notes*

# Notes

# Notes

# *Notes*

# *Notes*

# *Notes*

# Notes

# Notes

# Notes